Pawns of War

The Vietnam Experience

Pawns of War

Cambodia and Laos

by Arnold R. Isaacs, Gordon Hardy, MacAlister Brown,
and the editors of Boston Publishing Company

* חחח09*

Boston Publishing Company / Boston, MA

Time-life 1990
Mar 18 30

Boston Publishing Company

President and Publisher: Robert J. George
Vice President: Richard S. Perkins, Jr.
Editor-in-Chief: Robert Manning
Managing Editor: Paul Dreyfus
Marketing Director: Jeanne Gibson

Series Editor: Samuel Lipsman
Senior Editor: Gordon Hardy
Design Director: Lisa Bogle
Senior Picture Editor: Julene Fischer
Senior Writer: Denis Kennedy

Picture Editor: Lanng Tamura
Picture Coordinator/Researcher:
Rebecca Black

Text Researchers: Michael Hathaway,
Nicholas Philipson

Business Staff: Amy Pelletier, Amy Wilson

Special contributors to this volume:

Picture Editor: Wendy Johnson

Text Research: Katharine Brady, Jason
Brown, Matthew Hong, Kenneth Jacobson,
Steven W. Lipari, Jonathan Mark, Jennifer
Smith, Michael Youmans

Design: Sherry Fatla, Lynne Weygint

Picture Research: Lauren Chapin, Shirley L.
Green (Washington, D.C.), Kate Lewin
(Paris), Nana Stern, Ron Sternberg (Tokyo)

Editorial Production: Dalia Lipkin, Patricia
Leal Welch, Theresa Slomkowski

Index prepared by Steven Csipke

About the editors and authors:

Editor-in-Chief: *Robert Manning*, a long-time journalist, has previously been editor-in-chief of the *Atlantic Monthly* magazine and its press. He served as assistant secretary of state for public affairs under Presidents John F. Kennedy and Lyndon B. Johnson. He has also been a fellow at the Institute of Politics at the John F. Kennedy School of Government at Harvard University.

Authors: *Gordon Hardy* (who wrote chapters 1 and 3) is senior editor of Boston Publishing Company. Previously, he edited *Above and Beyond*, Boston Publishing Company's history of the Medal of Honor, and he has written for and edited a variety of periodical publications. *Arnold R. Isaacs* (chapters 4, 5, and 6) served as a war correspondent in Indochina for the *Baltimore Sun* from 1972 to 1975. The author of *Without Honor: Defeat in Vietnam and Cambodia*, he is currently a freelance writer living in Maryland. *MacAlister Brown* (chapter 2) is professor of political science at Williams College. He is coauthor of *Apprentice Revolutionaries: The Communist Movement in Laos, 1930-1985* and *Communist Indochina and U.S. Foreign Policy: Postwar Realities*.

Consultants: *Joseph J. Zasloff*, a specialist in Laos and Southeast Asia, is professor of political science at the University of Pittsburgh. His most recent book (coauthored with MacAlister Brown) is *Apprentice Revolutionaries: The Communist Movement in Laos, 1930-1985*. *William Shawcross*, a British journalist, has covered Southeast Asia since the early 1970s. His books include *The Quality of Mercy: Cambodia, Holocaust, and Modern Conscience* and *Sideshow: Kissinger, Nixon and the Destruction of Cambodia*.

Picture Consultant: Born in Cambodia in 1942, *Dith Pran* worked as an interpreter until 1973 when he became a stringer for the *New York Times*. Remaining in Cambodia after Pol Pot's takeover, Pran witnessed firsthand and experienced the horror of life under the Khmer Rouge. He left Cambodia in 1979 and became a staff photographer for the *New York Times* in addition to lecturing about his experiences. His ordeal was portrayed in the 1984 movie, *The Killing Fields*.

Cover Photo: A Vietnamese soldier patrols the walkway leading to Cambodia's ancient temple, Angkor Wat, in 1980. Vietnam invaded neighboring Cambodia in late 1978, toppling the murderous regime of Pol Pot and replacing it with a pro-Vietnamese puppet government.

Library of Congress Catalog Card Number: 87-072417

ISBN: 0-939526-24-7

10 9 8 7 6
5 4 3 2 1

Contents

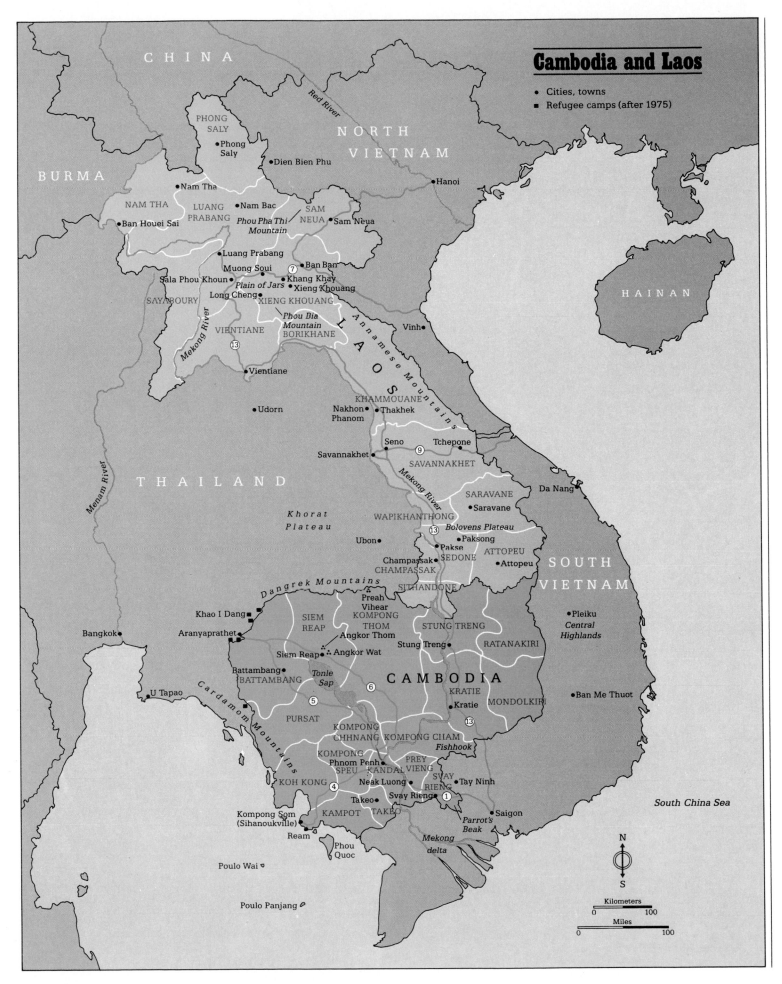

Cambodia and Laos

- Cities, towns
- Refugee camps (after 1975)

CHINA

NORTH VIETNAM

BURMA

PHONG SALY

•Phong Saly

•Dien Bien Phu

•Hanoi

•Nam Tha

NAM THA

LUANG PRABANG

•Nam Bac

Phou Pha Thi Mountain

SAM NEUA

•Sam Neua

•Ban Houei Sai

•Luang Prabang

Muong Soui•

⑦ •Ban Ban

Sala Phou Khoun•

Khang Khay

•Vinh

Plain of Jars •Xieng Khouang

SAYABOURY

Long Cheng•

XIENG KHOUANG

Mekong River

Phou Bia Mountain

BORIKHANE

VIENTIANE

⑬

•Vientiane

•Udorn

KHAMMOUANE

Nakhon Phanom•

•Thakhek

Annamese Mountains

Seno• ⑨ •Tchepone

THAILAND

Savannakhet•

SAVANNAKHET

•Da Nang

Menam River

Khorat Plateau

SARAVANE

•Saravane

WAPIKHANTHONG

⑬ *Bolovens Plateau*

Ubon• •Paksong

•Pakse

ATTOPEU

SEDONE

Champassak•

CHAMPASSAK

•Attopeu

SOUTH VIETNAM

SITHANDONE

•Pleiku

Central Highlands

Dangrek Mountains

Preah Vihear

KOMPONG THOM

STUNG TRENG

SIEM REAP

Khao I Dang■

Angkor Thom

RATANAKIRI

Aranyaprathet•■

•Stung Treng

Bangkok•

Siem Reap• ∴Angkor Wat

CAMBODIA

Battambang•

Tonle Sap

•Ban Me Thuot

BATTAMBANG

KRATIE

⑤ ⑥

•Kratie

MONDOLKIRI

U Tapao•

Cardamom Mountains

PURSAT

⑬

KOMPONG CHHNANG

KOMPONG CHAM

Fishhook

KOMPONG SPEU

Phnom Penh•

PREY VIENG

SVAY RIENG

KOH KONG

KANDAL

•Tay Ninh

④

Neak Luong•

•Svay Rieng

Takeo•

①

Kompong Som (Sihanoukville)•

KAMPOT

TAKEO

•Saigon

Ream•

Parrot's Beak

Phou Quoc

Mekong delta

Poulo Wai ◌

HAINAN

South China Sea

N S

Poulo Panjang ◌

Kilometers
0 ————— 100

Miles
0 ————— 100

Roots of Conflict

The two takeovers could not have been different. The first was peaceful, almost prosaic. On December 1, 1975, a secret Congress of People's Representatives met in Vientiane, the sleepy administrative capital of the Southeast Asian nation of
Laos. Two hundred-sixty-four delegates—Buddhist
monks, intellectuals, Communist ideologues, and
many others—gathered at Vientiane's old American
school. In two days of deliberations they completed a
revolution thirty years in the making. They abolished Laos's 600-year-old monarchy and affirmed a
new Socialist government for the nation, a Lao People's Democratic Republic. They declared their titular leader, a sixty-six-year-old prince of the royal
court named Souphanouvong, president of a Supreme People's Assembly and chief of state. The
actual wielder of power, General Secretary Kaysone
Phomvihan of the Communist Lao People's Revolutionary party (LPRP), became prime minister.

It was a remarkable moment, made all the more so
by the fact that the assembly also announced that

the deposed king, Savang Vatthana, would be retained as a "supreme counselor" to President Souphanouvong. Joining the king as an adviser to the government was Prince Souphanouvong's half-brother and long-time rival for power, the non-Communist former prime minister, Prince Souvanna Phouma. The calm turnover of power, and the positions accorded the two former leaders, seemed to promise a genuine reconciliation among Laos's warring factions. In fact, not all of the Communists' erstwhile enemies were treated so well. Many members of the old royal government had already fled the nation, and many who remained in Laos would be subjected to imprisonment and a cruel process of "reeducation." Nonetheless, it was as if, when the change finally came, some measure of reason had triumphed over the bitterness caused by many years of war.

Three years later, a far bloodier takeover took place just south of Laos. On December 21, 1978, troops of the Vietnam People's Democratic Republic crashed through the border of Communist Cambodia (or, as its leaders called it, Democratic Kampuchea). Their mission was to overthrow the bloodstained regime of Democratic Kampuchea's leader, Pol Pot. Vietnamese tanks, troops, and aircraft pierced deeply into the country along three fronts, pushing back Pol Pot's Khmer Rouge fighters. Just over two weeks later, they entered the deserted Cambodian capital, Phnom Penh, and announced a revolutionary council headed by a Khmer Rouge rebel, Heng Samrin. The regime renamed the country the People's Republic of Kampuchea.

The Vietnamese invasion was not an end to the killing in Cambodia, just as the establishment of the Lao People's Democratic Republic had not solved that country's problems. What both events marked instead was the triumph of Vietnamese rule in Southeast Asia. Prince Souphanouvong and Kaysone Phomvihan of Laos had long depended on Vietnam's Communists for support and military backing, and the Cambodian Heng Samrin was rightly considered a puppet of the Vietnamese. After thirty years of war, Vietnamese Communists had not only won their own revolution; they had gained hegemony over Cambodia and Laos as well.

Yet it was not the first time that Vietnam had done this. Indeed, the outcome was sadly familiar. Cambodia and Laos had often suffered at the hand of Vietnam, their far more populous and powerful neighbor. Time and again, their histories have been adjuncts—side shows—to the larger game being played to their east. Vietnam's domination of Cambodia and Laos in the 1980s was only the latest chapter in a long history of conflict, a history that begins with the coming of all three peoples—Cambodians, Laotians, and Vietnamese—to Southeast Asia.

Foundations of culture

Modern Cambodia and Laos emerged from a welter of ancient tribes and small states that rose along the Mekong River valley of Southeast Asia. Both peoples came originally from the mountains of southern China. The Cambodians, or Khmer, were the first of the two to arrive. Following the natural corridor formed by the Mekong River valley and surrounding mountains, they migrated south into the upper Mekong, to present-day Laos, a few centuries before the beginning of the Christian era. Among their neighbors were the Funanese, a Malayo-Polynesian people who occupied the southern Mekong River basin in what is now Cambodia, and the Vietnamese, who had migrated south from China through another valley to the Red River delta.

The early Cambodians borrowed much of their culture from the great civilization of ancient India. In the first centuries A.D., Indian traders, who were already doing business with Greece, Rome, and other Western empires, spread their mercantile network deeply into Southeast Asia. They brought not only commerce but teachers and missionaries who spread Indian religion, science, philosophy, and other learning eastward to the foothills of the Annamese mountain range. In a few centuries the Khmer (and later, the Lao) adopted from the Indians Hinduism, Buddhism, a code of law, political and social organizations, art and architecture, poetry, and systems of writing. To this day, Cambodian and Lao culture reflect these Indian roots.

Just over the Annamese Mountains, however, India's influence was far less significant. This created a great cultural difference between the Mekong River peoples and their eastern neighbors. Separated from the rest of Southeast Asia by those inhospitable hills, the Vietnamese of the Red River valley did not receive Indian culture directly. Instead, for 1,000 years another great ancient civilization dominated them—Imperial China. The difference in their cultural roots marks a profound separation between Vietnam and Cambodia and Laos and contributes to their long-standing hostility. Not only are their people separated by political borders; they are divided by cultural and social barriers more than 2,000 years old.

After establishing themselves in small villages on the upper Mekong, the Khmer began to infiltrate Funan, the kingdom to their south. Like the Khmer, the Funanese were thoroughly Indianized, but their state was far more powerful than the nation of the Khmer (called Chenla). In the sixth century, however, Funan suffered serious internal upheavals. As the nation waned in influence, Khmer power rose. At last in A.D. 540 Bhavavarman, a warrior and pretender to the Funanese throne who was married to a

---

Khmer princess, seized power in both Funan and Chenla. Funan broke apart over the next century as the Khmer flocked south into the wide Cambodian plain. By A.D. 635 Khmer control extended throughout Funan.

For 600 years, the Khmer kingdom (by then called Angkor) was an important power throughout the Cambodian plain and surrounding areas. Two great accomplishments of the Angkorean kings, still visible on the Cambodian landscape, give evidence of the nation's power. On the Angkor plain, near present-day Cambodia's "Great Lake," or Tonle Sap, King Indravarman (877-889) constructed a sophisticated hydraulic complex of dikes, channels, tanks, and reservoirs to hold water from the annual monsoon rains for use in the dry season. This system allowed year-round rice production, which in turn created a much stronger economy, allowed the population to grow, expanded transportation and communications networks, and fostered a complex society of craftsmen and other specialized laborers. Two centuries later King Suryavarman II (1113-1150) began the second great project, the most enduring symbol of Khmer civilization: the huge, extraordinarily beautiful temple called Angkor Wat.

Despite its power and advanced culture, Angkor (or Kambuja, as some Khmer inscriptions called it) suffered from upheavals within and pressures without. Other peoples made war upon the state: In turn, the Khmer fought the Vietnamese, a people living on the central Vietnamese coast called the Chams, and others. But it was the Thai, a people from a mountain state in China called Nan Chao, who finally destroyed the Khmer state.

In the early 1200s a band of Thai warriors seized power in a Khmer vassal state called Sukothai, in the upper Menam River valley of what is now Thailand. A few years later, when the Mongols of central Asia overran Nan Chao, more Thai flooded southward into Sukothai, and the new state grew rapidly. Then in 1275 a Thai prince named Rama the Brave began to raid other Khmer lands. He and his successors, capitalizing on Angkor's weakened state, spread the new Thai empire in several directions. The Khmer resisted for over a century, but their degenerating state was no match for the vigorous newcomers. In 1431 and 1432, a Thai army burst onto the Angkor plain, sacked the Khmer capital, and destroyed the Khmers' great irrigation system. Beaten and discouraged, the Khmer kings abandoned Angkor, moving their capital eastward several times, eventually to the site now called Phnom Penh. Although the Khmer would continue a fitful resistance against the Thai and others (even briefly restoring their capital to the Angkor plain), the Cambodians would never regain the full glory of their empire.

In the middle of the eighth century, about a century before the rise of the Khmer empire, a new people entered the valley of the Mekong from the north. They were the Lao, cousins of the Thai who came from central China. Pushed south by the Chinese, the Lao had lived for years in

The carved face of the Bodhisattva Lokesvara, the Buddhist god of compassion, gazes through the overgrown roots of a Bombox tree at Angkor.

southern China, until a legendary leader named Khun Barom had led them south to the banks of the Mekong. There they had dwelled unobtrusively, first under the rule of Angkor, then under the Thai kings of Sukothai. They lived as vassals until 1353, when Fa Ngum, a Lao prince who had been raised in the court of Angkor, mounted an expedition to the Lao-inhabited region near present-day Luang Prabang. Aided by the Khmer, Fa Ngum proclaimed the area free from the Thai. He called his state Lan Chang, "the kingdom of a million elephants." Fa Ngum occupied the city of Vientiane, on the Mekong south of Luang Prabang, and conquered a large portion of the Khorat Plateau, west of the Mekong, and the mountains east of the river as far as the Annamese watershed.

Though ethnically and linguistically Thai, Fa Ngum set the Lao apart from the Thai by pursuing the culture he had learned at Angkor. His Lao subjects, located almost entirely in the Mekong Valley and the Khorat Plateau, were much less belligerent than their Thai relatives; instead of aggressiveness, they cultivated gentleness and courtesy.

Angkor Wat

by Melanie Billings-Yun

Melanie Billings-Yun holds a Ph.D. in history from Harvard University and was director of research at the John F. Kennedy School of Government at Harvard.

In January 1861, after a harrowing month of trudging through the leech-infested swamps and jungles of central Cambodia, French naturalist Henri Mouhot discovered a temple complex whose decayed and crumbling beauty repaid in an instant all his pains. "It is grander than anything left to us by Greece or Rome," he wrote, "a temple to rival Solomon's and erected by some Michelangelo." Inscribed on its stone in an ancient language was the name Angkor Wat.

In the next century archaeologists, historians, engineers, and architects sought to unravel the mystery of Cambodia's pre-eminent monument. When Mouhot found Angkor Wat, Buddhist monks had taken over parts of the temple, yet except for some more recent statuary, the complex had no connection to Buddhism. The monks believed it had once been a palace: "Angkor Wat" means "palace-city that has become a Buddhist temple."

No Cambodian Mouhot spoke to could tell him who had built the fabulous edifice. Instead they recounted one of four legends: "It is the work of Pra-Eun, the king of the angels"; "It is the work of giants"; "It was built by the Leper King"; or "It made itself." Mouhot believed it was the creation of a lost great race whose name had long been forgotten.

In fact, as scholars gradually deciphered the monument's carvings, they found that Angkor Wat dates from the reign of Suryavarman II (1113-1150), who ruled at the height of the Angkor empire. A devotee of the Hindu god Vishnu, Suryavarman II built the monument as a temple to his patron deity. Other nearby monuments, such as the Buddhist Bayon (funerary temple) at Angkor Thom, are nearly as impressive as Angkor Wat. What sets Angkor Wat apart is its grand scale, its delicacy, its distinct design, and, most important, its excellent state of preservation.

The outer walls of the complex measure more than a kilometer each, surrounded by a moat stretching to nearly six kilometers. Inside are three concentric galleries adorned by an unbroken frieze of bas-reliefs three meters high. Nearly 20,000 animal and human figures loom from the once-polished sandstone. The innermost gallery rises to a seven-meter pyramid, graced by four corner towers and a central tower that once housed a giant statue of Vishnu. The statue is now gone, as is the gilding on the temple's twelve towers and the white paint that once covered the stone walls. Many of the bas-reliefs have been damaged by war and creeping jungle growth. However, perhaps because it was taken over by a thriving Buddhist community shortly after Suryavarman II's death, Angkor Wat survived as Cambodia's best-preserved Angkor monument.

Because Cambodia's tropical climate and the insects that thrive in it have destroyed almost all Angkorean documents and literature, Angkor Wat's bas-reliefs provide historians with some of their few glimpses into ancient Khmer life. Culturally, the carvings attest to Cambodia's large debt to India, for nearly all of the temple's bas-reliefs depict scenes from Hindu religious epics surrounding Vishnu. Even these, however, reveal a classical simplicity distinct to Khmer artistry. Politically, the fact that such a vast monument, with its 10,000 ridge crests, copious carvings, and massive construction, could be built in four decades attests to the kingdom's sophisticated organizational and economic structure—not to mention its large slave-labor pool.

For years, scholars argued over more arcane matters, such as the meaning of the temple's orientation. Angkor Wat is the only major structure in the ancient capital that faces west, the direction traditionally associated with death. Moreover, its bas-reliefs read right to left, another symbol of death. So, scholars asked, was the ancient palace actually a tomb? The probable answer is that it was both: a temple to Vishnu and the tomb of his incarnation on earth, Suryavarman II.

In the 1970s Elizabeth Moron discovered a striking pattern in the measurements of the shrine's principal axis. Using the ancient Khmer measure, the *hat* (approximately half a meter), she calculated the distance from the western entrance to the central tower as 1,728 *hat*, a figure that corresponds to 1,728,000—the number of years believed by the Hindus to have been the length of the first golden age. Distances to each of the galleries correlates in order to the lengths of the three remaining "ages" of Indian thought. Thus, as one enters Angkor Wat and walks toward the statue of Vishnu in the central tower, one passes symbolically from death, back through the ages, to the golden moment when time began.

For years after the Khmer Rouge revolution in the 1970s, Angkor Wat's fate was unknown. Reports coming out of Cambodia told of heavy damage to the temple during the fighting and widespread looting of statuary by starving Cambodians who hoped to barter the relics for food in Thai refugee camps. Then, in October 1986, a new Cambodian government, installed by the Vietnamese after their overthrow of the Khmer Rouge in 1979, invited a team of Indian archaeologists to resume restoration work on Angkor Wat. At the same time, the government opened Angkor Wat to visitors for the first time in more than a decade.

The archaeologists discovered that some parts of the temple had indeed been damaged by warfare in the 1970s. Far more destructive, however, were Angkor Wat's natural enemies—seeping water, jungle growth, and acidic bat droppings. The team began a major restoration effort, expected to take six years, to return the entire temple and its moat to their former glory. Chheng Phon, Cambodia's minister of information and culture, described the government's desire to restore Angkor Wat. "We still remember the high civilization of Angkor," he said. "What we had 1,000 years ago we must make alive again today."

In a contemporary illustration, French marines drive Cambodian rebels from the fort at Oudon, forty-five kilometers northwest of Phnom Penh.

Their kingdom also included a large population of non-Lao peoples, indigenous tribes who lived isolated in the mountains east of the Mekong, who worshiped spirits, spoke hundreds of different dialects, and practiced a nomadic slash-and-burn agriculture. Their high mountain homes formed a barrier between the Mekong-dwelling Lao and the Vietnamese of the Red River.

The Lao kingdom's peace ended, however, when the Vietnamese asserted their own growing power. After throwing off Chinese rule in the tenth century A.D., Vietnam's rulers were eager to expand their kingdom. First they pushed south to Annam, the mountainous central region occupied by the Chams, and then into Khmer territory, until they occupied the coast as far south as the edge of the Mekong Delta. Next they turned on Lan Chang, invading the Lao kingdom in 1478. Taking Luang Prabang the following year, they demanded and received tribute from the kingdom.

But Vietnam soon began to suffer internal problems. Revolts and power struggles erupted in the next century, and the country split into two quarreling kingdoms. The northern kingdom came under the control of the Trinh family; the southern kingdom was ruled by another family, the Nguyen. Once they established their rule, the Nguyen family pushed farther south, into the vast Mekong Delta. The delta had long been Khmer territory, but it had never been exploited to any degree by the Cambodians. To the

Vietnamese, the delta was a tempting, fertile frontier for their growing population. They colonized it rapidly, pushing back the weakened Khmer.

The Vietnamese invasion of Lan Chang and later expansion southward into Khmer territory, like the earlier Thai invasion of Angkor, confirmed a lasting pattern. For the next 300 years the Thai and Vietnamese (and occasionally the Burmese) exercised control over Laos and Cambodia. Confusing alliances were made and broken; as one nation rose in power, it would seize Cambodia and Laos or strike deals that pushed the weaker states further into vassalage. By the early 1700s Cambodia was being dismembered by the Vietnamese, while in Laos, the old kingdom of Lan Chang was broken up into three rival Lao states: Luang Prabang in the north, Vientiane in the center, and Champassak in the south, near the present Cambodian border. It seemed as if the Khmer and Lao, trapped between stronger nations, were doomed always to suffer one Southeast Asian master or another. Yet even as Siam (the Thai kingdom) and Vietnam quarreled over their territory, the Lao and Khmer were about to become pawns in an even larger game.

The French colonial era

The creation of a French empire in Southeast Asia in the mid-nineteenth century changed the balance of power between Cambodia, Laos, and their neighbors. By seizing control of both countries and Vietnam, France saved Laos and Cambodia from obliteration by their more powerful neighbors. It was, of course, not a matter of altruism:

despite protestations of a *mission civilisatrice* (civilizing mission), the French created their Indochina Union for the good of France.

The first French in Southeast Asia were missionaries who joined Portuguese Jesuits in Southeast Asia in the early 1600s. Almost immediately they ran into trouble. Their remarkably successful efforts at converting the population to Christianity alarmed both the Trinh and Nguyen rulers of Vietnam, who began to expel the priests and to suppress the religion violently. The French government, preoccupied by conflicts in Europe and elsewhere, chose not to fight Vietnam over the issue.

Another opening for the French came in 1802, when a Nguyen prince, aided by a shrewd French priest named Pigneau de Behaine, suppressed a thirty-year-long peasant rebellion and reunited Vietnam. Partly out of gratitude toward Pigneau de Behaine, the new emperor, Gia Long, allowed the French far greater influence in his country. When he died, however, his successors renewed the suppression of Christianity. In 1856, Emperor Louis Napoleon III of France, sensing an opportunity in these depredations, declared that violence against Christians in Vietnam was an insult to the honor and prestige of France. He sent a naval expedition under Admiral Regault de Genouilly to punish Vietnam—and not incidentally, add it to the French Empire if possible.

At first, the expedition was plagued by disease, tropical heat, and bad planning. Admiral de Genouilly, though, was determined to achieve some kind of victory. Gathering his forces, he attacked the southern city of Saigon. On February 17, 1859, the citadel there fell to his men. From this base, the French gradually asserted control over all of Vietnam; by 1884 the whole nation was in French hands.

Once established in Vietnam, the French sought to expand their empire into both Cambodia and Laos. At the time Cambodia was weak; a long and exhausting war between Vietnam and Siam had resulted in an uneasy joint rule under a Cambodian king named Norodom. Wanting Cambodia as a buffer state between their Vietnamese territories and the growing British presence in Burma and Siam, the French began to pressure King Norodom into acknowledging French "protection." Norodom was in no position to resist: In August 1863 he signed a treaty granting France control of Cambodia's foreign policy, the right to install consular posts, and the establishment of a French *resident superieur* at the capital, Phnom Penh. The French mollified the Thai by granting them control over the western Cambodian provinces of Siem Reap and Battambang.

Laos was taken by the French thirty years later. At first the colonizers were not much interested in the remote Lao kingdoms but then decided that, like Cambodia, Laos would make a useful buffer state. The only problem was that Laos was still under Siamese rule. The French solved this simply by claiming that the northern Lao kingdom,

Luang Prabang, still owed allegiance to Vietnam and thus, by extension, to France.

In 1886 French authorities appointed Auguste Pavie to a vice-consulate in Luang Prabang. Pavie skillfully won over the Lao by convincing them that a French protectorate would rid them of the hated Siamese. He curried the favor of Lao royalty and organized expeditions to explore the Mekong and spread French good will. When the Thai resisted, Pavie was ordered to claim all Thai territory east of the Mekong. The colonial administration in Vietnam sent three columns of soldiers across the mountains and deployed a naval force in front of Bangkok. The Thai had no choice but to relinquish their claims; on October 3, 1893, they recognized France's Lao protectorate. Fourteen years later, after adding two provinces west of the Mekong to Laos, the French completed their Indochina Union by abruptly retaking the Cambodian provinces of Siem Reap and Battambang from the Thai.

Because the colonizers regarded the more populous, economically exploitable Vietnam as their greatest asset in Southeast Asia, they hardly touched the Khmer way of life. Cambodia's 1 million inhabitants seemed less industrious than the Vietnamese, and their land afforded fewer resources that the French wanted. The French felt no need to alter the fundamental elements of Khmer society: subsistence farming, Buddhism, and divine kingship.

Through daring and ingenuity, French diplomat Auguste Pavie brought the Lao kingdom of Luang Prabang into France's Indochinese empire.

Under the French, King Norodom played the role of god-king with enthusiasm, if not always to good effect. He enjoyed broad powers within the country but used them less to help his people than to help himself. The common people accepted his divine will without question, even though many in the elite bureaucracy and the royal court were less impressed. In 1883 Norodom's half-brother, Prince Si Votha, staged a rebellion when the king signed a treaty turning French "protection" into outright control. Many peasants, fearful that the French would seize their lands, joined Si Votha's armed guerrilla bands and fought effectively against the French until Norodom falsely announced that the French had restored control to him. The French bought off Norodom by keeping him on the throne but surrounded him with their own sympathizers. Thinking the Cambodians inept as executives, they also began to import Vietnamese—some 60,000 by 1908—to administer the country.

Despite such heavy-handed political maneuvering, the French colonial setup benefited Cambodia in several ways. The French improved transportation and communications and turned Phnom Penh into a charming colonial city. The Khmer increased rice production, and as a partial result, the population tripled. There was another vital benefit: Under the French, the Cambodian people were united for the first time in years. Inadvertently, French efforts to create a subject state fostered a sense of nationhood in a people long enslaved by their neighbors.

The Cambodians' sense of nationhood was especially aided by the French-led restorations of Angkor Wat and seventy-one other ruins of ancient Cambodia in the nineteenth and early twentieth centuries. The deciphering of Angkor's reliefs and inscriptions by French archaeologists awakened long-dormant feelings of national pride in Cambodians, and this reinforced the sense of unity that the imposition of a colonial administration had started. That renewed nationalism, and the sense of rebellion that flowed from it, was slow in coming but, once started, would acquire a momentum of its own.

In Laos, French colonialism was also benign. Except as a buffer state between Vietnam and Siam, Laos seemed of little use to the French. There were few resources the French wanted, little land suitable for agriculture, and formidable natural barriers within the country that discouraged creation of an elaborate transportation or communications network. For their part, the Lao people accepted French rule without evident protest.

France unified the country in 1893, placing Vientiane, Champassak, Xieng Khouang, and other provinces under the king of Luang Prabang. A French *resident superieur* took office in Vientiane, but the colonialists retained much of the existing system of local government and allowed the

Europeans gather on the steps of an Angkor temple for an afternoon among the Khmer ruins.

Lao to take an active role in their own administration. The French controlled trade and the judicial and educational systems but with a lighter hand than they showed elsewhere in Indochina. Even their numbers were small: in 1940 the Lao nation of 1 million was administered by less than 600 French officials.

By and large, the Lao cooperated with French rule. Occasionally a tribal chief in the mountains would resist. Chinese bandits, too, were sometimes nettlesome. But the only major protest by ethnic Lao themselves was raised when the French proposed to annex Laos to Vietnam. Already upset by the presence of imported Vietnamese administrators, the Lao vigorously opposed the measure. Wisely, the French dropped the idea.

Beyond that, very little changed in Laos during the period of French rule. The French built only one major road, down the Mekong from Luang Prabang to the southern town of Pakse, and some smaller ones running east to Vietnam. They also tried raising coffee on the Bolovens Plateau in the south and mined for tin in Khammouane. The Lao, for their part, exhibited little of the restlessness of their Cambodian or Vietnamese neighbors. This stable situation might have lasted indefinitely, had not outside forces once again intervened.

Communism and a world war

After World War I, the victorious Allied powers met at Versailles to plan the outlines of the postwar world. During the conference a slightly built, twenty-nine-year-old Vietnamese calling himself Nguyen Ai Quoc (Nguyen the Patriot) presented the conferees with a petition calling for the independence of Vietnam. His suit was quickly dismissed, but the issue he raised did not die. Vietnam was restive under colonial rule; many bureaucrats and intellectuals trained by the French to run the colonial administration longed for self-determination. Nguyen Ai Quoc, a nationalist who had embraced communism while studying and working in Paris, had dedicated himself to this cause. Although he would not see his homeland for another twenty years, he would one day lead the movement for independence. By that time, he would be known by a more familiar name: Ho Chi Minh.

For a decade Ho Chi Minh worked as a Communist bureaucrat in Moscow and elsewhere. Then, on February 3, 1930, he met with other Vietnamese students and intellectuals in Hong Kong to organize the Indochina Communist party (ICP). In their blueprint for revolution, the ICP's founders had first favored a purely Vietnamese party but then agreed to a Comintern order to include Cambodia and Laos. Although Vietnam's independence was paramount, they realized, as a party newspaper noted, that "If the Vietnamese revolution succeeds but French imperialism is lurking in Laos and Cambodia, the revolutionary power in Vietnam will be shaky."

At first, the ICP had difficulty winning Cambodians and Lao over to their cause. One reason was the history of enmity between the peoples: Cambodians and Lao had little love for the Vietnamese, who dominated the ICP. The semifeudal Khmer and Lao also did not readily understand the ICP's leftist rhetoric and anticolonial message. With little prospect of success among the Khmer or Lao themselves, the ICP's organizers began to recruit candidates from a more receptive group: Vietnamese living in Cambodia and Laos.

The first Communist cells in Cambodia and Laos were made up almost entirely of Vietnamese residents of those lands. Communist agents from Vietnam infiltrated west to Cambodia in the early 1930s; by November 1934, there were five Communist cells operating in Cambodia, all made up of local Vietnamese (and occasionally ethnic Chinese). A few Khmer did join, but on balance the groups remained non-Khmer. In Laos, the same pattern emerged: Communist Vietnamese organizing small bands among their own kind. Expanding membership beyond ethnic Vietnamese was difficult in Laos, too: a 1934 party report on Laos stated that "our Laos section seems little more than [an ethnic Vietnamese] subdivision of the Communist Party." French officials, for their part, suppressed the Communists with arrests and jailings. Throughout the 1930s they reported nothing but "the most perfect calm" in Laos.

Things were less calm across the border in Vietnam. There, the ICP and other groups staged uprisings against French rule all through the decade. Each time, though, French armed might and French secret police managed to preserve colonial rule. By the end of the decade, the ICP still had little real power to use against the French. The coming of another world war, however, would shatter the seeming iron hold of France on all of Indochina.

In the spring of 1940, when France's home army was easily crushed by Adolph Hitler's tanks and troops, an ally of Germany cast a covetous eye on Indochina. Imperial Japan, desiring strategic gain and use of Indochina's natural resources, clamored for a presence there, and Germany agreed. In September 1940, with the acquiescence of the French collaborationist government, thousands of Japanese troops marched into Vietnam from China. They set up military bases but allowed the French colonialists to continue their civil administration. By 1941 all of Indochina was ruled by this uneasy joint control of French and Japanese.

The Japanese takeover of French Indochina sparked events that shocked Cambodia. In November 1940 the Thai, with Japanese support, invaded Cambodia and seized the western provinces of Siem Reap and Battambang. Four months later the Japanese signed a treaty with

Lao colonial officials oversee the construction of a bridge in Laos in 1923. The country's terrain made road building difficult, and the French installed only one major route.

Siam approving the takeover. Then in May 1941 two Japanese divisions arrived in Phnom Penh. Its commanders announced that European control over Asian nations was at an end.

The Japanese entry and the Thai takeover of the western third of their country traumatized Cambodians. French "protection" of Cambodia was obviously a fraud. The educated, modern urban elite, who had supported the French, felt betrayed. So too did the traditional Cambodian Buddhist hierarchy, who had never liked the French. In their anger, the two groups, usually at odds, formed an alliance against the outsiders.

Leading them was a dynamic Khmer nationalist named Son Ngoc Thanh. Thanh was a Khmer Krom, an ethnic Cambodian born and raised in southern Vietnam. An urban intellectual and newspaper publisher, Thanh was a fervent nationalist respected by both the Buddhist nationalists and the urban elite. He was also close to the Japanese and believed their rhetoric about freeing Cambodia from France. Thanh used money obtained from elite Khmer to finance Buddhist monks as they traveled around Cambodia, preaching the gospel of nationalism to ordinary Khmer.

The French, naturally, were worried by this alliance of Cambodia's monied class and religious leaders. On July 18, 1942, they arrested Hem Cheav, a popular and eloquent nationalist monk. Seizing the moment, Thanh called for a protest, and two days later, 1,000 to 2,000 people, including hundreds of Buddhist monks, marched in Phnom Penh protesting the arrest—the first large-scale anticolonial protest in Phnom Penh's history. The French police overreacted, beating the peaceful protesters and making arrests. To Thanh's dismay, Japanese officials, who had quietly encouraged his movement, simply stood by and watched. Now a wanted man, Thanh fled Cambodia for Japan, still convinced that a Japanese victory in the war would mean freedom for his country. Hundreds of other nationalists were forced to escape from Phnom Penh.

Thanh's protest dramatically illustrated the depth of anticolonial sentiment the occupation had bred in Cambodians. Although his movement faltered, other anticolonial organizations remained active. The ICP, which was still dominated by the Vietnamese, cultivated its strength among ethnic Vietnamese and small bands of Khmer Communists in eastern Cambodia. Its organization was the Vietminh, a front of many groups led by the ICP under Ho Chi Minh. In western Cambodia, a non-Communist Khmer Issarak (Independence) movement was formed with Thai patronage. Larger than the ICP in Cambodia, it was also looser and less disciplined and included nationalist elements of many different stripes.

The war years brought another change to Cambodia. In April 1941 the aged King Monivong, a member of the Sisowath branch of the royal family (and nephew of King Norodom) who had been on the throne since 1927, died.

Desiring a new king who would work their will, the French passed over Monivong's nominal heir and selected as king an eighteen-year-old great-grandson of King Norodom named Sihanouk. Norodom Sihanouk, a lycée student in Saigon, had a reputation as a playboy and a lightweight—just the sort to sit on the throne and not cause trouble. And trouble was what the French dearly wanted to avoid, for, as the war dragged on, it became evident to them that the Cambodian nationalist movement would not simply fade away after the Japanese left.

Cambodia: toward independence

By early 1945 the war was going badly for the Japanese. The Americans and their allies were closing in on the home islands, and Japan was running out of men and materiel. Desperately needing Indochina's resources and strategic position, the Japanese military decided that it could no longer afford its *modus vivendi* with the French colonial administration. On March 9, 1945, Japanese troops staged coups against the French in Vietnam, Cambodia, and Laos. Some French resisted, but most were caught off guard. Thousands were disarmed, arrested, and jailed. On March 13, the Japanese forced the young King Sihanouk to declare Cambodia independent of France. Son Ngoc Thanh returned from exile on May 30, and Sihanouk, again under intense Japanese pressure, named him to the post of foreign minister.

In one stunning stroke, the Japanese had ended French rule. But the Japanese version of "independence" was harsh. They imposed direct military rule, pressed 7,000 Khmer into military service, and demanded involuntary labor from others. They forced students to learn Japanese and suppressed any moves toward genuine independence. At the same time, they permitted the Thai to strengthen their grip on the northwestern provinces.

Many were dissatisfied. Sihanouk seemed a callow collaborationist, willing to bend to any foreign master. Some nationalists wanted Thanh to lead the country. Emboldened by their support, Thanh gradually challenged the king more and more. At last, on August 9, 1945, his allies stormed the royal palace and staged a coup against the king. The Japanese, who were only days away from surrender to the Allies, did not resist. Thanh, now prime minister, pledged to resist the return of French rule.

The French were not so easily cowed. After the Japanese capitulated, they returned to Indochina in force. On October 10, 1945, British, Indian, and French troops entered Phnom Penh. They arrested Thanh on October 15, shipped him to Saigon, and then to Paris. King Sihanouk was allowed to remain on the throne, provided he acknowledged French control. This he did, for reasons of purest expediency. "We are too poor to support or defend ourselves," he later explained. "We are a nation of 3 million people sandwiched between 20 million and 12 million Siamese." Already, Sihanouk was earning a reputation as a survivor.

The end of the war left Indochina in turmoil. In Vietnam, Ho Chi Minh had declared an independent republic on September 2, 1945. Facing rebellion in their principal colony, the French tried to keep Cambodia calm by holding elections. The Cambodians responded enthusiastically. In September 1946 the Democratic party, a collection of moderate Thanhists, urban intellectuals, and other democratic, independence-minded elements, swept the elections. Their leader, a royal prince of the Sisowath family branch named Youthevong, became prime minister in a consultative assembly. The assembly began to fashion a modern, constitutional government for Cambodia and appealed to the French to grant the country independence under their guidance before radical elements took the country by force.

King Sihanouk loathed the Democrats, since their program threatened the Khmer king's traditional powers. Then fate, or perhaps conspiracy (it was never clear which), intervened on Sihanouk's side. In July 1947, Prince Sisowath Youthevong died mysteriously in a French hospital. With Sihanouk's connivance, the French named a conservative prime minister who replaced Democratic members of the cabinet with ministers loyal to the king.

Backed by the French, Sihanouk now had the upper hand. However, he still had to face opposition from urban nationalists, Communists, and the non-Communist Khmer Issarak in the northwest. The Issaraks were still the largest independence group, but they were dependent on Thailand's progressive postwar leader, Pridi Phanomyong, for support. Pridi, who had earned international favor by returning Battambang and Siem Reap provinces to Cambodia in 1947, considered Sihanouk a collaborationist. With his help, the Issaraks seemed well positioned to challenge the king.

But once again, forces worked in Sihanouk's favor: In August 1947 Pridi resigned. Right-wing military men took over and suspended his support of the Issaraks. Without Thai help, the Issaraks dissolved into separate factions. So did the Democratic party, which never recovered from the death of Prince Youthevong. The disunity of the Issaraks and Democrats left the king as the only strong non-Communist figure on the national scene. Wisely, King Sihanouk realized that the demise of these forces did not mean that his subjects no longer wanted freedom. In a few

The end of Japanese occupation. Their own war lost, two Japanese soldiers sit and watch fighting between Vietnamese and French and British troops in Saigon in October 1945.

years, the shrewd monarch would himself embrace independence, moderation, and good relations with all neighbors—a course that, ironically, could have been drawn up by the Democrats.

While the Democrats and Issaraks struggled against the French and Sihanouk to build a non-Communist power base in Cambodia, other Khmer sided with the Vietminh to foment revolution. Among these were leftists who, having fled Cambodia during the war, had recruited for the ICP among the Khmer Krom of southern Vietnam. By 1947 these revolutionaries were filtering back to Cambodia, where they established "liberation committees." Prominent among these revolutionaries was Achar Mean, a former teacher who had changed his name to Son Ngoc Minh (a combination of Son Ngoc Thanh and Ho Chi Minh). Son Ngoc Minh was the first Khmer to join the ICP after the war; by 1949 French intelligence reported that he led a "well-armed band of about three hundred" leftist revolutionaries inside Cambodia.

Son Ngoc Minh's band, along with similar groups, formed the basis for a permanent Communist movement in Cambodia. On April 17, 1950, Son Ngoc Minh and 200 other delegates (including 105 Buddhist monks) met in southwestern Cambodia for a First National Congress of Khmer Resistance. The Communists declared a Unified Issarak Front (UIF), appointed a revolutionary government, and declared "independence" from France. The next year, 1951, Son Ngoc Minh and other Cambodians took the first steps to found a formal Communist party, which they called the Khmer People's Revolutionary party (KPRP). Son Ngoc Minh became chairman; a former teacher and monk named Tou Samouth became his deputy.

The party's actual power was minimal, for the Vietnamese Communists controlled the Cambodian movement. It was the Vietnamese-led ICP that had ordered the creation of the KPRP; one year later, these same Vietnamese informed the KPRP that eventually "the three revolutionary parties of Vietnam, Cambodia, and Laos will be able to unite to form a single Party: the Party of the Vietnam-Khmer-Laotian Federation." So pervasive was Vietnamese control that when the Khmer Communists founded the KPRP, Vietnamese Communists wrote the party statutes and draft platform in Vietnam, then sent it to Cambodia for translation. The Vietnamese even asserted (in a document from November 1951) that "the Vietnamese Party reserves the right to supervise the activities of its brother parties in Cambodia and Laos."

Despite Vietnamese domination, Son Ngoc Minh had already taken pains to gather more native Khmer under his banner. Throughout the late 1940s and early 1950s he and other Khmer Communist leaders organized and trained Khmer Communists in party schools inside Cambodia. Although dependent on the Vietnamese, there were Khmer leaders determined to build a native Cambodian Communist party.

In the late 1940s King Sihanouk was in a delicate position. The French, his nominal allies, were fighting difficult wars against the Vietminh in Vietnam and against the Communists and various Issarak factions in Cambodia. In Cambodia they had resorted to more violence, increasing the size of "free-fire zones" and forcibly relocating hundreds of thousands of peasants into fortified villages. The violence and relocations only increased anti-French sentiment, especially among the peasants, who were Sihanouk's natural constituency.

To make matters worse for Sihanouk, in 1951 new elections returned the Democrats to power, and the next month the old nationalist Son Ngoc Thanh returned to Cambodia from exile in France. Thousands cheered him wildly in Phnom Penh before he disappeared into the bush to join a force of Issarak guerrillas fighting the king. The situation degenerated: Several months later the French estimated that the Phnom Penh government controlled only one-third of the country. In May 1952 student demonstrations broke out in Battambang, Kompong Cham, and Phnom Penh. The central authority seemed to be crumbling everywhere.

The deteriorating French position concerned Sihanouk deeply. As king, he still had the sentimental support of the Cambodian masses, but as a political leader he could not ignore the growing national call for independence. Faced with such pressures, Sihanouk engineered an incredible turnaround. In June 1952 he dismissed his cabinet, made himself prime minister, and promised the people of Cambodia that they would be independent within three years. Asking full powers to run the country, he pledged to submit his actions to a "people's court" after that period.

The dramatic move paid off. The National Assembly granted Sihanouk his powers, while the Issaraks and Democrats fell into confusion. Despite vigorous protest from some quarters, Sihanouk's bold move saved his position in Cambodian politics. Seven months later, he dissolved the National Assembly, arrested prominent Democrats, and declared martial law. The next month he left on a world tour to convince France and other nations that Cambodia must be granted independence before the Communists seized power.

Sihanouk's "Royal Crusade for Independence" was another brilliant act of self-preservation. He played cleverly to each audience: In France, he tempted the government with promises of strict neutrality in its conflict with Vietnam. In America, he begged for support against the stubborn French colonialists. Returning to Cambodia, he took up "internal exile" in Siem Reap, swearing to remain until independence was achieved. Issarak factions flocked to him, and Khmer troops under French command defected to

King Norodom Sihanouk, the shrewd, mercurial leader of Cambodia, sits in full ceremonial court dress at the royal palace in 1953.

him. Soon his personal army numbered over 30,000 troops and police. The French, reckoning that Sihanouk would protect French business interests in Cambodia, negotiated a settlement. On November 9, 1953, the French transferred all powers to him, and colonial troops marched out of Phnom Penh.

Sihanouk had achieved an extraordinary political feat: independence without revolution and on his own terms. Even the leftists had trouble opposing him. When in spring 1954 a coalition of leftist Khmer and Vietminh troops attacked his forces, the king ordered a successful counterattack, at the same time scorning the Khmer Communists as Vietnamese puppets. By outmaneuvering the French and denouncing the Vietnamese and their Khmer allies, the king had embraced the most elemental positions of Khmer nationalism. As other events took over in the spring of 1954, Norodom Sihanouk had earned the right to call himself the father of Cambodian independence.

Laos: World War II and beyond

The years between the beginning of World War II and 1953 worked as many changes in Laos as they had in Cambodia. Laos was calmer than Cambodia during the war, but, just as in Cambodia, the Japanese-French joint rule stimulated disillusionment and nationalist sentiment. Like Cambodia, the country lost territory: when the Japanese first came, they forced the French and King Sisavang Vong of Luang Prabang to cede the Lao regions west of the Mekong to Thailand, an area of 54,000 square kilometers.

These events sowed the seeds of a revived Lao nationalism. Other events raised Lao consciousness. Many more Lao entered the national administration, which had been dominated by imported Vietnamese. In 1941 the first Lao-language newspaper was published and the first Lao radio station opened. The educational system was upgraded, and a National Renovation Movement made up of native, educated Lao was organized to celebrate Lao literature and arts. With such a movement the Lao, though ruled jointly by French and Japanese, began to believe more and more that they should shape their own destiny.

Although the country was quiet, some Lao resisted both the Japanese and the French. In northeastern Thailand, the Thai regent Pridi Phanomyong organized a Lao Seri (Free Lao) movement. These guerrillas, primarily Lao who had fled to Thailand at the beginning of the war, formed small bands armed and supported by the United States and Great Britain.

In March 1945 the Japanese staged a coup against the French administration, just as they had in Cambodia, and forced the king to declare independence. The coup left Lao nationalists in a difficult position: they welcomed the end of French rule but had little love for the Japanese. Trying to solve this situation was Prince Phetsarath, a member of the royal court who served as viceroy (a sort of deputy king) and prime minister under both the French and the Japanese. Phetsarath was an able prime minister and a dedicated nationalist. (It was he who had brought many native Lao into his administration to offset French and Vietnamese influence.) His solution was to wait: believing the Japanese would lose the war, he cooperated with them while laying the groundwork for a daring postwar move.

When the Japanese capitulated to the Allies in August 1945, Phetsarath bid swiftly for Lao independence. In Vientiane he informed the French *resident superieur* that he had no authority to resume power. On September 1, 1945—one day before Ho Chi Minh declared Vietnamese independence from France in Hanoi—Phetsarath issued a proclamation to the French population of Laos declaring that, since France had been unable to defend Laos from the Japanese, the ties between their nations were ended. Two weeks later he announced the union of the kingdom of Luang Prabang and the southern districts into a single kingdom of Laos. In these moves, he was strongly supported by other nationalists, including the Lao Seri guerrillas filtering across the Mekong from Thailand.

King Sisavang Vong, however, supported the returning French. On September 17 he informed Phetsarath that he considered the French protectorate agreement still in force; on October 10 he stripped the prince of all his offices. The nationalists gathered around Phetsarath in Vientiane were furious. On October 12 they announced the creation of a provisional constitution and a people's assembly and nominated a rebel government called the Lao Issara (Free Lao). When Sisavang Vong refused to back the new government, they voted to depose him.

Phetsarath's Lao Issara government included an extraordinary collection of diverse and mutually distrustful nationalist groups. Some enjoyed Chinese support, others Thai, and still others were backed by the Vietnamese. Among those also involved were two brothers of Phetsarath who would soon follow very different paths to power in Laos: Prince Souvanna Phouma and his half-brother, Prince Souphanouvong.

Souvanna Phouma had joined the independence government with some reluctance. Born in 1901, he studied engineering in Hanoi and France. In 1931 he returned to Laos, where he rose quickly in the public works section of the civil service. During the war, he had supervised road construction in northern Laos. He was regarded as a moderate, a technocrat brought into the Lao Issara government to administer public works and transportation.

His half-brother Souphanouvong followed a similar path at first: born in 1912, schooled in Hanoi, university trained in Paris. Dynamic, self-assured, good at sports and studies, he exceeded his half-brother's accomplishments in almost everything. When he returned to Laos, however, he received a much lower civil service job than Souvanna Phouma—engineering work in Vietnam. There he met and married a Vietnamese woman named Le Thi Ky Nam. She

A Cambodian soldier of the French colonial army sips muddy water from a rice field while on patrol during the French Indochina War in 1952.

was intelligent, ambitious, and strongly anti-French, a stance that reinforced Souphanouvong's own considerable ambitions, anticolonialism, and left-leaning sentiments. His sympathy for the Vietnamese, rare in a Lao, made him the ideal candidate when Ho Chi Minh needed someone to communicate with Phetsarath's Lao Issara government at the war's end.

Ho Chi Minh realized the strategic importance of Laos to the battle for Vietnamese independence. As the Japanese occupation faltered, Vietminh cadres infiltrated into the country, arming the local Vietnamese. Later, Vietminh troops entered border areas in large numbers; some had even clashed with Free Lao troops in the south. Ho decided that with Prince Souphanouvong's help, he could end the fighting and unite Lao and Vietnamese anticolonial forces.

At Ho's request, Souphanouvong returned to Laos in early October 1945 with a guard of Vietminh troops. The local Lao in the southern town of Savannakhet greeted him warmly. He traveled north to Vientiane, where he met with Lao Issara officials and offered to join them—on condition that he be named foreign minister and commander in chief of the armed forces. Knowing that the powerful Vietminh backed him, the Lao Issara ministers gave him both jobs. In the next month, the prince staffed his military command

with experienced Vietminh officers and raised large numbers of troops among both Vietnamese and Lao. On November 5 he departed for the south to defend Laos from the returning French.

Just then, Ho Chi Minh unexpectedly sabotaged the Lao Issara's resistance efforts. On March 6, 1946, he signed a *modus vivendi* with France. In exchange for French recognition of Ho's Democratic Republic of Vietnam as a "free state" within the Indochina Federation, Ho agreed to allow a French military presence in northern Vietnam for five years. Ho's action doomed the Lao Issara; without Vietminh support, it was too weak to prevent a French return to Laos. The Lao Issara government made some conciliatory moves, such as restoring King Sisavang Vong to the throne, but they were isolated and unsupported. Resistance crumbled as French troops entered the country from Vietnam, joining armed Frenchmen who had fought as guerrillas against the Japanese. The only significant opposition they met was in Thakhek, where on March 21 Vietnamese and Lao troops under Souphanouvong fought

a savage battle against them. It was the prince's first taste of combat, and he directed his troops with great courage. But his forces lost the battle, suffering over 1,000 casualties. Souphanouvong himself was badly wounded by aerial strafing as he crossed the Mekong River into Thailand.

The Lao Issara position crumbled. On April 24 French troops occupied Vientiane; on May 13 they took Luang Prabang. The Lao Issara's leaders fled to Bangkok and set up a government-in-exile. Joined there by Souphanouvong, they plotted fitfully and organized small armed raids into Laos.

Meanwhile, the French had decided to work with King Sisavang Vong. On August 27, 1946, they reached a *modus vivendi* with the royal government that recognized a unified kingdom under Luang Prabang but also restored French control. To sweeten the deal, they convinced Thailand in 1947 to return the territories west of the Mekong they had seized during the war. They held elections for a constituent assembly, and another constitution, promulgated May 11, 1947, declared Laos an independent state within the French Union. The French, though, still controlled the nation's most important business.

When the French returned to Laos in 1945 and 1946, thousands of local Vietnamese, fearing retribution for their wartime support of the Japanese, fled to Thailand. This huge exodus—some 80 percent of the prewar Vietnamese population in Laos—decimated the Communist movement in Laos, which for years had recruited almost exclusively among the Vietnamese. The remaining ICP Communists in Laos, utterly dependent on the Vietminh, began to seek out new recruits. They also joined forces with Prince Souphanouvong.

At the time, Souphanouvong was in Bangkok, trying to gain American support against the French. It was a reasonable bid: President Franklin Roosevelt had said during the war that the French should not return, and American OSS agents in Vientiane had been openly hostile to the returning French. But Roosevelt was dead, and the new administration was preoccupied with containing international communism. U.S. officials told the prince that anticommunism took precedence over support for anticolonial movements.

Meanwhile, the rest of the Lao Issara government-in-exile was quarreling itself into impotence. The demise of Pridi Phanomyong's progressive Thai government in late 1947 threw the Lao Issara into further disarray. The next spring the new military government ordered exiled Lao soldiers to leave Thailand. When an amnesty was declared in 1949, the Lao Issara split into two factions. Prince Souvanna Phouma, among others, returned to Laos and joined the royal government. Others joined the Vietminh, who were fighting the French after the breakdown of Ho's 1946 agreement. Weakened, beset by problems, the Lao Issara officially dissolved on October 24, 1949.

Prince Souphanouvong had already distanced himself from the Lao Issara leadership during the years of exile. On March 26, 1949, he had resigned his posts. Accusing the Lao Issara of being a "government of children" and "retarded fossils," he resolved to continue his fight against the French. Since Western support was not forthcoming, the prince turned again to the Vietnamese.

By 1949 the Vietminh were fighting a full-scale guerrilla war against the French. To harass the staging areas used by the French in Laos, they were once more infiltrating Laos's border provinces. There, aiding the few Lao Communists still in the country, they vigorously recruited among the local population—the non-Lao tribal groups who had always resented Vientiane's nominal rule. Souphanouvong joined the Vietminh and Lao Communists near the border. Within a year, he and his comrades were ready to declare an open resistance movement.

From August 13 to 15, 1950, they held a Laos National Assembly, with over 100 Lao of different backgrounds in attendance. The Vietnamese discreetly stayed in the background as the assembly denounced the 1949 declaration of independence and called on the people to resist the French. The assembly also formed a resistance government, with Souphanouvong as president and foreign minister. At the bottom of the assembly's manifesto was the name by which the resistance movement would come to be known: Pathet Lao (Land of the Lao).

Souphanouvong was not the actual leader of the Pathet Lao, although his energy and dynamism made him an important figure in the movement. Real power rested with the Communist leaders of the so-called Committee of the East, who had been organizing revolutionary groups in Laos since the end of the war. The prince was a tremendous asset to them, for his popularity and royal blood lent legitimacy to the Pathet Lao in the eyes of ordinary Lao.

Kaysone Phomvihan, defense minister in the new government, was the movement's real leader. Half-Vietnamese by birth, Kaysone was an ICP-trained revolutionary who had studied law in Hanoi during World War II and later had been active in Savannakhet. Another leading Communist, Nouhak Phoumsavan (economy and finance minister), was an ICP member closely connected to the Vietminh. Phoumi Vongvichit (interior minister) was a Souphanouvong lieutenant who had been a governor of Sam Neua Province. These men—Kaysone, Nouhak, Phoumi Vongvichit, and others—were in some respects more important revolutionaries than Souphanouvong himself. Their commitment to communism was far clearer than the prince's. Throughout the movement's life, Souphanouvong would act as something of an able, involved figurehead, while actual power stayed in the hands of the ICP veterans.

Geneva

French Indochina was convulsed by revolution. Eight months before the Lao Communists formed the Pathet Lao, Ho Chi Minh had called on the nations of the world to recognize Vietnamese independence. Communist China and the Soviet Union immediately responded. In retaliation, on February 7, 1950, the United States, which had reluctantly continued to support the French, recognized the Western-aligned governments of Vietnam, Laos, and Cambodia. The U.S. was in a difficult position: When Secretary of State Dean Acheson complained that the French were "stalling" in granting independence, the French responded that theirs was a fight against international communism—an argument the U.S. found hard to counter. The French stance took on added force when the Korean War broke out in the summer of 1950. Since global anticommunism was its principal aim, the U.S. increased its support for the French war effort. To help further, on September 9, 1951, it signed an aid agreement with the French-backed government of Laos.

But aid was not keeping the Vietminh out of Laos. Large Vietnamese units operated freely in the border provinces, especially Sam Neua. Pathet Lao forces were still insignificant—only about 300 troops in Sam Neua—but its allies, the Vietminh, fought hard against French outposts in Laos. In April 1953, there was a sharp increase in Vietminh infiltration and violence: Fifteen battalions of Vietminh captured the provincial capital of Sam Neua, destroyed a column of retreating French Union soldiers, then linked up with another Vietminh column and advanced on Luang Prabang. They were stopped just thirteen kilometers from the capital by stiffened resistance and the threat of monsoon rains. The United States rushed aid to Laos, including six large C-119 military transport planes with civilian crews, and stepped up aid to Thailand and to French forces fighting in Vietnam.

In the meantime, Souphanouvong's half-brother, Prince Souvanna Phouma, had risen to the post of prime minister of Laos. Like Sihanouk in Cambodia, he urged the French to negotiate complete independence in order to blunt the Communist drive. The French government continued to stall, but their military situation was eroding rapidly. Even with greater U.S. backing (by September 1953 the United States was paying 70 percent of the cost of the war) they could barely hold on. At last, the French decided to cut their losses by freeing Laos and concentrating on Vietnam.

Another round of independence negotiations between Laos and France opened up on October 15, 1953. A week later they produced a treaty that declared the kingdom of Laos a fully independent and sovereign state. The two

Left. *A helicopter lands to pick up Franco-Vietnamese troops wounded at Hine Siu village in Laos during the battle for Seno airstrip in January 1954.*

Above. *Led by a French officer, Vietnamese soldiers of the 3d Parachute Battalion counterattack Vietminh troops in Hine Siu, January 1954.*

Below. *A French Union soldier stops to take the gun of a dying Vietminh as Franco-Vietnamese forces clear the jungle surrounding Seno airstrip.*

countries pledged themselves to a mutual defense—a move that, in effect, allowed French troops to stay in the country to fight the Communists. They were needed: In late 1953, after the rainy season's end, the Vietminh renewed their pressure on the Lao-French alliance. In the south a column crossed the Annamese Mountains and briefly occupied the southern Mekong towns of Attopeu and Thakhek. Infiltration also increased in the north.

The French, obliged to defend Laos, sensed a double opportunity. Their commander in Indochina, General Henri Navarre, wanted to break the nine-year cycle of guerrilla war by luring the Vietminh into an all-out battle. To draw Ho Chi Minh's troops into a trap, and at the same time block the traditional invasion route from northern Vietnam to Laos, Navarre garrisoned a remote, inaccessible valley just inside the Vietnam border. Ringed by mountains, it was named Dien Bien Phu.

When Navarre occupied Dien Bien Phu with six paratroop battalions in late 1953, the commander of the Vietminh, General Vo Nguyen Giap, did not respond as the French expected. Instead of rushing into a pitched battle, he quietly surrounded the isolated post with two divisions of infantry. In February 1954 he emplaced 105MM artillery pieces, which had been painfully wrestled through 800 kilometers of jungle by peasant-porters, on the mountain crests overlooking the valley. By March, Giap had almost 50,000 combat troops and 31,500 logistical personnel near Dien Bien Phu, more than six times Navarre's 13,000 men.

The French were trapped. Supplied only from airstrips hundreds of kilometers away, their garrison was pounded day and night by Giap's artillery. Instead of a sturdy blockade between Laos and Vietnam, Dien Bien Phu became a nightmare for France. As French troops fell back into an ever-shrinking perimeter, the government in Paris appealed for help from the United States. Secretary of State John Foster Dulles suggested that the U.S. might intervene, but Congress, top military men, and, ultimately, President Dwight Eisenhower opposed him.

The Vietminh siege of Dien Bien Phu destroyed France's political position. The French people were weary of war. In February 1954 the government accepted a Soviet proposal to end the war with a peace conference at Geneva, Switzerland. They would be joined at the conference (which was also convened to end the Korean War) by other involved parties: the United States, the United Kingdom, the Communist Chinese People's Republic, Sihanouk's Cambodian government, the royal government of Laos, the Vietminh, and the French-supported government of the Emperor Bao Dai in Vietnam. The conference began in early May, one day after the last French positions at Dien Bien Phu were overrun.

The big powers that assembled at Geneva in 1954 to make peace in Indochina had many different agendas. France wished to find an honorable way out of its terribly expensive and bloody colonial war. The Soviet Union,

emerging from the Stalin era, wanted to ease international tensions and cultivate better relations with the French. Communist China wanted to protect its southern flank from the United States and demonstrate that it was a rational world power committed to peace. For its part, the Eisenhower administration wanted to protect the non-Communist royal governments in Vietnam, Laos, and Cambodia. The United Kingdom stood somewhere in the middle, firmly backing Western intentions but also wanting to prevent a wider war in Southeast Asia. And allied to these big powers were the indigenous forces: three royal governments backed by the West on one side, the Vietminh and its much smaller Khmer and Lao Communist allies backed by China and the Soviet Union on the other.

Strangely, although everyone realized that the most important Indochinese conflict was in Vietnam, the conference's first concerns were about Cambodia and Laos. The Vietminh insisted that the Free Khmer (Son Ngoc Minh's small band of Cambodian Communists) and the Pathet Lao were legitimate liberation governments that deserved equal representation at the conference. Negotiators for King Sihanouk and the Lao royal government scorned these assertions, claiming (rightly) that the indigenous Communists amounted to little more than a few hundred Vietnamese-backed rebels. They and their Western allies asserted that Cambodia and Laos would be at peace if the Vietminh left their territory. This argument lasted all through May and into June until China and the Soviet Union, realizing that the talks might break down on this point, agreed to by-pass the issue. Angered by their patrons' flexibility, the Vietminh nevertheless capitulated.

The next debate covered the political future of Cambodia and Laos. Again, the talks might have ended over this point had not the larger Communist powers decided that their own security took precedence over the wishes of their Indochinese clients. Chinese premier Chou En-lai indicated on June 16 that, since Cambodian rebel forces were small, a political settlement there would be "easily" achieved; he added that while resistance forces were larger in Laos, a regroupment of those forces to the provinces bordering Vietnam (Sam Neua and Phong Saly) was possible. When asked about Vietminh objections, Chou said it would "not be difficult" to persuade Vietminh "volunteers" to leave Cambodia and Laos if it was understood that all foreign forces would be withdrawn. The Soviet Union also agreed to this formula.

In making these concessions, the Soviet Union and China had all but abandoned the rebel movements in Cambodia and Laos. The Vietminh, deeply dependent on China for supplies and political support, had little choice but to comply; so, in turn, did the Khmer and Pathet Lao

---

Premier Chou En-lai, China's representative to the international peace conference on Indochina at Geneva, strides toward a meeting at the Palais des Nations in 1954.

forces dependent upon the Vietminh. Chou En–lai's desire to avoid a conference breakdown cleared the way for agreements on political and military settlements in Cambodia and Laos. As the details of Franco-Vietminh cease-fires and disengagement in Vietnam were worked out, the Laos-Cambodia arrangements were also completed.

The agreements on Cambodia included the removal of foreign troops, including Vietminh and French Union troops (but not French military advisers), within ninety days of a July 20, 1954, cease-fire; demobilization of native insurgents, with a guarantee that they could participate in national elections in 1955; the establishment of an International Control Commission (ICC) to enact the agreements; and a guarantee from Sihanouk's government that it would not permit foreign military bases or join military alliances "not in conformity with the principles of the Charter of the United Nations."

The Lao agreements were similar: removal of foreign forces, a withdrawal of the Pathet Lao to Sam Neua and Phong Saly, a government pledge of "special representation" for the Pathet Lao in those provinces, and national elections open to all political factions. In addition, the royal government was permitted to retain 1,500 French "advisers" at two bases. As in Cambodia, the royal government was allowed to import arms only for "self-defense," although the government made clear that, as in Cambodia, it would import arms and make alliances whenever it felt its security was threatened. Lastly, an international commission and a joint commission of royal government and Pathet Lao representatives were established to supervise the accords.

The agreements were a great success for both King Sihanouk in Cambodia and Prime Minister Souvanna Phouma in Laos. The Vietminh, too, had achieved much for themselves: control over the northern half of Vietnam, a French withdrawal south of the seventeenth parallel, and a guarantee of elections in 1956 that they were sure would bring all of Vietnam under their control. The Chinese also fared well, gaining a Communist state (North Vietnam) to their south and reasonable assurances of Lao and Cambodian neutrality.

But the Pathet Lao had gained little from the accords and the Khmer Communists even less. The Pathet Lao were merely allowed to regroup in territory they already controlled. The Khmer Communists were not even granted that much. They felt the Russians, Chinese, and Vietnamese had sold them out for their own purposes. That sense of betrayal, deep and enduring, reinforced Khmer Communist suspicion of outside powers and sowed the seeds of a bitter harvest in the months and years ahead.

French soldiers bury their dead at Dien Bien Phu in December 1953. By January 1954, the Vietminh had surrounded the French garrison. In May they overran it, effectively ending the French war in Indochina.

The Heritage

The lands of Cambodia and Laos only entered Western consciousness in the nineteenth century, and even then they remained little known. Well into the twentieth century American maps labeled these regions simply "French Indochina." Such ignorance obscured the varied populations, divergent histories, and rich heritages that have shaped the two countries.

The inhabitants of present-day Cambodia and Laos are descendants of peoples that migrated from southern China beginning in the first centuries A.D. These settlers—the Khmer in Cambodia and the Lao, hill-Tai, Mien, and Hmong in Laos—came to a hot, tropical land of valleys and mountains. They soon adapted to the seasonal changes that govern life on the Indochina Peninsula: six months of dry, temperate weather followed by six months of harsh, prodigious rainfalls. All learned to subsist on the foods that thrive in a watery environment: rice and fish.

Under the influence of Indian Hinduism and Buddhism, the Khmer and Lao developed the concepts of divine kingship, royal authority, and social hierarchy that were central in the formation of the kingdoms of Angkor and Lan Chang (early Laos). Education, government, and the arts flourished in these kingdoms, and beautiful *wats* (temples) constructed in that time still dot the two lands. But while Angkor united the Khmer, Lan Chang did not assimilate its varied mountain dwellers into Lao culture. Ethnic diversity has remained the norm in Laos, precluding a strong sense of nationhood.

A row of carved demons lines the walkway to the south-gate entrance of Angkor Thom, one of Cambodia's ancient architectural masterpieces on the Angkor plain.

Cultural Divide

Above. *A dirt road winds through the mountains near Long Cheng in northern Laos. The country's topography—steep, forested mountains and narrow valleys—isolated Laos's ethnic communities and discouraged national unity.*

Right. *Residents of Luang Prabang walk toward a new year's celebration along the Mekong River. Over the years, three Lao kingdoms arose on the banks of the mighty Mekong—Luang Prabang, Vientiane, and Champassak.*

Indian Influence

Cambodia and Laos both have deep roots in the advanced civilization of ancient India. The Khmer adapted the customs of Indian merchants and priests who traveled to the region starting in the second century A.D., and the resulting Indianized society provided the framework for the Angkor empire.

In Laos, Prince Fa Ngum, who was raised at Angkor, gathered Buddhist monks, scholars, and craftsmen at Luang Prabang after 1353. He made India's Therevada Buddhism—a school stressing simplicity, contemplation, and personal responsibility—the central teaching for lowland Lao.

Above. *A bas-relief from the temple of Angkor Wat (built between 1113 and 1150 A.D.) depicts a scene from the Hindu epic poem, Ramayana.* Right. *A huge Buddha statue sits inside a cave in Pak Hou, downstream from the royal capital of Luang Prabang in Laos.*

Royal Capitals

Laos and Cambodia have beautiful royal cities that once sparkled with traditional Buddhist festivals. Luang Prabang, whose name means Town of the Golden Buddha, became the royal court of Lan Chang in 1353 and remained the royal seat of Laos, though Vientiane later became the country's administrative center.

In contrast, Phnom Penh's reign as Cambodia's royal city has been brief. Angkor was the heart of Cambodia's ancient kingdom, but as a result of Thai invasions the capital was moved to Oudong and finally to Phnom Penh in the nineteenth century.

Left. *Laotians celebrate the end of the year with a colorful procession to be followed by prayers and festivals along the streets of Luang Prabang in April 1968.*
Above. *A parade of elephants passes the Khmer king's viewing stand during a royal ceremony inside Phnom Penh's palace grounds, February 1968.*

Following page. *Cambodian merchants crowd the street at an open-air market in downtown Phnom Penh in March 1980.*

Spirits and Amulets

While Buddhism is the religion of the lowland Lao, many of Laos's hill and mountain tribes—more than half the population—remain adherents to animism. For these high-ground dwellers the trees, mountains, rivers, and animals of Laos are alive with spirits, called *phi*, which can control external events. Angry *phi*, for example, can cause disease or ruin crops. They therefore need to be supplicated with sacrifices and rites. Customs often vary from village to village, with each having its own forbidden areas, unlucky words, and bad omens.

A Mien woman carries her sleeping child in an ornate backpack. The Mien (also known as Yao) migrated to Laos in the middle of the nineteenth century from southern China and settled along the country's lower mountain slopes.

Cambodia is predominantly Buddhist, although the Khmer are also extremely superstitious. They find room in their Buddhist faith to worship animist spirits similar to those revered by the tribesmen of Laos. For most Cambodians, especially those in the countryside, Buddhism is a way of life, not a strict religion, and folk practices, such as wearing magic scarves, sucking holy amulets, and being tattooed with magical designs, do not conflict with it. They blur beliefs together, making little distinction between Buddhist and animist practices.

A Cambodian refugee in Thailand in 1979 displays his tattoos, written in Sanskrit, which are meant to guard against bullet and knife wounds.

Buddhism

Above. *Lao youths wearing Buddhist robes sit before a relief inside Wat May, a Buddhist temple in Luang Prabang.*

Right. *Buddhist monks stroll near the western entrance to the temple of Angkor Wat. Buddhism was a primary target for the victorious Khmer Rouge regime after 1975. The Communists disrobed monks, burned religious books, and destroyed Buddhist statues and temples. They could not, however, destroy the Buddhist faith. Many Cambodians, in fact, turned to Buddhism for spiritual strength against the murderous Khmer Rouge revolution.*

The Delicate Balance

King Sihanouk and his negotiators had achieved all they could have hoped for at Geneva. Cambodia's territory would be cleared of Vietminh troops, it was free to seek outside military support if threatened, and its independence had been tangibly demonstrated. Left-wing opposition groups, already stripped of the anticolonialism issue by Sihanouk's campaign against France in 1953, would have to focus their attacks on social and economic problems, which were abundant. Yet even amid these problems, most Cambodians showed little desire to alter their government. Sihanouk remained the one towering legitimate figure of national leadership.

Under Cambodia's constitution, however, the monarch was expected to be nonpartisan. To lead his country into the future, Sihanouk realized that he would have to enter the political arena in a partisan way. Accordingly, in March 1955 the forty-three-year-old king announced a dramatic move: he would abdicate the throne in favor of his father, Norodom Suramarit. Now, as Prince Sihanouk, he was free to

run for elective office. He began by organizing a political front, the Sangkhum Reastr Niyum (Socialist Community). Officially a "national rally which fights against injustice, corruption, exaction, oppression and treason," its purpose was to translate Sihanouk's political skills and popularity into concrete, constitutional power. In the months before the September 1955 elections required by the Geneva accords, the movement campaigned on the dual themes of socialism and democracy. Adherents from all parts of the political spectrum were welcomed.

The prince claimed the reason for this extraordinary political redefinition was that he would otherwise be shut off from knowing the true situation among his people. As he said in a broadcast, "The palace is stuffed full of a hierarchy of court mandarins and intriguers. They are like bloodsucking leeches that attach themselves to the feet of elephants." Sihanouk would break out of his palace cocoon by leading a political movement of national dimensions. He traveled frequently to the provinces to meet the people, entering villages by car or helicopter, making speeches, and chatting with peasants.

His electoral opposition was fragmented, split between small right-wing parties and the leftist Pracheachon party, a legitimate, aboveground party organized by local Communists (including members of Son Ngoc Minh's KPRP) after the Geneva Conference. During the campaign Sihanouk's police harassed his opponents mercilessly, even beating and jailing leftists throughout the country. The outcome was never in any doubt. In the September 1955 balloting the Sangkhum garnered 83 percent of the vote, winning all ninety-one seats in the National Assembly. Its founder-leader became prime minister.

Winning the elections had been simple, but energizing a poorly educated civil service and inspiring a sense of popular participation in government was another matter entirely. To accomplish this, the resourceful prince devised another instrument of leadership by creating a biannual national congress of the Sangkhum. These meetings, held on the open grounds next to the royal palace and lasting several days, provided an occasion for thousands of citizens, many listening by radio, to hear issues raised and complaints lodged against government ministers. The parliamentary National Assembly was then obliged to address and implement these matters. Sihanouk took pride in the direct democracy that these congresses provided and stage-managed the meetings personally.

But along with his political strength and virtuosity, Sihanouk displayed some serious weaknesses. He could play the prince of darkness as well as Prince Charming. Raised in a royal household, he lacked the capacity to brook criticisms of his policies, because he saw them as

attacks on his person. Even at the Sangkhum congresses, where complaints were allowed against individual ministers, direct criticism of Sihanouk was risky. And, although he claimed to be just a "simple citizen," Sihanouk also enjoyed the lingering aura of his semidivine heritage: he often treated his ministers and even foreign ambassadors in a commanding fashion, subjecting them to bouts of manual labor during symbolic trips to the countryside or to organized sports for his own amusement.

Sihanouk's tolerance for corruption as virtually a method of government baffled some foreign observers, who expected better of a modernizing prince. Outsiders were also thrown off stride by the contrast between his childlike enthusiasm for the arts—filmmaking, saxophone playing, and jazz composition—and his extreme aggressiveness in political matters. He was quite confident of his political abilities but suspicious and hypersensitive to what he saw as insults or diplomatic slights. His verbal tirades, published in his own press or delivered to foreign journalists, contributed to a reputation for verbosity, egocentric histrionics, and indiscretion. Such behavior generated frequent charges that he was unpredictable, unreliable, and arrogant.

Despite the success of his Sangkhum movement, Sihanouk still faced serious challenges to his personal populism both from the radical left and the traditionalist right. His long-time adversary, the conservative, pro-American Son Ngoc Thanh, lurked in exile in Thailand with a mercenary band of about 3,000 followers, called the Khmer Serei (Free Khmer). On the left was the Pracheachon, which included both veteran Communists and some young Cambodians who had studied abroad (with government assistance) and returned home infected with what Sihanouk called "international progressivism." In March 1958 Sihanouk called for the second election since his abdication. The prince personally chose all the candidates for office from the ranks of the Sangkhum. The Pracheachon party fielded several candidates, but once again they suffered from fraudulent vote counting and considerable harassment by Sihanouk's police. The prince's list officially won 99 percent of the vote, and the National Assembly remained composed of Sangkhum members.

Having again suppressed the leftists, the prime minister moved against his conservative opponents and also against his traditional foreign enemies, Thailand and South Vietnam. The reason he gave was the "Bangkok Plot" of March 1959. Sihanouk described the plot as a conspiracy to overthrow him hatched by three prominent conservatives: Sam Sary, a veteran politician who wanted to form a pro-Western political party; Son Ngoc Thanh, in Thailand; and Governor Dap Chhuon of Siem Reap Province, a former Khmer Issarak who led a sizable private army in Cambodia's northwest. Sihanouk accused the three of attempting to infiltrate Khmer Serei troops into Cambodia. He charged that Thailand was funding the

Norodom Suramarit is crowned Cambodia's new king outside the Royal Palace in March 1955, following Prince Sihanouk's decision to abdicate the throne and run for public office.

plan, with help from the United States Central Intelligence Agency and South Vietnam. When Sihanouk announced that he had information linking Sam Sary to the CIA, Sary fled the country. The prince then ordered the arrest of Dap Chhuon (who was soon shot "while trying to escape") and smashed his private force.

The incident quieted the right wing in Cambodia for several years and demonstrated to Sihanouk the political potential of denouncing outside threats to his rule. A few months later, a second incident reinforced Sihanouk's claims of foreign intrigue. A postal package bomb exploded in the antechamber of Sihanouk's mother, Queen Kossamak. The queen was not hurt, but even the most skeptical observers were hard put to dismiss the prince's denunciations of his perceived enemies abroad.

The next year Sihanouk orchestrated two events that entrenched his power still further. In June 1960, he held a national referendum to choose the nation's foreign policy. The voters were offered four choices: a photograph of Sihanouk (representing neutrality), a photograph of Son Ngoc Thanh (representing alliance with the United States), a red ballot (for communism), or a blank one (no opinion). Ninety-nine percent of the voters chose the picture of the prince. In the meantime, Sihanouk's father, King Suramarit, had died on April 13, 1960. The National Assembly, the

armed forces, and government ministries called upon Sihanouk to become the chief of state. After pro-Sihanouk demonstrations outside the National Assembly, the constitution was duly amended to provide for this new office, while the throne remained unoccupied. Notwithstanding the crude methods used to effect the constitutional revision, Sihanouk had scored another brilliant political improvisation. He was now chief of state and prime minister, combining both the highest formal status and also administrative control. He kept the monarchy in reserve and later designated one of his sons as the future chief of state.

At the same time that he maneuvered against his conservative foes, Sihanouk sought to disunite his leftist opposition by co-opting some of its members. After the 1958 election, for example, he brought into his cabinet certain prominent, French-educated young Cambodian leftists. Among these was Hou Yuon, who had written a noted doctoral dissertation exposing the exploitation of Cambodian peasants by the urban elite; he became minister of commerce and industry. Hu Nim, a former Democratic party member turned Socialist, also joined Sihanouk's government. Later, in the 1962 elections, Sihanouk allowed leftists to run for office as members of the Sangkhum. Hou Yuon became finance minister, and Hu Nim briefly served as minister of commerce. He was replaced by Khieu Samphan, a leftist assembly member who had returned from study in France in 1959 to become editor of the French-language *Observateur.* Khieu Samphan had also written a provocative dissertation, one which asserted that Cambodia must end its dependence on the international economy and move, under state management, from its current agricultural base to an industrial economy. In the cabinet, both Hou Yuon and Khieu Samphan pushed for reforms of Cambodia's economy.

Although the leftist intellectuals were eventually forced out of the government by right-wing pressure, some of their thinking was adopted by the chief of state. Even though he was well accustomed to Cambodia's time-honored government corruption, he was prepared to nationalize the import-export sector, as well as banking, in order to keep private entrepreneurs from reaping illicit profits from foreign financial aid. Sihanouk also shared the leftists' distaste for dependence on Western aid, with its attendant political strings and threats to his foreign policy of neutrality. His suspicion of Western political motives, exacerbated by growing difficulties between his nation and two American allies, set the stage for a dramatic break in the coming years.

Foreign policy of maneuver

Notwithstanding its diplomatic success at the Geneva Conference, Cambodia in 1954 faced an insecure future squeezed between two hostile neighbors. Thailand, which had seized Cambodian territory in World War II, now aligned itself with the United States against communism. Vietnam, which had pushed the Khmer empire out of the Mekong Delta, was now bitterly divided between north and south, each with its external patrons. Thailand and South Vietnam both had disputed borders with Cambodia. North Vietnamese forces, moreover, might intrude into Cambodian territory if they resumed fighting in the South. In guarding against Thai or Vietnamese encroachment, Cambodia might seek help from larger powers, but at the expense of its neutrality. Prince Sihanouk tried to answer all these problems by adopting a course of neutrality. In practice, his policy consisted of repeatedly veering back and forth between the West and the Communist states throughout his years in power.

At Geneva, Cambodia's leaders had explored the prospects for an American guarantee of their nation's security. No formal commitments were reached, but just after the conference, America promised protection to Cambodia indirectly by means of the Manila Pact. Signed on September 8, 1954, the pact was a collective security treaty between the United States, the United Kingdom, France, Australia, New Zealand, Pakistan, Thailand, and the Philippines. It provided for the united action against Communist aggression that had been lacking at the time of the French defeat at Dien Bien Phu. In a separate protocol to the pact, the new treaty partners, who called themselves the Southeast Asia Treaty Organization (SEATO), unilaterally extended their collective security pledge to Cambodia, Laos, and the Republic of Vietnam (South Vietnam). By this means the three states, which were obliged by the Geneva accords to refrain from military alliances so long as their security was not threatened, gained SEATO's protection nevertheless.

In December 1954, Sihanouk proclaimed neutrality as the foreign policy of his government. On a visit to Peking in early 1955, he had publicly rejected SEATO's unsolicited offer of protection. (The offer, however, was not withdrawn by SEATO, so in effect the prince was able to have it both ways.) A few months later, in April 1955, the prince strengthened his commitment to formal nonalignment in conversations at the Bandung (Indonesia) Conference of Non-Aligned States. At the conference Chinese foreign minister Chou En-lai encouraged Sihanouk to deny military bases to the United States. The foreign minister of North Vietnam, Pham Van Dong, added his pledge of peace, friendship, and respect for the territorial integrity of Cambodia, so long as it pursued neutrality.

Meanwhile, relations between Cambodia and its neighbors Thailand and South Vietnam were worsening. Both countries seized upon Sihanouk's 1955 Peking visit as an occasion to close their frontiers with Cambodia, thereby denying Cambodia the vital port of Saigon, upon which it depended almost totally. The quarrel between Bangkok and Phnom Penh was fueled both by the activities of Son Ngoc Thanh's Khmer Serei and also by Thailand's failure to relinquish the ancient Khmer temple at Preah Vihear, on the border of the area it had occupied during World War II. On October 23, 1961, following an exchange of mutually hostile and unacceptable remarks by both chiefs of government, Cambodia broke diplomatic relations with Thailand. The situation was not improved when, on June 15, 1962, the International Court of Justice ruled that Thailand must return Preah Vihear to Cambodia. The Thai leadership found it galling to lose to their weaker neighbor; the fact that a former American secretary of state, Dean Acheson, argued Cambodia's case before the court made the matter all the more perplexing to them.

On its eastern frontier, Cambodia faced other threats to its sovereignty. In 1959 the Communist leadership in Hanoi decided to resume armed struggle for unification of Vietnam. As part of their war plans they began to build the Ho Chi Minh Trail, which was to become a complex network of roads, paths, and way stations through southeastern

Cambodians kneel before Prince Sihanouk in a traditional deferential pose during the former king's visit to their village in 1961.

Laos and eastern Cambodia. The trail soon became the main supply route for Communists fighting in the South. Supplies and eventually North Vietnamese soldiers traveled down the trail to secret Communist base areas along the ill-defined Cambodian-South Vietnamese border.

Even prior to this infiltration, South Vietnamese government forces had entered Cambodia. In addition to raids over territorial disputes, the South Vietnamese had violated Cambodian territory in pursuit of its non-Communist domestic opposition—the political-religious sects that operated in the area in the 1950s and 1960s. When the Ho Chi Minh Trail was built, Sihanouk and others feared that North Vietnamese and Vietcong intrusions into Cambodia might precipitate even more counterattacks or "hot pursuit" by the South Vietnamese. The South Vietnamese intrusions, as displayed in the Cambodian press, tended to reinforce the proposition that national independence required opposition to both South Vietnam and Thailand. Rather than joining them in defensive alignment with the United States against communism, Cambodia sought broader support for its neutrality and independence.

United States-Cambodia relations

In the mind of U.S. Secretary of State John Foster Dulles, neutralism between communism and the free world was immoral, and alliances were a constructive means of avoiding war rising out of regional imbalances of power. Sihanouk's reluctance to ally his country with SEATO and the U.S., therefore, exacerbated existing misunderstandings and bolstered elements within the American government determined to reorient the wayward nation into solidarity with the anti-Communist bloc. Sihanouk was reluctant to diminish his freedom of action by joining the Western camp. He was also doubtful that U.S. policy would prevail in the region. Neutrality had become a rallying cry for his people, a symbol of national independence that Sihanouk skillfully used to bolster his popular leadership. Yet the more he stressed his independence, the more he antagonized American policymakers.

Sihanouk was distressed by the fact that SEATO's protection extended to his hostile eastern and western neighbors, Thailand and South Vietnam. He worried about the generous American backing of Thai and South Vietnamese military security programs and also about the clandestine role the CIA played in subsidizing Son Ngoc Thanh's Khmer Serei. (Such was his anger against the U.S. intelligence service that, in later years, he wrote a bitter retrospective on foreign policy entitled *My War with the CIA*.) He considered Robert McClintock, U.S. ambassador to Cambodia in 1955, a CIA agent and was equally suspicious of the American ambassador in Bangkok, John Peurifoy (who had been in Guatemala during the CIA-orchestrated overthrow of the government there in 1954). The "Bangkok plot" of 1959, the package bomb sent to

the royal palace a few months later, and Khmer Serei radio propaganda transmitted from South Vietnam and Thailand also implicated the United States in a campaign to do away with Sihanouk and his neutral Cambodian policy. The fact that hostile intentions could be denied by the United States government made no difference in Sihanouk's eyes.

At one time, however, Cambodia's relations to the United States had been fairly good. Once the 1954 Geneva settlement removed the Vietnamese Communist military presence from his territory, Sihanouk had accepted American military assistance, including thirty American weapons instructors. Secretary Dulles had even traveled to Phnom Penh in February 1955 to negotiate military assistance for Cambodia. The nation also accepted some economic project assistance, such as the "Friendship Highway" connecting Phnom Penh with the seaport of Kompong Som and financing for consumer goods imports. About 30 percent of annual Cambodian police and military budgets was covered by the U.S. assistance, and the economic aid amounted to about $25 million per year.

American military aid, however, came with conditions that Sihanouk found insulting. He resented restrictions on the use of American weapons—they could not be used against South Vietnamese army forces that entered Cambodia—and end-use inspections by the American military mission. In addition, the United States evaded Sihanouk's diplomatic initiatives to convene a conference to provide international verification and guarantee of his borders. Sihanouk's exasperation on these issues made him ready to renounce American assistance. The November 1963 murders in Saigon of America's political clients (President Ngo Dinh Diem and his brother) by America's military clients (South Vietnamese army officers) convinced the prince to make a break with Uncle Sam. Although he maintained diplomatic relations, he terminated all U.S. aid programs in November 1963.

The end of American aid struck severe blows to both the economically privileged class and the armed forces elite. The notoriously corrupt elites could no longer enjoy the fruits of import rights and real estate deals extended to them by American aid administrators. Cambodian army officers also felt deprived as training assignments in the United States and handsome provisions of military equipment ended.

At the same time that Sihanouk veered away from the United States, he warmed up to Peking. Within a month of the cutoff of U.S. aid, China had picked up some of the slack by extending military assistance. In the next year and a half Sihanouk seemed to confirm the widespread American perception that he was a Communist Trojan horse, by staging massive anti-American demonstrations outside the U.S. Embassy in Phnom Penh in March 1964. Meanwhile, Vietcong and North Vietnamese Army units frequented Cambodian border areas in growing numbers, and the U.S. Air Force, assisting South Vietnamese army units, periodically penetrated Cambodian airspace. The issue of border violations was aired inconclusively at the UN Security Council in May 1964, and in October 1964 the Cambodian National Assembly threatened to break diplomatic relations with the U.S. over the matter. On May 3, 1965, following an alleged U.S. air strike in the Parrot's Beak area of Cambodia, Sihanouk bitterly severed all but consular relations with the United States.

Sihanouk later explained his break of relations with the U.S. as a "politically imperative" response to the indignation and fury of the peasants who were "subject to daily bombings and shellings." Yet even if he was shoring up his patriotic appeal to a portion of the rural population, Sihanouk was feeding the suspicions and resentments of his right-wing opponents within the army and the urban elite. These two groups—the army officers and elites who had gained so much from American economic assistance—never lost their resentment of Sihanouk after the cutoff of American aid.

Evolving Khmer communism

The intricate balancing act performed by Sihanouk involved not only his neighbors and their great-power backers but also the political factions within his nation, which were constrained but not eliminated by his highly personalized leadership. One of those factions was the Communist party of Kampuchea (CPK). This highly secret party had led a life of peril, persistence, and intrigue throughout its short life.

During the mid-1950s, the radical leftist opposition in Cambodia experienced two contrasting migrations. The first was a move from the countryside of Cambodia to refuge in North Vietnam. When the Vietminh left Cambodia for North Vietnam as part of the 1954 Geneva cease-fire agreement, the Vietnamese Communist leadership decided to include in the withdrawal about 1,000 Khmer national resistance fighters. Almost 200 of the departing stalwarts were members of Son Ngoc Minh's KPRP (Son Ngoc Minh himself went to North Vietnam directly from Geneva). After arriving in North Vietnam, the Khmer Communists received further revolutionary training. With their exit, though, the party at home suffered. The KPRP members who left for Vietnam included the revolutionaries best known by the people (and, not incidentally, by the police), and their exit left the party's internal leadership to less-experienced and lesser-known figures.

With Son Ngoc Minh and other Khmer Communists in North Vietnam for an indefinite period, a temporary Central Committee took charge of the revolutionary struggle in Cambodia. This opened the way to the Cambodians of the second migration—the younger generation of leftists who had gone to study in France, been radicalized there, then returned to their native country to take up revolutionary

struggle. These former students formed the core of what was to be a new Communist party in Cambodia, one with very different origins from the ICP-dominated party of Son Ngoc Minh.

Particularly important among the new recruits to the now-bifurcated party were two former students named Saloth Sar and Ieng Sary. Sar came from a landowning family. After an only ordinary performance in carpentry school, in 1949 he was given one of the few dozen Cambodian government scholarships to study radio electronics in France. A year later Ieng Sary, a Khmer Krom originally from southern Vietnam, arrived in France to study commerce and political science. Sary was a veteran of the postwar independence movement. He had organized the first student demonstrations against the French in Phnom Penh after World War II.

While in Paris, the two young men became friends and joined a study circle of Cambodian Marxist-Leninists. There they met other Cambodian students and leftist intellectuals (such as those who would serve briefly in Sihanouk's government, Hou Yuon and Khieu Samphan).

Cambodian men wash their clothes in a stream in 1957. The cotton material was one of the many goods imported by Cambodia thanks to U.S. financial assistance in the 1950s.

Sary and Sar were exposed to the radical ideas of the French Communist party and other foreign students. Youth conferences and work camps in East Germany and Yugoslavia also shaped their thinking. In time, they also became brothers-in-law, for they both married sisters from the well-placed Khieu family. The Khieu sisters, themselves leftists, recorded better academic records than their husbands and became involved in radical activities when they returned to Cambodia.

Saloth Sar first challenged the royal government at home by signing an open letter denouncing then-King Sihanouk's dissolution of the National Assembly. In 1953, after also failing his exams, he was denied further scholarship support. He traveled home in time to join the underground ICP and participate in a minor way in the Vietminh's Cambodian campaign during the months preceding the Geneva Conference. After the 1954 cease-fire and the exit of the leading Khmer Communists to North Vietnam, Sar remained in Cambodia. He smuggled himself into Phnom Penh with twenty fellow students and became active in the city's Communist party committee. Ieng Sary returned from France in 1957.

To operate under Sihanouk's rules of the game in independent, post-Geneva Cambodia, the veteran Communists and newly arrived student radicals founded the Pracheachon party, fought for political power, and protested what they saw as lingering colonialism and feudalism. The Vietnamese Communist government in Hanoi, however, gave them scant support, finding it more expedient to encourage Sihanouk's neutralism in the hopes of keeping the American military out of Cambodia. The Vietnamese preferred to postpone domestic revolutionary challenges in Cambodia until they achieved their goal of uniting Vietnam.

While the Vietnamese Communists thus restrained their Khmer comrades, Sihanouk routed them physically and politically. During the late 1950s, his police pacified or killed 90 percent of the party's membership, while his Sangkhum party dominated them politically. Under these circumstances, the morale of the clandestine party in Cambodia tumbled. Unlike their Communist comrades in Vietnam or Laos, the KPRP could claim no territory under their control, no armed force, and no guaranteed political rights. The editor of the party's weekly journal, *Pracheachon*, was assassinated in October 1959. The next year thirty other leftist editors, including Khieu Samphan, were arrested, beaten by the police, and held for three weeks while their newspapers were banned. Some regional party leaders surrendered to the government, and the leading old-guard Communist remaining in Cambodia, Sieu Heng, defected to Sihanouk in 1959, after having worked

Cambodians march in an anti-American demonstration staged by Prince Sihanouk outside the U.S. Embassy in Phnom Penh in March 1964.

four years as a secret agent for the police. The rural network of the party was torn apart, and the urban element was held together only by inexperienced hands.

To assess the near-fatal damage of the Sieu Heng betrayal, the KPRP convened its Second Congress for three days in late September 1960 in empty railroad cars warehoused at Phnom Penh's Central Station. Twenty-one delegates were present, from a party reduced to less than 800 nominally active members. Fourteen of those delegates came from the rural network and seven from urban areas. During the congress, the urban-oriented former students proposed more active struggle; they were implacably opposed to Sihanouk, no matter what the Vietnamese Communists said. The North Vietnam-oriented veterans, however, supported Hanoi's restraining advice. The congress ended in a stalemate between these groups. Even though three urban radicals—Saloth Sar, Ieng Sary, and another former student named Moong—were elected to the number-three through five positions in the party's Central Committee, the policy line adopted, after some debate, went only so far as to "prepare for armed struggle," not to launch it. The name of the party was changed to the Worker's Party of Kampuchea, in accordance with the designation that the Vietnamese Communists had adopted for themselves in 1951. The former monk Tou Samouth, an old-line party

stalwart who had worked with Son Ngoc Minh and the Vietminh since the earliest days of the postwar revolutionary movement, was chosen general secretary.

Less than two years later, Tou Samouth was apparently arrested and disappeared without a trace. The party's number-three member, Saloth Sar, was elected secretary general in February 1963 by a third party congress. Ieng Sary was promoted to the party's Politburo, and five former students joined the twelve-man Central Committee. The breach between the younger hard-line revolutionaries and veterans of the Vietminh-inspired party began to grow. Some have even suggested that Sar betrayed Tou Samouth to the police, but the truth may never be known.

Within a few years the party's name was changed again, this time to the Communist party of Kampuchea. The former students began to dominate the party's structure, so much so that in later years, party historians would refer to the 1960 railroad car congress as the first and founding meeting of the Marxist-Leninist party of Kampuchea. By the summer of 1963, Saloth Sar and Ieng Sary had left Phnom Penh to set up underground headquarters in the northeast, along the South Vietnamese border. Another associate from Paris, Son Sen, abandoned his teaching job to go underground one year later. (Their wives joined them in September 1965.)

In late 1964 Saloth Sar started a long march up the Ho Chi Minh Trail to Hanoi and thence to China. In both capitals he was cautioned against, but not deflected from, his resolve to overthrow Sihanouk. The Chinese made clear their support for Sar's party, with an eye to separating him from dependence on the Vietnamese comrades—a position he was already inclined to avoid. Meanwhile, the security police at home did their utmost to hunt down those whom Sihanouk labeled Khmer Rouge (Red Khmer), and the Communists began to heed Saloth Sar's advice to take to the bush. For his part, Saloth Sar became a shadowy figure. He would not emerge in public for many years. By then, he would be known by a different name—Pol Pot.

Thus, as the 1960s wore on, Cambodian politics became more polarized, both in relation to domestic issues and external alignment and hostilities. Sihanouk could try to hold the middle ground, but he was being squeezed from the right, which wanted a renewal of U.S. aid and support, and from the left, where power had passed from old-line leftists to Saloth Sar and other radicals dedicated to violent revolution and Communist rule. Both groups would continue their pressure on the prince. For the moment, however, Sihanouk maintained his own power and his country's precarious neutrality.

Laos: pending a settlement

In the decade following the Geneva accords of 1954, the kingdom of Laos, like Cambodia, maintained a delicate balance between competing political forces. Unlike its

Soldiers and officials of the Pathet Lao disembark a riverboat in northeastern Laos, a Communist stronghold, in the early 1960s.

southern neighbor, however, Laos had no Sihanouk to dominate the political landscape. Instead, the struggle between leftists, rightists, and neutralists took on a wearying seesaw rhythm, with no side gaining a decisive advantage until many years had passed.

The Agreement on Cessation of Hostilities in Laos had designated for the Pathet Lao (PL) two northeastern provinces (Phong Saly and Sam Neua) adjoining North Vietnam in which the PL could concentrate their fighting forces, "pending a political settlement." This vague formula left dangerously undetermined the status of both the PL and the Royal Lao government in these provinces. Although the royal government had unilaterally declared its resolve "to integrate all citizens, without discrimination, into the national community," using "general elections by secret ballot," the settlement lent itself to a virtual partition of the country, if the Pathet Lao chose to insist upon the ambiguities in their favor—which they did without hesitation.

While the People's Army of Vietnam began to withdraw according to the cease-fire timetable, Prince Souphanouvong negotiated with the Laos government concerning the regroupment of PL troops into the two designated provinces. But it became quite clear that the PL was not ready to see the royal government's writ run into "their" area until a political settlement was reached. Nor were members of the International Commission for Supervision and Control (ICSC), the supervisory commission set up by Geneva, able or willing to clarify the issue by entering and surveying the area. Prime Minister Souvanna Phouma was known to believe that Lao personalities, freed from external interference, could reconcile their differences in a truly patriotic spirit. Souvanna seemed to believe that the hardcore Communists among the Pathet Lao were not numerous enough to control Souphanouvong or the destiny of the resistance movement. By October 1954, however, Souvanna had resigned the premiership. A few weeks earlier, his moderate minister of defense, Kou Voravong, while visiting the home of Foreign Minister Phoui Sananikone, was killed by a sniper firing through a window. Souvanna was replaced by a militant pro-Western politician, Katay Don Sasorith.

Despite the Manila Pact protocol that extended SEATO's protection to Laos, and the small French military force that remained in Laos after Geneva, American military planners and Secretary of State Dulles still saw little chance of "saving the situation" there. State Department prodding, however, and a visit by Dulles to Laos in February 1955 brought the U.S. government into direct budgetary and training support of the Royal Lao Army. Prime Minister Katay was encouraged enough by the U.S. actions to launch commando operations against the Pathet Lao in the two disputed provinces.

Notwithstanding the reported withdrawal of Vietminh forces from Laos, the Royal Lao government complained without satisfaction to the ICSC about the presence of

A commissar of the Lao People's Revolutionary Party exhorts villagers to support the Pathet Lao during a political meeting in the early 1960s.

Vietnamese "volunteer" officers holding official posts in Sam Neua Province. It also protested the continuing presence of Vietminh troops in Laos, the "forced recruitment" of natives into the Pathet Lao forces, and the illegal introduction of arms for the Pathet Lao. The Vietnamese presence was particularly troublesome. Not long after the Geneva Conference the North Vietnamese command headquarters for Laos, know as Doan (Group) 100, was moved to Ban Na Meo, directly on the border, a short walk from the PL headquarters in Sam Neua Province. As many as 300 North Vietnamese advisers may have worked at Doan 100, with two-thirds assigned to military functions and one-third to political tasks. With their help, the Pathet Lao grew from between 1,500 and 3,000 at the time of the Geneva settlement to 6,000 three years later.

On March 22, 1955, in a bamboo building at the Pathet Lao's base in Sam Neua, a hard core of twenty-five Laotian veterans of the Indochina Communist party held a constituent congress of the Lao People's Revolutionary party (LPRP). Such a party had been in preparation since 1951, when the ICP had ostensibly dissolved in favor of separate national revolutionary parties. Kaysone Phomvihan was named general secretary of the new all-Laotian party.

The secret party followed the technique that Ho Chi Minh had used in Vietnam during World War II: it organized a broad, progressive national front that was secretly directed by Communist party leadership. Thus, on January

Laotian civilians use their feet to smooth an airstrip in Sam Neua Province in 1959. The airfield was used to resupply RLA troops stationed in Communist-controlled eastern Laos.

6, 1956, the revolutionaries held a national congress to create the Lao Patriotic Front, or Neo Lao Hak Sat (NLHS). As described in retrospect by Phoumi Vongvichit, the fourth-ranking leader:

We learned that our side had won victories, but our forces remained weak; the enemy had been defeated and compelled to withdraw his troops from our country, but the United States—a stronger and more affluent country—became involved in our affairs. Thus it was absolutely necessary for us to change our fighting objectives and expand our national front.

The leading role of the Communist LPRP in the new front, however, was not revealed, even though it "acted as the backbone of the Front." The political appeal of the NLHS was designed to compete nationwide for popular support among both the peasants and the commercial classes. Prince Souphanouvong was prominently featured as the elected president of its Central Committee. The front's slogan called for a "peaceful, independent, neutral, democratic, unified and prosperous Laos." Support for the monarchy as well as the Buddhist religion was included with this stance. The NLHS built up the conventional subgroups of a national front with a Youth Union, Women's Union, trade unions, Buddhist Association, Christian Association, Farmer's Association, and tribal associations. Thus, a public progressive and patriotic movement paralleled the secret network of Laotian party cells. The LPRP, meanwhile, manipulated the larger movement to its own ends, namely thwarting the counterrevolutionary efforts of

the "American imperialists" and expelling the "U.S. interventionists" and "traitorous lackeys" from the country.

When the Katay government lost its parliamentary support on February 22, 1956, the more pliable Souvanna Phouma returned as prime minister. He pledged to give highest priority to national reconciliation. His half-brother Souphanouvong proposed a resumption of direct talks, and Souvanna accepted. In August, they declared jointly for a durable "cessation of hostile acts," legal entry of the NLHS into political activity, and the integration of the two northeast provinces and PL troops under royal government authority. Supplementary elections were to be held (with female suffrage, a long-time goal of Souphanouvong) and the NLHS was to be represented in a national union government, which would follow a policy of peace and neutrality. By the end of 1956 the two princes announced that a united government would be formed even before the supplementary general elections and that the two northern provinces and PL forces would be placed under the authority of the new government immediately after its formation. Both Peking and Hanoi expressed their approval of the arrangement by issuing declarations of respect for Laotian independence and territorial integrity.

The U.S. Embassy in Laos, under an aggressive ambassador, Graham Parsons, however, found the new government quite distressing, since it legitimized Communist participation in the Laotian government. On April 16, 1957, the U.S. government, joined by the British and French, addressed identical notes to the royal government expressing gross disapproval of the "extraneous conditions" (such as accepting aid and diplomatic representation from Communist states) being exacted by "dissident groups enjoying no constitutional status" for their reintegration into the national community. Ambassador Parsons later testified to Congress that he "struggled for sixteen months to prevent a coalition government." Yet the National Assembly and Souvanna ultimately could not be deterred from reaching a compromise with their countrymen in the Pathet Lao.

After a visit to Washington in January 1957, the rightist former prime minister Katay launched a violent propaganda campaign against the Lao Patriotic Front. Americans made known that economic aid could not be taken for granted by a government that included the NLHS. For lack of firm National Assembly support, Souvanna Phouma resigned as prime minister. Katay, however, was unable to form a new cabinet, and Souvanna returned as premier in August. Finally, on November 12, 1957, he and Souphanouvong reached agreement on a symbolic return of the two PL provinces to the Royal Lao government and the entry of two Pathet Lao into a coalition government.

Under the agreement, Souphanouvong swore allegiance to the kingdom for himself and his front and became minister of reconstruction and planning. Phoumi Vongvichit took over the ministry of religion and fine arts. A small contingent—1,500 soldiers—of the Pathet Lao military forces were to be integrated into the 23,650-man Royal Army, while the remaining 4,280 PL soldiers would be demobilized.

Election shock and a move right

In May 1958 a special election was called in Laos to fill twenty-one out of fifty-nine assembly seats. During the election the NLHS worked closely with another party, the Santiphab (Peace party), established in 1956 by Quinim Pholsena, a protégé of Souvanna Phouma. The NLHS posted only thirteen candidates and won nine seats, while the Santiphab posted five and won four. Thus the combined left wing obtained thirteen seats out of the twenty-one available and more than half the total votes cast. In Vientiane, the popular Souphanouvong won the largest personal poll of any candidate. When the new National Assembly convened, he was elected chairman.

The success of the left in the election delivered a brutal shock to the American embassy, which had spent over $3 million on Operation Booster Shot, a high-visibility set of economic aid projects. Americans also provided cash and merchandise for progovernment candidates to distribute to influential villagers. In air-dropping tons of supplies with

U.S. Air Force planes, however, the operation exposed America's Laotian allies to charges of "U.S. domination" and "governmental corruption." The U.S. aid policy since 1955 had already generated negative side effects, since it emphasized roads and airfields over other aid. The U.S. had also financed the importation of consumer items to soak up inflationary demand created by swollen army salaries. The luxury acquisitions by military officers, black marketeers, and some Lao officials tended to confirm the Pathet Lao propaganda that a new form of colonialism and corruption was growing in Vientiane and the Royal Army.

The results of the May election also brought about a new political force on the right in Laos. Encouraged by the CIA (which worked outside of ambassadorial guidelines), the new group grew out of the Junior Chamber of Commerce and the army's officer corps. In June 1958 these so-called young ones created a Committee for the Defense of National Interests (CDNI), which pronounced itself in favor of civil service reform and a hard line in dealing with the Pathet Lao. Prime Minister Souvanna supported them at first, but as he began to form a new government, the CDNI, with U.S. backing, demanded important ministerial posts, even though it held no seats in the National Assembly. When Souvanna resisted, a well-funded CIA effort actively encouraged deputies to oppose a government led by Souvanna. Blocked in the National Assembly, Souvanna gave way to a right winger, Phoui Sananikone.

Phoui formed a government with CDNI members in four out of eight ministries and announced as his primary objective "the struggle without fail against the implantation of the Communist ideology in Laos." With the national elections now completed, the ICSC voted to adjourn *sine die*. The stage was set for a sharp departure from the neutrality pursued by Souvanna Phouma in favor of ruthless opposition to any Communist political foothold within the body politic. The new government upgraded relations with Thailand, established consular relations with Nationalist China and South Vietnam, and invited American military instructors to work in Laos. U.S. military aid increased by nearly 40 percent (while French aid diminished as France gradually withdrew from Laos), and U.S. economic aid also resumed, with emphasis on visible civic action projects relying heavily on Army personnel. Selected junior officers were to be trained in the United States. In the meantime, "Communist sympathizers" were purged from the Laotian civil service.

When a Lao military patrol was fired upon in December 1958 in a remote frontier district near the demilitarized zone separating North and South Vietnam, Phoui Sananikone's government raised cries of alarm about a brewing insurrection and frontier violations by North Vietnam. The National Assembly granted the government emergency powers for twelve months. Sananikone shuffled his cabinet to include Colonel (later General) Phoumi Nosavan and two other army officers, all adherents to the CDNI.

The move right continued. In February 1959 the government declared, with subsequent American support, that the Geneva prohibition against military buildup with outside aid was no longer binding. The Soviet cochairman of the Geneva Conference protested, but his British counterpart rejected the suggestion that the ICSC should be reconvened. In March, the government banned the NLHS newspaper, *Lao Hak Sat.*

Pressing its advantage, the government prepared in May 1959 to absorb (and thus neutralize) the two PL battalions designated to enter the national army. The critical issue regarding the PL battalions was the number of officer ranks the PL would retain in the Royal Army. The government agreed to PL demands, expecting that the PL officers, many of whom were uneducated hill tribesmen, would be weeded out later by examination requirements. The two PL battalions in question, however, refused to assemble for conferring of ranks without their own commanders. Rightist army battalions responded by encircling the two battalions. On May 14, the government ordered the PL battalions either to submit to integration, resign, or be declared rebels. At the same time, the NLHS's top leaders, including Souphanouvong, were put under house arrest in Vientiane. Three days later the first battalion, near Luang Prabang, submitted, but during the night of May 18 the entire 700-man second battalion escaped the royal troops. Encamped east of Luang Prabang on the Plain of Jars (a broad plateau named for the large earthenware vessels found there by the French), the battalion stealthily slipped into the forest with their families, arms, livestock, and household possessions. The government declared the battalion's behavior an act of rebellion for which there could only be a military solution. Three weeks later, the Hanoi press trumpeted the battalion's return to "its former revolutionary bases" in Sam Neua.

In the face of swelling rumors of rebel attacks on mountain villages, the U.S. government endorsed another expansion of the Royal Army (to 29,000 men) and sent more than 100 more military advisers, out of uniform, to the so-called Program Evaluation Office in Vientiane. Four days later, Souphanouvong—the symbol of coalition and reconciliation—was charged with treason and imprisoned with fifteen of his PL colleagues. Armed conflict was now inevitable.

Armed struggle

By virtue of vigorous recruitment methods in the two PL-controlled provinces, the Pathet Lao armed forces had grown by 1957 to 6,000 soldiers. Reports of rebel attacks on misty villages in Sam Neua Province grew to a crescendo in the summer of 1959. The rumors may have been groundless—they were never verified by Western journalists who stayed in Vientiane—but many in the West took the royal government's exaggerated claims at face value. In partic-

ular, the report of "a full-scale artillery-backed invasion from Communist North Vietnam" in the *Washington Post* of September 5, 1959, caught American attention. The day before, the Royal Lao government had asked the United Nations to send an emergency force to "stop the aggression and prevent it from spreading." The UN Security Council agreed to send a fact-finding subcommittee to Laos. Its prompt arrival in Vientiane caught the Royal Lao government without documentation of their charges. Subsequent reports failed to convince the subcommittee that any organized invasion had occurred.

There were logical reasons for the growth of the Pathet Lao in the northeastern provinces. A U.S. intelligence estimate later observed that tribal people of the area were traditionally "antagonistic toward the Lao people and government" and susceptible to "rumors, propaganda and intimidation." Thus, psychological warfare had been "at least as effective as armed action in the current effort." There was "no conclusive evidence of participation by North Vietnamese," although they were almost certainly involved in coordination, communication, and military advisory roles. The report also estimated that the Laotian Communists could capture Sam Neua and Phong Saly provinces without the use of regular North Vietnamese units, if they made a "vigorous effort."

While discounting the wild alarms raised in Vientiane, the U.S. government did increase its military assistance to the Royal Lao government at the end of August and initiated U.S. military training for Lao combat troops in a program later called White Star. Pathet Lao propaganda later labeled this period as the beginning of the American "special war" in Laos.

Prime Minister Phoui Sananikone, in failing health, faced a Royal Army swelling with confidence derived from mounting U.S. aid. When he tried to switch to a more moderate foreign minister, the right-wing CDNI ministers, encouraged by the CIA, refused to agree. After he reshuffled anyway, the army blockaded his house and five days later occupied the key communication centers in the city. The CIA station chief in Vientiane had outmaneuvered his own nominally superior ambassador in dealing with the CDNI and army leaders who opposed Phoui's movement toward a more neutral foreign policy. Nonetheless, the American, British, French, and Australian ambassadors appealed to King Savang Vatthana not to name a military man to replace the resigning prime minister. The king responded with Kou Abhay, whose ten-man cabinet contained three CDNI members, including Phoumi Nosavan.

The new government felt itself able to conduct national elections in April 1960, notwithstanding the control exerted by the Pathet Lao in the northeastern provinces and the

Royal Lao Army sentries keep watch for Pathet Lao guerrillas at a remote royal army outpost near Sam Neua in northeastern Laos, 1959.

White Star in Laos

by Colonel Rod Paschall

Colonel Rod Paschall, former commander of Delta Force, served in Laos in 1964.

When Lieutenant Colonel Arthur "Bull" Simons arrived in Laos in July 1959 with his 107-man Special Forces contingent, he was a bit upset. He had just learned that the arrival of his American training team had been publicly announced in a joint Lao-French communiqué. Simons's U.S. superiors had told him that his mission was secret and that it was important for the Special Forces troopers to be in civilian clothes. Apparently, the French did not regard his mission as a confidential one, or else American and French coordination had been poor. Simons would have a difficult time keeping the American Special Forces effort in Laos quiet.

But quiet was what U.S. President Dwight Eisenhower wanted. Lao leaders had told him that the North Vietnamese were not abiding by the 1954 Geneva agreements and that further appeals to the UN were hopeless. Eisenhower believed that Laos had to serve as a buffer state between North Vietnam and the rest of Southeast Asia. Because the French were not providing enough support to the fledgling Royal Lao Army, Eisenhower decided to assist the Lao government with U.S. support and training. Since he did not want to create a confrontation with the Chinese, he chose a low-visibility operation—Simons's.

Simons dispatched three of his eight-man teams north to a training center in Luang Prabang. Other teams went south to Savannakhet and Pakse, while the last of the twelve teams settled in at the training center on the outskirts of Vientiane. Together with their French army counterparts, the Special Forces officers and men began their training task.

When Captain Kong Le's coup d'état in August 1960 shook the relative tranquility of Vientiane, Simons's men acted as advisers to rightist General Phoumi Nosavan's troops. Parachuting in north of the capital with the 1st and 3d Lao Parachute battalions, Simons's men assisted

A U.S. Special Forces team directs soldiers recruited from the Kha tribes of the Bolovens Plateau in southern Laos as part of the White Star program in 1962.

Phoumi's capture of Vientiane in December 1960. As Kong Le escaped north along Route 13, the Americans and rightists attempted to cut him off. The rebel captain, however, reached Vang Vieng, where the Russians established a supply base for him. Pathet Lao troops also rushed there from the Plain of Jars, and an impasse developed along Route 13.

Shortly thereafter Eisenhower's successor, President John F. Kennedy, opted for a higher-visibility U.S. presence in Laos. In a televised address on March 28, 1961, Kennedy said that a Communist takeover there would "affect the security of the United States" and that the U.S. response would be "suitable, selective, swift, and effective." The president authorized U.S. Air Force C-130 flights into Laos and rushed in sixteen H-34 helicopters for the civilian contract airline, Air America.

In May 1961 the U.S. began equipping Hmong tribesmen behind Communist lines. Two months later the government increased the strength of the U.S. program, now called White Star, to 154 men. By October, the size of the force had doubled to over 300. Led by Simons, the teams recruited and trained Kha tribesmen in the Bolovens Plateau area to contest the North Vietnamese and Pathet Lao along the Ho Chi Minh Trail. A new feature of the program underscored Kennedy's more

public commitment: U.S. soldiers put on their uniforms.

White Star's progress was uneven in the winter of 1961-1962. In northern Laos, two White Star detachments advised lackluster Lao commanders at Muong Sai and Nam Tha. After concerted Pathet Lao attacks the whole enterprise collapsed in an ignoble retreat to the Mekong.

In the south, Simons experienced greater success. By May 1962 twelve companies of Kha soldiers had swept the west and center portions of the Bolovens Plateau and brushed up against NVA units along the Ho Chi Minh Trail. Just a few months later, however, the leaders of the Laotian factions, along with Washington, Moscow, and others, reached agreement on the neutralization of Laos in the Geneva talks of 1962. Suddenly, White Star was finished: in compliance with the accords, 512 Special Forces officers and men departed Laos by October 1962.

The story of White Star is not one of unblemished success. President Eisenhower's original concept—to protect South Vietnam and Cambodia by providing Laos with volunteer professionals who would work in the background of a shadow war—was abandoned in the new Geneva accords. As the organization disbanded, many of its members traveled south, to where a bigger war was brewing.

traditionally anti-Vientiane region of the Bolovens Plateau in the south. The government revised electoral districts to break up previously concentrated zones of NLHS influence, doubled the deposit required of candidates, and set minimum educational standards designed to exclude Pathet Lao leaders with no schooling. The Royal Army staged military raids to reassure the population, protect the government's candidates, discipline rebels, and generally create a "favorable climate for elections." Substantial financial assistance from the CIA also helped General Phoumi to wage a potent propaganda campaign. The rigged election results, a foregone conclusion, completely frustrated the fourteen Lao Patriotic Front and Peace party candidates. In Sam Neua Province, which was barely accessible to the royal government, the official count listed 13 votes for the NLHS candidate out of 6,000 cast. Nevertheless, the major Western ambassadors again persuaded the king not to elevate General Phoumi to prime minister.

Before a new government could take office in June, Prince Souphanouvong and his imprisoned comrades pulled off a startling escape. Over nine months the sixteen prisoners had gradually struck up communication with their guards and worked on "awakening" them through secret political study groups. On May 23, the eight most sympathetic guards assumed the night shift and provided the prisoners with gendarme uniforms. Souphanouvong and his comrades simply walked away from prison. Four Buddhist monks from a nearby pagoda helped the escapees to evade a military camp and to rendezvous with thirty-six PL soldiers in the forests outside Vientiane. Several months later, Souphanouvong reached PL headquarters in Sam Neua, after organizing supporters along the mountainous way.

The Kong Le coup

A second dramatic turn of fortunes for the Pathet Lao occurred on August 9, 1960, when the 2d Royal Lao Paratroop Battalion of Captain Kong Le suddenly seized key government offices and communications centers in Vientiane and broadcast an appeal for an end to fraternal bloodshed and governmental corruption and the adoption of a genuine Lao neutrality. Their leader, Kong Le, was a diminutive, animated, twenty-six-year-old who had served ably in the Royal Lao Army since 1951. He had developed a distaste for the fratricidal (yet often sham) battles that he had been asked to conduct against the PL and their Vietnamese backers. Simple, self-disciplined, he resented the corruption and self-seeking politicians in Vientiane. His fervent peasant rhetoric in addressing the people generated immediate enthusiasm for his seizure of power. With most of the cabinet away in Luang Prabang in conference with the king, Kong Le consulted Quinim Pholsena, a leader of the Santiphab, on how to establish a government of neutrality. Working through Souvanna

Phouma, forty-one deputies met to consider the vociferous demands of Kong Le and his zealous backers. They voted "no confidence" in the existing government, then dispatched a delegation to Luang Prabang to urge the king to appoint Souvanna Phouma prime minister. With the king's agreement, Souvanna formed a new cabinet on August 16. Kong Le declared that his coup d'état was terminated.

In Washington there was general relief that the captain had been deflected, but the Pentagon was uneasy at the new political atmosphere of neutralism that he had created. General Phoumi Nosavan, with the support of four out of five regional military commanders and the backing of U.S. military advisers, declared martial law on August 15 in southern Savannakhet, using an American-supplied radio transmitter. In Luang Prabang on August 31, Souvanna met Phoumi's opposition by reenacting the assembly's approval of the new cabinet. He also offered General Phoumi the vice-premiership and the interior ministry.

General Phoumi was unenthusiastic. With the approval of American military and CIA personnel, he insisted upon receiving the defense ministry portfolio. His Thai cousin, Marshal Sarit Thanarat, the chief of government in Bangkok, encouraged him by channeling military supplies into Savannakhet, while closing off cross-river traffic carrying food and fuel to Vientiane. On September 10, Phoumi announced that a new revolutionary group, headed nominally by Prince Boun Oum of the southern Champassak dynasty, was seizing power. U.S. policymakers found themselves in a crossfire of conflicting preferences: for Souvanna and constitutional legality or for Phoumi and anticommunism.

All of this was a windfall for the Pathet Lao, which radioed its full support for Souvanna's proposed policy of neutrality and reconciliation. At the same time, attacks by guerrillas in eastern provinces and their outright seizure of Sam Neua City in late September increased the pressure on Souvanna to seek an accommodation with his half-brother. On the southern front General Phoumi's forces were moving haltingly north toward Vientiane, using Thai territory when convenient. Souvanna pleaded with U.S. officials for help in coping with the Thai blockade of fuel and food needed in Vientiane. When Washington rejected his requests, he announced on September 30 his readiness to establish relations with the USSR. Four days later, he began negotiations with the Pathet Lao about political reconciliation. With the Thai blockade of Vientiane continuing, Souvanna announced in late October that he would be "very happy" to accept Soviet offers of assistance. At this point the badly divided bureaus and agencies in Washington agreed that Souvanna was too compromised and must be replaced.

General Phoumi's rightist forces finally overran Vientiane on December 16, 1960, after four days of erratic fighting. An estimated 800 surviving Kong Le and Pathet Lao irregulars made an orderly withdrawal north to the

Laos Cease-fire

May 1961

---- Approximate cease-fire line

▨▨▨ Area of Pathet Lao control

In May 1961 the Royal Government of Laos and the Pathet Lao agreed to a cease-fire, to be followed by negotiations toward a unified government.

Plain of Jars. A weary Souvanna had flown to respite in Phnom Penh, but Quinim Pholsena as his acting chief of government worked out an alliance of Kong Le's troops and the Pathet Lao. Phoumi Nosavan had arranged in Savannakhet a vote of no confidence in Souvanna Phouma by thirty-eight visiting members of the National Assembly, a move endorsed by the king. The U.S. government promptly announced its full support on December 15 of the ensuing new provisional royal government, under Prime Minister Boun Oum. Now labeled "pro-Communist rebels" by the Western press, Kong Le's forces captured the central airfield in the Plain of Jars at the year's end. Pathet Lao forces invested the province capital at Xieng Khouang, at the southern end of the Plain of Jars.

In late February 1961, Souvanna Phouma returned from Phnom Penh to join Souphanouvong at Khang Khay, a village on the Plain of Jars, where they shared an old French barracks. Souvanna's neutralist government-in-residence consisted of four ministers. The neutralist troops of Kong Le were reorganized and equipped with Russian

weapons, which the allied but separate Pathet Lao units also carried. A North Vietnamese regiment was present to fuse extra backbone into PL units.

Since December 4, the Soviet Union had provided an emergency airlift of food and fuel from Hanoi to the neutralists and Pathet Lao; military equipment was added on December 11. The Soviet Union established an embassy near the office of Souvanna Phouma, whom they recognized as the legitimate neutralist prime minister. China also agreed to diplomatic relations with Souvanna's government and set up an economic mission in the province capital. North Vietnamese air field technicians, guards, advisers, and other aid personnel, including clandestine weapons specialists, maintained a military camp in Khang Khay to back up the leftists and their neutral allies.

The potential for dangerous civil war now existed in Laos, with two rival governments each recognized and assisted militarily by rival camps among the great powers. An escalation of the contest could bring the United States and the Soviet Union into direct confrontation. The Eisenhower administration, about to be replaced after eight years, pondered a variety of military deployment options. Nonetheless, the door was kept open to diplomacy.

Geneva once again

The incoming American president, John Kennedy, was shocked and angered by the news President Eisenhower delivered to him just one day before Kennedy's inauguration in January 1961. The situation in Laos was critically bad—a "mess" in the old general's words. "You may have to go in there and fight it out," he told the president-elect.

Kennedy's distress was all the worse because the Laos crisis was so unexpected. The Laos situation had swollen in importance during the last months of the Eisenhower administration. The remote, politically inchoate buffer state between Vietnam and Thailand had become a battleground in which the two superpowers had seriously committed themselves to unpredictable armed rivals in a brewing civil war. The Soviet Union, with North Vietnamese cooperation, maintained an air supply operation of the highest priority to one side. The United States, committed through SEATO to protect Laos and Thailand, was deeply concerned with maintaining a friendly security zone east of the Mekong River. The new American president's mettle was untried, and the State and Defense departments and the CIA could not agree on a course of action. A collapse of the feckless American-backed royal government in Vientiane would seriously damage the credibility of the new administration in dealing with Communist-supported wars of "national liberation." Acutely aware of the larger

Spearheading the successful drive of General Phoumi's right-wing army against the allied troops of the Pathet Lao and Kong Le, a tank rumbles into Vientiane on December 13, 1960.

implications, John Kennedy devoted more time to Laos during his first two months in office than to any other issue.

Kennedy immediately sought advice from his military and diplomatic subordinates. The U.S. Joint Chiefs of Staff were split between all-the-way-or-not-at-all sentiments in the Army and bomb-the-source advocates in the Air Force. In the State Department, some feared that China would move to defend its borders if the U.S. entered Laos in force. Other nations weighed in with various ideas. India suggested a reactivation of the ICSC. Cambodia proposed a conference of fourteen regional states and great powers. The Asian members of SEATO wanted reassurance through strong American action. And the Soviet Union, while continuing its airlift, indicated that it was willing to reconvene the Geneva Conference. In the midst of all the conflicting advice, President Kennedy set up an interdepartmental task force to sort out the options.

Notwithstanding the new president's inaugural promise to "pay any price" to preserve liberty worldwide, he began to lean away from the military track, particularly after learning that it would take the Army fifteen days to airlift one division with equipment to Laos from the United States. And although his joint Laos task force had devised a seventeen-step escalation ladder (leading to all-out use of force), the failure of Phoumi's rightist army even to advance against the Plain of Jars raised questions about the military seriousness of the ally the U.S. would be "rescuing." During March 1961 the new president's advisers pressed for increased military aid and a demonstration of strength. Kennedy insisted on getting the Soviets to end their airlift, which was delivering fifty tons of supplies a day to the Communists and neutralists on the Plain of Jars.

Eventually, Kennedy gravitated toward a moderate course: a cease-fire and termination of the Soviet airlift, followed by an international conference to settle the situation. But he clothed his flexibility in a grim and foreboding news conference on March 28, 1961. With a map illustrating the growing area of Pathet Lao control, he talked ominously of America honoring "its obligations." Yet he supported "constructive negotiations" among Lao leaders toward a "neutral and independent Laos," and he significantly omitted any insistence on an end to the Soviet airlift.

The Soviet Union responded positively to the press conference, as well as to the alerting of 4,000 U.S. troops in Japan and Okinawa for possible dispatch to Laos. The test of wills over an issue of secondary importance was coming into proper proportion. On April 1 the Soviets expressed their willingness to join the United Kingdom in appealing for a cease-fire that could precede an international conference. Determined diplomatic initiative by Souvanna Phouma and Souphanouvong in Moscow, Peking, and Hanoi finally produced a cease-fire order on May 2. The reactivated ICSC verified the cease-fire sufficiently on May 11 for a fourteen-nation Geneva Conference to begin.

Before reaching this diplomatic track, President Kennedy had received eight different proposals for military operations. Appalled by the dissonance and uncertainties, he had settled on preparation for air strikes and deployment of combat brigades to northeast Thailand and South Vietnam. He also authorized intelligence and sabotage missions into North Vietnam and southeastern Laos. In a show of determination, following his anti-Castro fiasco at Cuba's Bay of Pigs in mid-April, Kennedy ordered the 400 American "civilian" advisers in Laos to don their military uniforms and to accompany the Royal Lao Army to the combat areas. None of these steps provoked a countermove by Moscow. Even at the stormy summit meeting between Kennedy and Khrushchev at Vienna in early June, they agreed that Laos should be neutralized.

A diplomatic solution now depended heavily upon the correlation of local forces and the willingness of the three Lao factions to compromise. Each was represented by a royal personality of distinctly different political orientation: Prince Souphanouvong, secretly relying on the North Vietnamese; Prince Souvanna Phouma, preferring national nonalignment but supported by the Russians and Chinese; and Prince Boun Oum, deviously encouraged by the Thais and some Americans. Even the question of seating all three parties at the Geneva Conference was initially in dispute. By the end of June, however, the three princes had agreed in principle to call upon the king to form a tripartite provisional government. It took another twelve months of diplomatic and military manuever, however, with occasional meetings of the princes, before this could be translated into an actual distribution of ministries and a conference declaration on the neutrality of Laos.

While the princes haggled over portfolios in the new cabinet, the great powers met in Geneva. Essentially, they did little more than indicate their willingness to endorse a neutralized coalition government for Laos. The conferees conducted thirty-six plenary sessions in two months, followed by forty-three private sessions. Great Britain and the Soviet Union, cochairmen of the 1954 Geneva Conference, alternately presided. The conference concluded in July 1962 after eighty-seven sessions, during which the participants resolved many differences.

During this period U.S. Special Ambassador Averell Harriman and the U.S. ambassador to Laos, Winthrop Brown, gradually built up support in Washington for Souvanna Phouma as a responsible non-Communist leader on whose patience and persistence the United States would have to rely. At the same time, the wily ambition and erratic leadership of General Phoumi gradually disillusioned his numerous champions and encouragers among American military and CIA advisers. His resort to military "probing actions" in October 1961 set back three-party negotiations, and his prolonged holdout (through Prince Boun Oum) for control over the defense and interior ministries delayed agreement for many months.

Prince Boun Oum, Prince Souvanna Phouma, and Prince Souphanouvong (left to right) shake hands after agreeing to form a tripartite government for Laos, June 1962.

Ultimately, Phoumi's lack of military prowess undid him. In early 1962 he dispatched 5,000 troops to the vulnerable village of Nam Tha, located twenty-four kilometers south of the Chinese border. The Pathet Lao responded by closing in on the town, mortaring the defenders, and taking the airport Phoumi had used to garrison the town. On May 6, 1962, Nam Tha's defenders abandoned their posts. Twelve American White Star advisers had to be evacuated by helicopter. Phoumi's soldiers fled west as far as the Mekong River, some even crossing into Thailand.

The United States responded to the Nam Tha debacle by dispatching 3,000 troops to Thailand. Secretary of State Dean Rusk formally agreed with his Thai counterpart that the U.S. would help defend Thailand independent of its SEATO obligations. In the meantime, Ambassador Harriman was finally able to deal decisively with General Phoumi. Previously, he had seen to the transfer of the CIA station chief in Vientiane (whom he blamed for encouraging Phoumi's folly) and had withheld U.S. economic aid to the rightists from January through May. Now, he got Thailand's Marshal Sarit to counsel his bootless cousin to give way to a coalition government.

Souvanna Phouma used his own diplomatic devices to press for a solution by announcing a deadline for his participation in the negotiations on the Plain of Jars—his daughter's wedding in France in June 1962. Under this combination of pressures, Boun Oum finally gave in to a balanced government formula. Souvanna would become

prime minister and minister of defense, while Phoumi Nosavan and Souphanouvong would become deputy premiers, each with a veto over cabinet decisions. In addition, Phoumi became minister of finance, and Souphanouvong assumed the ministry of economy and planning. The Pathet Lao and Phoumi supporters each received four portfolios in the new cabinet, while Souvanna's neutralists received seven, and "Vientiane neutralists" four.

With this unlikely bargain struck, the concerns of the Geneva conferees were finally wrapped into the Declaration on the Neutrality of Laos, signed by fourteen nations on July 23, 1962. It required all foreign military forces to leave the country and included provisions designed to avoid some defects of the 1954 Geneva agreements. It precluded the use of Lao territory for interfering in the internal affairs of another country—an effort to shut the Ho Chi Minh Trail. It seemed as though the Laos "side show" to the military struggle in Vietnam had been closed via diligent diplomacy and a gamble on Souvanna Phouma's nationalism and durability. The prospects for reconciliation in Laos were perhaps worth the gamble, but the chances that the North Vietnamese would stay out of eastern Laos while pressing the struggle for power in the South were less than gambler's odds.

Neutrality Lost

The peace that came to Laos after the 1962 Geneva accords was fatally fragile and tragically short. If any of the parties involved—Laotian rightists, leftists and neutralists, the United States, North Vietnam, and others—hoped for a genuine reconciliation, their hopes went unanswered. Almost overnight the agreement's flaws and the overriding interests of outside nations and inside factions doomed the country to another decade of grinding, debilitating war.

First to fail was the new coalition conceived by Souvanna Phouma, Souphanouvong, and Phoumi Nosavan. The Government of National Union was paralyzed by the veto power each man's faction held over major decisions. The proposed unification of Laos's military groups into one army of 30,000 (10,000 from each faction) foundered as the rightists, who had the largest force, dragged their feet. The weakness of the International Commission for Supervision and Control (ICSC) aggravated the situation. Its agents were unable to prevent cease-fire violations,

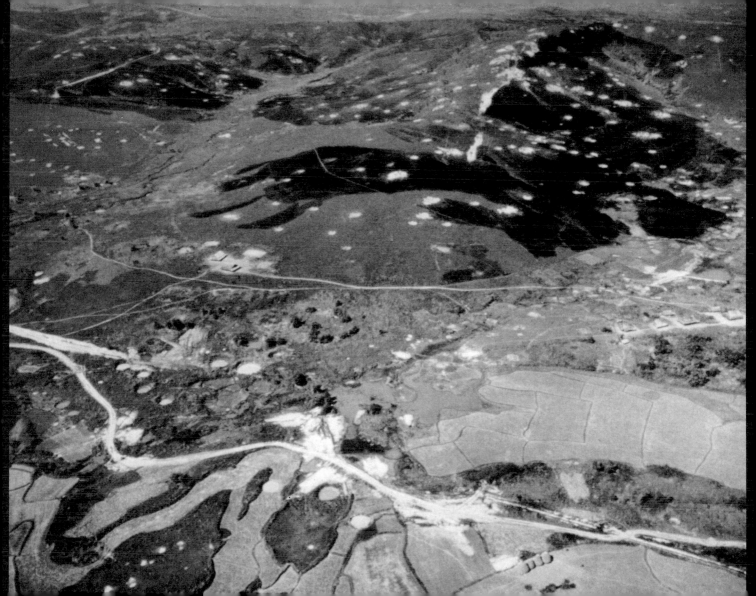

Outside powers, especially North Vietnam, did little to ease the situation. By the October 7, 1962, deadline for withdrawal of foreign forces, the ICSC reported that only 40 North Vietnamese military personnel had left the country through the commission's checkpoints. Some 6,000 North Vietnamese soldiers, according to U.S. intelligence, remained in the eastern half of Laos after October. There they continued to supply the Pathet Lao with advice, arms, and other material support. American officials complained publicly about these troops but lodged no official protest for fear it would destroy the brand-new accords.

The United States, however, also played a part in the agreements' eventual collapse. Even as it complied with the letter of the treaty—removing its 666 military advisers by the October deadline—it violated Geneva's spirit by increasing covert military operations. The CIA continued to supply anti-Pathet Lao villages inside Communist territory with food, blankets, medicine, and "hard rice"—weapons and ammunition—via its charter airline, Air America. The Communists charged that the CIA's military airdrops were violations. The U.S. responded variously that the supply runs were legal under the treaty's "national defense" clause or that they constituted "refugee" relief.

One of the first secret U.S. military aid programs began in October, when embassy officials in Vientiane established the Requirements Office. This bureau, supposedly under the U.S. AID mission, was in fact a covert military advisory operation staffed by twenty-six retired American military officers who reported on Royal Laotian military needs and arranged for delivery of supplies from Thailand. In addition to the Requirements Office, the embassy began to rotate unusually large numbers of military "attachés" through its offices in Vientiane and elsewhere.

For all the trouble, then, that went into the 1962 Geneva accords, they amounted to a dead letter within a few weeks. The Laotian factions continued to disagree, and outside powers substituted secret military operations for open ones. All that remained to kill the agreements was for a spark to ignite a new round of violence.

That spark came in October, when the Soviet Union announced that it would no longer airlift supplies to Kong Le's 4,500-man neutralist army on the Plain of Jars. The shutoff forced the neutralists to rely on supplies routed through North Vietnam to the Pathet Lao, with whom Kong Le shared an uneasy alliance. Within days, though, it was clear that the 7,000 Pathet Lao soldiers on and around the plain were not going to share these supplies equitably. Without the supplies, Kong Le's men would starve.

Not wanting to see the neutralist position erode, a reluctant Prime Minister Souvanna Phouma asked U.S. ambassador Leonard Unger for aid. Unger promptly author-

ized Air America to drop supplies to Kong Le's men. The Pathet Lao's General Singkapo, in command of Pathet Lao troops on the plain, denounced the airdrops as "subversive." Singkapo, who knew something about subversion (he had for some time been infiltrating men into the neutralist forces), announced that his men would fire on Air America flights bound for Kong Le.

At this crucial juncture, divisions appeared in the neutralist camp. Colonel Deuan Sunnalath, an ambitious subordinate of Kong Le, announced that his men also would fire on American supply flights. On November 27, Deuan's gunners shot down an Air America cargo plane. Infuriated, one of Kong Le's most trusted lieutenants, Colonel Ketsana, tried to arrest the gunners, but the Pathet Lao prevented him. Two months later another U.S. plane was downed. Then on February 11, 1963, Colonel Ketsana was assassinated by leftists. The murder of his aide infuriated Kong Le. He forbade Pathet Lao and Deuanists from entering neutralist areas. He also swore vengeance, a vow fulfilled when Foreign Minister Quinim Pholsena was assassinated in Vientiane on April 1. Quinim, a left-leaning, anti-American neutralist, was machine-gunned in front of his home by a soldier assigned to guard duty by none other than Kong Le.

The violence on the Plain of Jars and in Vientiane ruined what political cohesiveness was left in Laos. Prince Souphanouvong, who up to this point had remained in the capital as deputy prime minister in the coalition government, fled Vientiane shortly after Quinim's assassination. On April 19, 1963, he was followed by his associate, Phoumi Vongvichit. Their departure left just two junior Pathet Lao representatives in the rapidly unraveling coalition government.

In the meantime, heavy fighting broke out between Kong Le's men and the Deuanist/Pathet Lao alliance on the Plain of Jars. There was evidence that North Vietnamese troops were aiding the leftists: Kong Le's men reported radio combat instructions given in Vietnamese during the fighting, and French observers on the plain saw Vietnamese wearing Pathet Lao uniforms on the road between Khang Khay and Xieng Khouang. Badly outnumbered, Kong Le nevertheless skillfully consolidated his widely scattered men and withdrew to more defensible positions on the western third of the plain. There he was reinforced by his one-time enemies, troops from Phoumi Nosavan's Royal Laotian Army (RLA). Phoumi had little love for the neutralists but even less for the Pathet Lao. Others also came to Kong Le's aid: on May 12 Souvanna Phouma openly requested and received more U.S. arms and ammunition for Kong Le. The next month, citing the NVA's domination of the Pathet Lao, he cut off all government assistance to them.

Despite the renewed fighting, neither Souvanna nor Souphanouvong wished to disavow formally the Geneva agreements. Attempts were made at reconciliation: In

September 1963 members of the Pathet Lao's political wing, the NLHS, conferred with officials in Vientiane on a possible return to the government. Around the same time, Kong Le and General Singkapo met on the Plain of Jars in an effort to defuse tensions. In January 1964 Souvanna traveled to the Pathet Lao's stronghold in Sam Neua to negotiate with Souphanouvong; at these discussions the two men reaffirmed many principles of the Geneva agreements. Souvanna also proposed that, since Vientiane was under rightist control, the coalition government be moved to a neutral, demilitarized Luang Prabang. The two princes appeared to be edging toward a solution to Laos's crisis.

Subsequent actions by both the left and the right, however, again ruined the chances for peace. Just a few days after the January 1964 discussions, the Pathet Lao and North Vietnamese opened up a new offensive, pushing toward the Mekong Valley and battering Kong Le's forces on the Plain of Jars. Two months later General Phoumi—with dubious authority—agreed to let South Vietnam send troops into Laos in "hot pursuit" of Communist troops. While not particularly significant militarily, his move underscored how little authority the central government had over the rightist armies.

Souvanna Phouma made yet another attempt at reconciliation. On April 17, 1964, he, Souphanouvong, and Phoumi Nosavan met on the Plain of Jars. Souvanna pressed for a coalition in a demilitarized Luang Prabang, but Phoumi rejected all proposals. A dejected Souvanna returned to Vientiane and announced his intention to resign.

The government moves right

On April 19, one day after Souvanna's return, two rightist commanders stunned the capital by arresting Souvanna and announcing that a Revolutionary Committee controlled the government. Interestingly, the committee did not include Phoumi; the coup leaders, Generals Kouprasith Abhay and Siho Lamphouthacoul, who controlled their own factions within the right, may have staged the rebellion to take power from Phoumi. The coup, however, was short-lived. U.S. Ambassador Unger, who was in

South Vietnamese soldiers transported by a U.S. helicopter head for the jungle to pursue Vietcong guerrillas in Laotian territory, 1964.

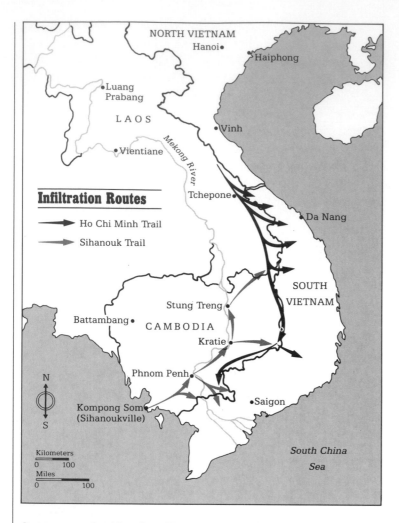

Infiltration Routes

→ Ho Chi Minh Trail
→ Sihanouk Trail

Saigon, rushed back to Vientiane to inform both Souvanna and the rebel generals that the United States continued to support the coalition government. Other Western nations, King Savang Vatthana, and even Phoumi also denounced the coup. Under tremendous pressure, the Revolutionary Committee backed down after just four days, and Souvanna returned to power.

Nevertheless, the abortive coup, short as it was, had a profound impact on Laotian politics. First, it affirmed the American government's support for Souvanna, just a few years after it had dismissed him as a tool of the leftists. Second, it caused the neutralists to shift political allies from the leftists to the rightists. As part of the price for returning to power, Souvanna agreed to give good assignments to eighty conservative junior officers associated with the coup. Then in May 1964, under further rightist pressure, he announced the political and military union of the rightists and neutralists against the left.

The merger of the center and right under Souvanna spelled the end of the coalition government. When Souvanna and Souphanouvong met once again on the Plain of Jars on May 4, the Pathet Lao leader accused his half-brother of being a "prisoner" of the rightists. On May 30 he instructed the last two Pathet Lao ministers to leave the coalition. A few days later he wrote the Geneva cochairmen that the NLHS no longer recognized Souvanna's government as the legitimate heir to the regime created by the 1962 agreements.

Events moved toward renewed conflict. Uneasy truces that had been arranged on the Plain of Jars collapsed after the sudden alliance of the rightists and neutralists. Many of Kong Le's troops, unwilling to join with the right, defected to the Deuanists and Pathet Lao. Fresh attacks by these self-styled "patriotic neutralists" and Communists drove Kong Le's remaining troops completely off the Plain of Jars by the end of May.

Souvanna answered these attacks by calling on the United States to support his new political alignment. The U.S. responded firmly: President Lyndon Johnson, who had taken the reins of government after the assassination of President Kennedy in November 1963, was eager to support a rightist-neutralist alliance in Laos. On May 19 the United States Air Force, at Johnson's order, began low-level Yankee Team reconnaissance flights over southern Laos. Two days later U.S. planes began flying over northern Laos as well. Johnson also authorized increased shipments of T-28 aircraft to Laos. Because there were few qualified Laotian pilots, these planes—bearing Royal Laotian Air Force markings—were manned by Thai pilots and U.S. civilians connected with the CIA's Air America. They bombed the Communists who pressed Kong Le's forces.

In July 1964 the Vientiane government, with U.S. help, launched Operation Three Arrows (also called Operation Triangle), a successful push to clear the Pathet Lao from Sala Phou Khoun, the critical junction where Route 7, which ran through the Plain of Jars, met Route 13, the north-south road from Luang Prabang to Vientiane. The U.S. role in Three Arrows was extensive. Before the operation, the Requirements Office in Vientiane supplied the RLA with materiel that some units had not received in years: weapons, clothing, and other supplies. U.S. planes transported troops and conducted reconnaissance flights before the operation. American military advisers helped coordinate Three Arrows, while other Americans functioned as ground controllers for U.S. and Thai air strikes. This last step—air strikes—reflected a change in American policy. It was the first step in what was to become the heaviest sustained bombing campaign in history.

"Armed reconnaissance"

Before the 1962 Geneva accords collapsed in the spring of 1964, the U.S. air role in the Laotian war had been quite limited. Communist provocations, however, combined with the new alliance in Vientiane, changed that role. First, on June 6, 1964, Pathet Lao gunners shot down a U.S. reconnaissance aircraft. The next day they shot down another. U.S. planes responded by bombing Pathet Lao positions for the first time. The attack alarmed Souvanna Phouma, who threatened to resign if U.S. flights were not halted. They were—for a few days. Then, after consultations with Souvanna (in which the Laotian leader was pressured to accept the American point of view), the United States announced on June 11 that the flights would resume. What was not announced was that the purpose of the flights had changed from reconnaissance to attack. For the next six years—until June 1970—the flights were publicly termed armed reconnaissance; in fact, they were an intensive bombing campaign against Communist positions throughout northern and southern Laos.

The "armed reconnaissance" missions started as observation flights, then took on new roles. In October 1964, U.S. planes began to fly cover for Laotian T-28s on their regular bombing runs against Communist positions in northern Laos. On December 14, 1964, the United States, with Souvanna's approval, initiated Operation Barrel Roll, purely American bombing missions in the north. One month later Operation Steel Tiger began, the bombing of southern Laos. Steel Tiger was another important change in U.S. policy, for while the targets in northern Laos had been primarily Pathet Lao, the target in the south was the supply route the North Vietnamese had been building to the battlefields of South Vietnam, the Ho Chi Minh Trail.

Barrel Roll and Steel Tiger were flown in secrecy (that is, secret to Americans) because the American government did not want to publicize its involvement in Laos while it was already deeply involved in South Vietnam. Secrecy also shielded Prime Minister Souvanna Phouma, who wanted U.S. help against the Pathet Lao but was loath to be labeled a U.S. puppet. Souvanna also reasoned (as many Lao did) that American air raids against the Ho Chi Minh Trail were part of the larger U.S.-North Vietnam conflict in South Vietnam. He dearly wanted to avoid that war. The consensus between Washington and Vientiane, then, was that the less Souvanna knew about the bombings in the south, the better.

The two bombing campaigns thus became, in effect, two separate wars. Officially, the northern operations were carried out at the request of the Laotian government. The southern operations, on the other hand, were essentially U.S-inspired and executed. There was, though, one unifying factor: all attack proposals for Laos were subject to the approval of the new U.S. ambassador there, a remarkable diplomat named William Sullivan.

Sullivan, who was to be ambassador from November 1964 to March 1969, had already spent years working on the Laos situation for the U.S. government. He had been Averell Harriman's second-in-command during the Geneva talks. He knew Souvanna well and had nudged U.S. policy from support of the rightists to the neutralist camp. Mindful of the uncoordinated U.S. response to events in Laos during the post-1954 period, Sullivan was determined to supervise his nation's actions in Laos precisely and completely. To a large extent, he succeeded.

Because the Geneva accords officially forbade an American military office in Laos, the ambassador was also in

Images of destruction. Houses and streets in Xieng Khouang Province lie in ruins as a result of the accelerated U.S. bombing campaign against Pathet Lao positions in northern Laos in 1969.

charge of the military aspects of U.S. aid. This Sullivan did with great thoroughness. He gave final approval to all target selection in Laos. It was a complicated job, partly because the CIA, the Air Force, and the American military command in Vietnam all demanded a say in the matter. There were other considerations, too: the American and Laotian governments wanted to minimize civilian casualties and avoid targets that could be embarrassing to a secret war, such as Chinese road-building gangs working in northern Laos. Sullivan kept absolute control over target selection, the level of bombing, and the rules of engagement under which U.S. military men flew against targets in Laos. He maintained a firm grip over the U.S. war, even though military men complained that his rules limited the effectiveness of air power against the enemy in Laos.

The military, however, did not hesitate to fulfill its bombing role under the guidelines set by Sullivan. The missions were carried out on a rotating basis by U.S. Air Force planes stationed in both South Vietnam and Thailand and by carrier-based Navy and Marine aircraft from the U.S. Seventh Fleet, which was stationed in the South China Sea off Vietnam. With all this firepower, the air war in Laos grew rapidly. From 1964 to 1966, there was a massive increase in the number of strikes; in the north, Barrel Roll went from about 2 strikes per week in 1964 to about 140 per week in 1966. The southern bombings were even more extensive: by mid-1965, American planes were already flying 1,000 sorties per month over the Ho Chi Minh Trail; that figure grew to 3,000 by 1967.

The organization of the bombing campaigns changed over the years. In December 1965, Steel Tiger was divided into two bombing campaigns after General William Westmoreland, commander of the Military Assistance Command, Vietnam (MACV), asked for control of bombing in that part of the trail contiguous with South Vietnam, claiming it as part of an "extended battlefield." His request was approved, and the region was separated from Steel Tiger and renamed Tiger Hound. MACV selected most of the targets in Tiger Hound, and allowed looser rules of engagement than those for the rest of Laos.

Despite the extent of the bombing, Barrel Roll, Steel Tiger, and Tiger Hound achieved little. In the south, the Ho Chi Minh Trail network survived and even expanded greatly after the U.S. committed ground combat troops to South Vietnam in 1965. One reason the bombing campaign failed was that the "trail" was in fact a multitude of intertwining roads and trails. When American target selectors discovered one trail, the Vietnamese moved to another trail or built a new one. A North Vietnamese strategist estimated that the trail eventually grew to more than 13,000 kilometers of roads and pathways.

Communist supplies headed for the war in South Vietnam are guided down a Laotian river on the Ho Chi Minh Trail in February 1971.

As the Ho Chi Minh Trail grew, so did the number of troops traveling down it to South Vietnam. In 1964, 12,000 troops went south; by 1968 that figure had ballooned to 200,000. Materiel transported grew from 100 tons per week in 1963 to 10,000 tons per week in 1970. Fully 80 to 85 percent of the materiel sent down the trail made it to South Vietnam. Likewise, casualties caused by bombing amounted to only about 2 percent of North Vietnamese soldiers traveling down the trail.

In northern Laos the bombings were also heavy, but they simply became part of the stalemate between the Communists and the royal government. North and south, each year brought more violence and more destruction, but to little military effect. Ultimately, the 2.75 million tons of bombs dropped on Laos during the war (at an average cost of about $1.14 billion per year) did little but destroy the landscape and disrupt the lives of the people who lived under the bombers' rain of fire.

Ground war stalemate

The war that sputtered on in northern Laos after the collapse of the 1962 Geneva accords became a seesaw, seasonal affair in which neither side made effective headway for several years. During the dry season (starting in November), the Pathet Lao launched offensives against government-held positions in the highlands east of the Mekong Valley. When the rainy season began in May royal government forces, having greater mobility and backed by air power, regained these positions. The Communists generally kept control of the Plain of Jars and eastern Laos. The Vientiane government held the Mekong Valley and other areas of western Laos. It was a frustrating, back-and-forth war, but if it satisfied no one, at least it served the purposes of outside powers on either side.

On one side, the Americans and their Thai allies wanted to keep the Communists out of the Mekong Valley. The U.S. government, preoccupied with the war in South Vietnam, was willing to avoid a major escalation as long as North Vietnamese and Pathet Lao forces remained in the mountains. Thailand also wanted to keep the Vietnamese out of the valley. Besides traditional concerns about Vietnamese expansionism, the Thais' Mekong border area was plagued by a nagging leftist insurgency that could easily be aided by a Communist presence in the valley. So, in addition to flying bombing missions against the Communists, the Thais, subsidized by the U.S., also maintained a significant troop presence in the valley.

North Vietnam, although it had very different aims in Laos, agreed with the United States: the real war was in South Vietnam. The DRV's main activity in Laos—maintaining the Ho Chi Minh Trail—served this end. Fighting the United States in Laos did not. Yet North Vietnam did not ignore the Pathet Lao's military efforts. For political reasons, the DRV preferred to let the Pathet Lao spearhead the Communist military and political effort in Laos, but it aided the Lao Communists in many ways. It supplied the Pathet Lao with Communist cadres who encouraged the growth of leftist ideology and organization in the hills. It provided military equipment and training and a limited number of combat troops—perhaps several companies of 125 men each—or even regiments that could appear when needed. Vietnamese political and military advisers also accompanied Pathet Lao units and maintained close relations with the leadership. In addition, a number of NVA units maneuvered secretly in northeastern Laos to defend the passes between Vietnam and Laos and to protect the Communist-held areas bordering the Plain of Jars. The number of NVA troops in Laos varied over the years but grew gradually from about 15,000 to almost 70,000 by decade's end.

With North Vietnamese assistance, the Pathet Lao's military wing (called the Lao People's Liberation Army, or LPLA, after October 1965) grew from a force of between 14,000 and 19,000 in 1962 to over 40,000 in 1969. Yet even the bonds of shared Communist ideology could not break the traditional stereotypes the allies in the leftist movement held of each other. The Vietnamese regarded the Pathet Lao troops as unaggressive and incompetent; the Pathet Lao tended to be suspicious of the driving, humorless Vietnamese. And when the time came for a genuine escalation in Laos, the Vietnamese would depend on their own troops far more than on the Pathet Lao.

The Pathet Lao succeeded in building and holding a base in the Laotian mountains for several reasons. First, although the political leadership of the Laotian Communist movement remained in the hands of lowland Laotians, a sizable number of Pathet Lao soldiers were highland tribesmen who lived in Communist-held areas on the Vietnamese border. These hill people had long resisted Vientiane's authority; Communist cadres played on their resentments and preached equality and solidarity to them. In addition to exploiting such hostilities, the Pathet Lao secured loyalty among the tribes by other means. They made allies of local chieftains, won the confidence of the people, cultivated their grievances against Vientiane, and used force (such as assassination of recalcitrant village chiefs) when other methods failed. Not that the leftists represented anything like an enlightened regime in eastern Laos: forced labor, taxes, and the presence of the roundly disliked North Vietnamese made life in the "liberated zone" difficult and uncertain.

In contrast to the Pathet Lao, the Royal Laotian Army was notoriously corrupt and inefficient. Its officers, largely lowland Laotians, treated their military regions as feudal fiefs, and some were known to flee battles even before

Members of the Pathet Lao print the official NLHS newspaper, Lao Hak Sat, *at a factory located inside a limestone cave in eastern Laos, January 1966.*

their men did (which was often). The lowland Laotian soldiers of the RLA and neutralist armies reinforced the hill tribesmen's anger by contemptuously referring to them as *kha* (slaves) and Pathet Lao soldiers *kap kap* (toads). Royal soldiers abused women and stole livestock and food in tribal areas. And while the Pathet Lao attempted to organize villages and regions into overlapping networks of communications, RLA units tended to remain isolated in garrisons and outposts, preparing for set-piece battles instead of the war that prevailed around them: small-unit actions, control of roads and strategic mountaintops, and hit-and-run ambushes.

While the RLA fought the Communists, Prime Minister Souvanna Phouma spent the mid-1960s fending off challenges to his authority. Although he never built an effective, nationwide political party, the fragmented parliament could agree on no one to replace him as head of government. Numerous coups also failed. In January 1965, the rightist leader Phoumi Nosavan was forced to flee to Thailand after a confused artillery duel between factions in Vientiane. In October 1966, a Laotian air force general, Thao Ma, bombed army headquarters near Vientiane in a

quixotic overthrow attempt, then also fled to Thailand with one-third of Laos's air force pilots. And in that month Kong Le, who had once represented many Laotian (and foreign) hopes for true neutrality, was pressured to leave the country as the rightists began to integrate his army into theirs. In typical RLA fashion, he was replaced by an egregiously corrupt colonel who promptly destroyed what morale was left among Kong Le's troops.

The American mission in Vientiane continued to grow through this period. In 1966 the United States initiated Project 404, in which 117 additional military advisers, wearing civilian clothes and called "attachés," were brought in to advise the Laotian army and air force. About 90 other military advisers, officially stationed in Thailand, were rotated into Laos on "temporary duty." These soldiers brought to over 500 the total number of American military advisers in Laos. There were other U.S. military personnel in Laos. In 1966 the first U.S. forward air controllers were

Lao Communist leader Kaysone Phomvihan gives a talk at the Khommadan School, the North Vietnamese-administered Pathet Lao officer training institute in Sam Neua Province, 1965.

stationed in remote Laotian navigational beacon stations, where they helped direct the bombing campaigns against North Vietnam and the Ho Chi Minh Trail.

Along with advisers, the U.S. provided the Laotian military with aid averaging some $80 million per year from 1963 through 1970. This aid, which included everything from blankets to aircraft, was the source of almost all the RLA's equipment. Economic aid told much the same story: at $700 million between 1954 and 1970, it dominated the Laotian economy, even though tremendous amounts were lost through corruption and Vientiane's incredibly inefficient bureaucracy. So thick was Laotian red tape that, at times, U.S. AID field workers simply by-passed the government, developing a parallel American government for aid distribution that reached down to the village level.

The secret army

Economic aid, equipment for the RLA, and massive bombing of Communist-held areas represented much, but not all, of the U.S. anti-Communist program in Laos during the 1960s. A fourth effort was the formation of a clandestine army trained and supervised in secret by the CIA. Unbeholden to the Vientiane government, it was led by General Vang Pao, a Hmong (sometimes called Meo) tribesman and veteran of the French colonial army. This army was mostly made up of Hmong, a people who occupied the mountains ringing the Plain of Jars. Martial, aggressive, regarded as troublemakers by the lowland Lao, the Hmong were nevertheless valued by the CIA and other Americans, who saw in them a dynamism conspicuously absent in lowland Laotians.

Beginning in 1959, a small group of Hmong and other tribesmen were trained by the CIA and U.S. Special Forces White Star teams to gather intelligence and to operate in small guerrilla bands. President Kennedy and his advisers, fascinated by "counterinsurgency" and other types of nontraditional warfare, supported the buildup of this force. When the 1962 Geneva accords obliged the U.S. to withdraw its military mission, the CIA turned the force into a sizable anti-Communist army under Vang Pao.

Trained, supplied, paid, and directed by CIA agents (who worked in the guise of AID employees or refugee workers), the secret army soon became the most effective military force on the government's side in Laos. In 1962 it numbered 15,000 men; eventually it reached almost 40,000, although probably only 30,000 of these could be considered effective. Vang Pao staged three monsoon counteroffensives against the Pathet Lao in 1964, 1965, and 1966 that allowed government troops to recapture outposts in the Communist strongholds of Sam Neua and Xieng Khouang provinces. The Hmong force also harassed Communist forces on the Plain of Jars. Most of these operations were directed from Vang Pao's secret headquarters at Long Cheng, a base built by the CIA in 1961 to 1963 on a remote

Lt. Col. Vang Pao, a veteran of the French colonial army and now leader of the CIA's secret Hmong force, observes the battlefield at Padong, Laos, in early May 1961.

mountaintop southwest of the Plain of Jars. Long Cheng grew from a small outpost to, by 1970, the second-largest city in Laos, with a population of 40,000.

Although the secret army benefited U.S. policy in Laos, it had a corrosive effect on traditional Hmong life. Vang Pao and his CIA cohorts drained the Hmong villages of young men, offering guns, rice, and money if they would join his army. If bribery did not work, brutality often did: Vang Pao's officers warned villagers that those who did not cooperate would be considered Pathet Lao, with dire consequences. The army also perverted Hmong agriculture. Before the war, the Hmong grew rice for food and cultivated opium as a cash crop. As more tribesmen joined the army, fewer were left to grow crops. The CIA responded by shipping large amounts of rice to Hmong villages. The villages quickly became dependent on U.S. rice and turned all their fields over to the more lucrative opium trade. Vang Pao soon took control of this trade. By some reports, he even used the CIA's Air America to transport opium from the mountains of Laos to heroin factories in Vientiane, where the drug was manufactured, then sent on to Saigon for sale to U.S. servicemen.

The turning point

The war in Laos, a stalemate throughout the mid-1960s, changed dramatically in 1968. Renewed Communist activity, coupled with developments in Vietnam, resulted in a tremendous rise in the level of violence and stunning setbacks for pro-American forces.

At the end of January 1968, Communist forces launched attacks against every major city and town in South Vietnam—the Tet offensive. To protect the Ho Chi Minh Trail during the attacks, the North Vietnamese also pushed against government forces in Laos. On January 13, Communist forces attacked royal troops in the Nam Bac Valley, a strategically important fertile region north of Vientiane. They seized ridge lines, mortared the airstrip, and forced RLA forces to flee into the hills at a cost of 2,000 government casualties. A few weeks later, the North Vietnamese sent three battalions against the U.S. navigational station at Phou Pha Thi, a cliff-sided mountain in Sam Neua Province just twenty-seven kilometers from the North Vietnamese border. Although U.S. planes showered bombs on the jungles around the mountain, the NVA overwhelmed the Hmong and Thai irregulars defending Phou Pha Thi on March 11 in vicious, hand-to-hand combat. The post fell on March 11; twelve American Air Force personnel were killed. Ironically, three weeks later President Lyndon Johnson announced a partial bombing halt over North Vietnam, a move that obviated the need for a navigational station at Phou Pha Thi.

Johnson's bombing halt over North Vietnam had dramatic consequences for the war in Laos. When the halt went into effect, U.S. Air Force bombers once destined for North Vietnam were simply redirected against Communist targets in Laos. No specific policy change had brought this about—the bombers were there, so they were used. As one U.S. official said, "We just couldn't let the planes rust." When a complete bombing halt over North Vietnam was announced at the end of October, bombings in Laos took another jump, to a staggering 600 strikes per day. In the north, the number of sorties doubled, to about 50 per day; one year later this figure doubled again. Along the Ho Chi Minh Trail, fighter-bomber sorties leapt from 4,700 to 12,800 between October and November 1968, while B-52 bombing strikes went from 273 to 600 in the same period. Yet the bombings failed to stop North Vietnamese traveling down the trail. Indeed, in the months before and after the start of the bombing campaign the number of NVA soldiers marching south to fight grew from between 60,000 and 90,000 in 1966 to about 200,000 in 1968.

As the bombing increased, so too did ground combat. The North Vietnamese, distrusting the military skill of the Pathet Lao, dominated the Communist efforts, relegating the Laotian Communists to a subordinate role. In January 1969 the NVA drove Vang Pao's men off of Phou Pha Thi, which they had briefly reoccupied. Then they pushed the Hmong army out of their base at Na Khang, fifty-six kilometers to the southwest. Pathet Lao and NVA troops seized many key airstrips in the north, cutting off the Hmong army from its sources of supply. Other Communist forces attacked targets in the Mekong Valley, near Vientiane, and pushed against royal troops in southern Laos. The Bolovens Plateau of southern Laos, long a fertile farming region, turned into a Communist area as royal troops became trapped in their garrisons.

The ground combat and bombing unleashed a flood of refugees. Twenty thousand farmers fled the Bolovens Plateau. Tens of thousands more fled areas of fighting in the north. Those who chose to stay in combat areas suffered terribly, living in caves and growing ever more dependent on outside aid as their homes and livelihoods were shattered by war.

The Vientiane government's military situation was deteriorating rapidly. In April the U.S., which had always resisted bombing the Plain of Jars, bowed to RLG entreaties to aid a government attack there. In a few months, the bombings turned the Plain of Jars into an uninhabitable wasteland. More people fled as, in the words of one refugee, "the planes came like birds and the bombs fell like rain." Yet the bombing did little to improve the government's position. In June two NVA battalions, spearheaded by Russian-made tanks, forced royal and neutralist troops out of the government stronghold of Muong Soui, near the Plain of Jars, for the first time ever. And in a new and frightening move, the North Vietnamese, instead of retreating when the monsoon rains came, kept most elements of their 316th Division in Laos.

Vang Pao's army was badly mauled by the fighting, but in August and September 1969, after more heavy bombing by U.S. aircraft, his troops swept onto the devastated Plain of Jars. The North Vietnamese, overextended and rattled by the ferocity of the bombing, retreated as Vang Pao reoccupied the plain. The victory was a hollow one, however, for the war had drained all the Hmong villages of fighting men. Edgar "Pop" Buell, an agricultural expert who had long worked with the Hmong and the secret army, summed up the situation in a conversation with Don Schanche of the Washington *Sunday Star*: "It ain't gonna last. Vang Pao's soldiers are mostly little kids and old men. They just ain't got the strength to keep going. They'll get pushed out soon, and I'll have another 70,000 refugees to take care of. It's like starting all over again."

Buell was right. When the North Vietnamese introduced a whole new division, the 312th, into the fighting in 1970, the Hmong army was forced to retreat from the Plain of Jars. The North Vietnamese, hidden from aerial view by the smoke from peasants' slash-and-burn agriculture, pushed the Hmong against the outskirts of their base at Long Cheng. For a time even Long Cheng was threatened, but after heavy bombings and the deployment of two battalions of Thai troops in front of the base, the few

Hmong troops still fighting were able to chase the Vietnamese back into the hills.

Things were no better in the south. The Communists drove government troops out of the garrison town of Attopeu at the end of April 1970; Saravane fell on June 10. Vientiane launched a disastrous attempt to retake Saravane, to no avail. By midyear, the government was in retreat everywhere, and 250,000 Laotian men, women, and children were refugees in their own land.

Cambodia: a balancing act

The war that ravaged so much of Laos in the late 1960s was avoided in Cambodia for a few brief years. Much of the credit for that delay must go to Prince Sihanouk, who maintained an extraordinary balancing act between left and right both inside and outside his country throughout the last half of the decade. But even as Sihanouk furiously upheld his neutralist, centrist vision of "Buddhist socialism," contradictions in that policy compromised his political power. When outside forces upset the balance in the late 1960s, Cambodia took the first steps down the road to an unimaginable horror.

In 1965, though, Sihanouk's neutralism was succeeding. Convinced that communism would ultimately triumph in Southeast Asia, Sihanouk protected Cambodia—and himself—by warming up to outside Socialist forces. In March 1965, for example, he held an Indochina People's Conference in Phnom Penh. There his own Sangkhum party joined representatives from North Vietnam, the NLF, and the Pathet Lao in calling for the withdrawal of U.S. troops, "liberation" of South Vietnam, and a new Geneva conference to guarantee Cambodia's neutrality.

Significantly, none of these outside Communist organizations disputed Sihanouk's claim to represent "progressive" forces in Cambodia. Saloth Sar, Ieng Sary, and the other leftist insurgents that Sihanouk had labeled Khmer Rouge were still small in number and received little backing from other Communists as long as Sihanouk remained in power. Indeed, the Chinese and North Vietnamese actively discouraged them from challenging Sihanouk, out of concern that the prince would cease his political support of their efforts against the U.S. in South Vietnam.

After he broke off relations with the United States in May 1965, Sihanouk continued his dalliance with the interna-

Hmong peasants evacuate their village in February 1970 during the Pathet Lao/North Vietnamese offensive that swept the Hmong army and civilians off most of the Plain of Jars.

tional left. In September and October 1965, he traveled to Communist China for an extravagant show of friendship and solidarity, including a tour of ten provinces and cities, pledges of mutual support, and a celebration of the sixteenth anniversary of the Communist takeover there. Sihanouk's relations with the Chinese had flowered after they supplied him with arms in the wake of his 1963 U.S. military aid shutoff. Now he leaned even closer, supporting China in its ideological dispute with the Soviet Union. When Soviet leaders indicated their displeasure, the prince abruptly canceled a visit to Moscow that was to follow his Chinese tour.

While he embraced outside Communists, however, Sihanouk moved to outflank leftists in his own country. In early 1966 he allowed his right-wing defense minister, General Lon Nol, to crack down on leftist activities. This Lon Nol did with relish, using widespread, indiscriminate violence against the left and arresting members of the legal leftist political party, Pracheachon. At the same time, Sihanouk took the political offensive against them. In long, intemperate speeches, the prince accused Pracheachon of subversion and subservience to North Vietnam. In spite of these attacks, though, the leftists maintained considerable strength among students, teachers, and other educated segments of society.

Sihanouk's attacks on "Vietnamese lackeys" bespoke his long-time anti-Vietnamese sentiments. The prince had reason to fear the Vietnamese: although supposedly aligned with the DRV against the United States, he knew the Vietnamese would do whatever they had to in Cambodia to prosecute their war in South Vietnam. Moreover, the Vietnamese Communists had considerable influence among Cambodia's 600,000 ethnic Vietnamese. In their wartime staging areas along the South Vietnamese border, the Communists pressed the local Vietnamese into labor gangs, taxed them, and spread Communist propaganda among them. Their influence grew after the 1965 American escalation of the war in South Vietnam, when they greatly expanded their base camps and troop presence along Cambodia's border with the south. Their efforts, though, were concentrated against America and the Saigon regime. Though not particularly friendly toward Sihanouk, they preferred to establish a modus vivendi that allowed the prince to keep his power while the Communists kept their bases.

Sihanouk knew a great deal about the Ho Chi Minh Trail and the Vietnamese bases in his country. However, since the North Vietnamese had the power to stay anyway (and since he assumed the Chinese would back him if the Vietnamese became overly aggressive), he tolerated their presence on Cambodian soil. Grudgingly, he also helped

the Communists to obtain supplies for their war. In 1966, at the request of China's premier Chou En-lai, he began to permit shipments of arms, ammunition, and other equipment to the Communists from the Cambodian ports of Sihanoukville and Ream. This supply line soon outstripped the Ho Chi Minh Trail as a source of Communist war materiel for the base camps. It also happened to profit the royal family, Cambodian army officers, and Chinese middlemen. The whole business distressed Sihanouk, but he saw little choice. "Two thirds for the Viet Cong, one third for yourself," he later said. "At that rate one sells oneself."

Others in Cambodia were making different deals with the Communists. Beginning in 1966, Chinese middlemen smuggled at least 100,000 tons of Cambodian rice to the Vietnamese Communists. This weakened the nation's economy, which was heavily dependent on rice for foreign export trade; it also cost the government, which taxed rice, tremendous amounts of revenue. Part of this revenue loss was the government's fault, for it paid only a low fixed price for rice, while the Vietnamese offered payment at the higher world price (and in American dollars). The dramatic drop in rice available for export—from 563,700 tons in 1965 to 199,049 tons in 1966—exacerbated an economic crisis that grew worse with each passing year.

The Battambang revolt

By mid-1966, Sihanouk was feeling the pressure of his centrist position. The Cambodian right was upset by his overtures to Communist countries while the left was alienated by his internal crackdowns. To respond to these pressures, and to charges of despotism, the prince declared that he would hold an election without endorsing any candidates. On September 11, for the first time in its history, Cambodia held an open election. It was not, however, a fair one. The wealthy right-wing candidates spent huge sums buying votes and harassing leftist candidates. When the polls closed, the conservatives had won nearly 75 percent of the seats in the National Assembly. Sihanouk's plan had backfired, but he could not turn away from the results. He told the new assembly to form a government without his interference. For prime minister, the conservatives chose Sihanouk's long-time minister of defense, Lon Nol. For his deputy they selected Sirik Matak, a member of the Sisowath branch of the royal family. Sirik Matak was a close friend of the Americans and an enemy of Norodom Sihanouk.

For his part, Lon Nol had been a leading, if limited, figure on the right wing for years. He first came to prominence as national police chief and head of a political party supported by large landowners in the early 1950s. First chief of staff then defense minister in every cabinet since 1955, he was regarded as a trustworthy subordinate to Sihanouk, even though he often disagreed with the

A Royal Lao Air Force T-28 prepares to make a second napalm strike against a Communist position on the northern branch of the Sihanouk Trail near Attopeu, November 1966.

prince's policies. Deeply religious and superstitious, he was a true reactionary, wanting to return Cambodia to its ancient roots as a Buddhist state. He was also ruthless, fiercely anti-Communist, and capable of considerable violence. Because he seemed such a mediocrity, people tended to underestimate him.

Sihanouk was in a bind. He had called elections in part to keep a balance between left and right. Now the right threatened it. To preserve his own authority in the face of the conservative's triumph, he leaned leftward, toward the very people he and Lon Nol had lately been repressing. He created an opposition "countergovernment" to monitor and criticize Lon Nol's government. Sihanouk's alternate "cabinet" included not only loyalists but also the well-known leftists (and former cabinet members) who had been elected to the assembly: Khieu Samphan, Hou Yuon, and Hu Nim. The countergovernment issued caustic daily bulletins accusing Lon Nol and his cabinet of corruption, inefficiency, and other crimes. These criticisms had their intended effect, giving Sihanouk a platform on which to challenge Lon Nol's political power.

One of Lon Nol's first priorities was to aid the economy—and distance Cambodia from the Vietnamese Communists—by trying to stop the smuggling of Cambodian rice to the Communist base areas in the east. Unfortunately for the peasants, his methods were extremely harsh. He sent soldiers into rice-growing areas to collect rice at gunpoint, paying farmers only the low government price instead of the high price offered by the Communists. This *ramassage du paddy* was bitterly opposed by the peasants. It caused widespread unrest, especially in the rice-rich western province of Battambang, where the left still had some organizational clout. Soon Communist-inspired leaflets began to appear all over Battambang, calling on the peasants to oppose Lon Nol's regime.

As trouble brewed in Battambang, Sihanouk left the country in January 1967 for a two-month "medical" visit to bathe in the mineral waters of southern France. By the time he returned, the left and the right were on the verge of civil war. Lon Nol, after establishing headquarters in Battambang in January, had unleashed violent repression against leftists and the resisting peasantry. More ruthless tactics were used to gather rice, and soldiers began killing captured rebels. The left, for its part, was in open revolt, not only against Lon Nol but in places against Sihanouk, whom it accused of complicity with the government and wanting only "to live the good life in France." Unrest began to trouble the cities as well. On March 11, two days after Sihanouk's return, Khieu Samphan organized a large demonstration outside the "countergovernment's" offices, demanding that Lon Nol resign and new elections be held.

If Sihanouk had an opportunity to re-create his centrist power base at this point, he failed. Instead of steering a moderate course, the mercurial prince suddenly sided with Lon Nol against the leftists. This choice may have been premeditated (he later said that Lon Nol's program had been "launched on my instructions"), but it was hardly in keeping with his long-time, careful balancing of left and right in Cambodia. In any case, his switch tipped the balance in favor of the right. He accused Khieu Samphan and the other urban leftists of fomenting the rebellion and called on Lon Nol to crush the uprising.

Battambang exploded. On April 2 peasants in the nearby village of Samlaut killed two soldiers and took their weapons. Others joined them. By the end of the day, 200 peasants bearing arms and anti-Lon Nol banners attacked a local garrison. Lon Nol launched another wave of repression. His men killed hundreds of peasants and laid waste whole villages as Lon Nol declared martial law. The government's violence worked. The revolt sputtered to an end as thousands of rebels fled to the forests.

Sihanouk continued his assault on the left by secretly ordering the executions of Khieu Samphan, Hou Yuon, and Hu Nim. The three leftists, however, had sensed the danger they were in and had fled Phnom Penh for the *maquis* before government soldiers could find them. Their disappearance caused many to assume that they had in fact been killed, provoking another political crisis and large demonstrations by the urban left. To calm the nation, on April 29 Sihanouk accepted Lon Nol's resignation for reasons of "ill health." Lon Nol left for France, ostensibly for a medical visit. With Lon Nol gone, Sihanouk formed a new cabinet that included both rightists and (in typical Sihanouk fashion) a few figures from the left whom he could use to play off the right.

The prince also used the fallout from the revolt to answer a challenge from another sphere, the economically powerful Chinese minority in Cambodia. In 1967 the People's Republic of China was convulsed in Mao's Great Proletarian Cultural Revolution. During the revolution, radicals inside the PRC attempted (with some success) to instill unrest among Cambodia's 400,000 ethnic Chinese: At their behest, some in the Chinese minority had spread prorevolutionary and anti-Sihanouk propaganda in Phnom Penh and elsewhere. Sihanouk seized this opportunity to crack down on them, closing Chinese schools, shutting down the leftist-dominated Khmer-Chinese Friendship Association, and arresting a few Chinese middlemen who controlled the rice trade between Battambang and the Communist base camps. It was a deft move, since Sihanouk's attacks on the Chinese furthered his political clout, gained more rice revenues for the government, and earned him political credit among conservatives.

Thus, for the price of aligning himself with the right, Sihanouk had stayed in power. By October 1967, things had calmed enough to allow him to invite Lon Nol back from France. But even though the prince had survived another challenge, his options had narrowed. Just as important, the leftists now had thousands more recruits to their cause. Lon Nol's repression of a large segment of the peasantry, tolerated (and perhaps initiated) by Sihanouk, laid the groundwork for future tragedy. In a very real sense, the horrific revolution that was to engulf Cambodia began in earnest at Battambang in 1967.

The gathering storm

After Lon Nol returned to Phnom Penh, Sihanouk continued his crusade against the left. The army and national police struck at supposedly leftist villages all over the country, bombing and burning villages and killing peasants on rather shaky evidence of subversion. At the same time, the government acquiesced in the continuing presence of large numbers of Vietnamese Communist soldiers in the east. Sihanouk understood that the bases were vital to their war effort, and he had enough troubles without prompting Vietnamese anger. He and the Vietnamese Communists arrived at some mutual understandings. For his part, Sihanouk continued to allow arms to be shipped to the bases from Cambodian ports (prompting some to speak of a "Sihanouk Trail" akin to the Ho Chi Minh Trail) and in June 1967 opened up diplomatic relations with both the DRV and NLF. For their part, the Vietnamese Commu-

nists formally recognized Sihanouk's version of the ill-defined border between Cambodia and Vietnam, agreed to avoid roads and population centers near NVA bases, and promised to withdraw from Cambodia when the war in the South was over.

Meanwhile, the still-small Khmer Rouge was trying, without much success, to organize a more significant rebellion. Sihanouk's decimation of the "traditional" left—the Pracheachon and other urban Communists—had allowed Saloth Sar and his comrades in the rural *maquis* to assume leadership within the Communist movement. Their rise among the left, however, was not well supported by fellow Communists, such as the North Vietnamese, who had their own agenda in Cambodia. Without much outside help, and without a following among the urban left, the radical *maquis* Communists needed another base from which to pursue their revolution.

They found it in the wilderness. As Lon Nol's repression grew, Khmer Rouge leaders, including Saloth Sar, fled

A Khmer Rouge cadre trained by the North Vietnamese attempts to enlist Buddhist monks into the fledgling Cambodian revolutionary movement in 1970.

from the lowlands to Cambodia's hilly northeastern provinces. There they found aid and comfort among the Khmer Loeu, a group of highland tribespeople. Darker skinned and primitive compared to the Khmer of the Mekong Basin, the Khmer Loeu were considered savages by their lowland countrymen; they had long answered that contempt with hostility toward Phnom Penh. Sihanouk had exacerbated their hatred when, in the 1960s, he attempted to collect the nomadic tribesmen into permanent villages and sent lowland Khmer colonists to live among them in the remote mountains.

The Khmer Rouge, who needed a following among the people of Cambodia, and the Khmer Loeu, who had a strong grudge against the central government, joined together. The Khmer Rouge drew close to the tribespeople, because in the inhospitable, malarial northeastern mountains, the Khmer Loeu treated them kindly, showed them hospitality, and protected them from the government troops who occasionally ventured into the mountains. Like the Pathet Lao in Laos, the Communists responded by feeding the tribes' anger against the central government. The situation in the hills also reinforced the Khmer Rouge's sense of mission. In Elizabeth Becker's words, "Sar went to the hills for safety and ended up adopting for his cause the hill people who needed revolution. When his troops won the war eight years later, witnesses remarked on the high proportion of dark-skinned tribals fighting in his ranks."

The revolution, however, was slow in coming. Outside its base in the northeastern hills, the Khmer Rouge had only small pockets of rebels scattered throughout Cambodia. Central organization and coordination were extremely difficult, especially in the face of Sihanouk's continuing repression. Regional sections of the Khmer Rouge tended to act in disjointed fashion, and loyalties were sometimes divided. The Khmer Rouge eastern section, for example, stayed in close touch with the Vietnamese Communists, while those connected to Saloth Sar's Central Committee felt the Vietnamese consistently betrayed them for the sake of their own revolution. In a sense they were right, for the Vietnamese Communists, not wanting to upset their *modus vivendi* with Sihanouk, continued to counsel patience while Saloth Sar thirsted for revolution.

Still, the Khmer Communists tried. Beginning January 17, 1968—just a few weeks before the Communist Tet offensive in South Vietnam—they launched numerous attacks, bombings, bridge blowings, and raids against government targets. Most of these were aimed at collecting arms rather than holding territory or killing large numbers of government troops. Sihanouk, however, reacted by stating that "total war" now existed in Cambodia and ordered more repression. The cycle of violence grew.

Under pressure from the rightists, the prince now began to reexamine his *modus vivendi* with the Vietnamese. Despite his own reluctance to confront them, he understood that they made convenient scapegoats for the na-

tion's internal difficulties. Turning against them also appealed to his countrymen's traditional hatred of the Vietnamese. Certainly, 40,000 Vietnamese in the eastern sanctuaries seemed more a threat to Cambodia than the 4,000 to 5,000 poorly armed, poorly trained Khmer Rouge rebels.

In the meantime, Lon Nol had continued to rise steadily in Sihanouk's government. On May 1, 1968, he was reappointed defense minister; in December he became acting prime minister; and on August 12, 1969, prime minister in a new Government of National Salvation. The cabinet was so named because of the worsening economic situation. By that time, however, another profoundly significant development had come to pass in the skies over the Vietnamese base camps on the eastern border.

"Menu" and Sihanouk's fall

When Richard Nixon took the oath of office as president of the United States on January 20, 1969, he carried with him a pledge to end the war in Vietnam—the war that had torn America apart as Lyndon Johnson's escalation failed to defeat the Communists. Coming to Washington with Nixon was Henry Kissinger, a Harvard professor and global strategist whom the new president had appointed his national security assistant.

Nixon and Kissinger were willing to consider almost any military move to end the war. When they asked for recommendations, the Joint Chiefs of Staff proposed renewed bombing of North Vietnam, which Johnson had halted in late 1968. The new president, however, rejected this course as politically impossible. Next, the chiefs sent Kissinger a recommendation that the Air Force bomb the Communist base camps along the South Vietnamese border in Cambodia. This idea had some appeal, especially since General Creighton Abrams, commander of U.S. forces in Vietnam, had also recommended a B-52 bomber strike against COSVN (Central Office for South Vietnam), the supposed Communist command center located just over the Cambodian border. There were just three problems with the proposal. First, COSVN was not the concrete-bunkered, nine-kilometer-square, easily bombed headquarters the U.S. military thought it to be. COSVN, such as it was, consisted of a mobile command unit that changed location every ten days or so. Second, such a move risked dragging Cambodia openly into the Vietnam War. Third, bombing raids into a neutral nation such as Cambodia could very well be construed a violation of international law.

Around the same time that the raids were being considered, the Vietnamese Communists launched a series of attacks in South Vietnam. President Nixon saw this as a test of his resolve. It prodded him to move forward with the bombing plan. In a meeting of his top advisers, Secretary of State William Rogers objected, fearing the certain diplomatic fallout. Also protesting was Nixon's defense secretary, Melvin Laird, who feared the political repercussions when the raids became known on Capitol Hill. But Nixon was determined. In strict secrecy, he authorized the first bombing raids over Cambodia. The attack was designated Operation Breakfast, after the morning meeting at which it was first outlined to Pentagon officials.

On March 18, 1969, sixty B-52 bombers, on loan from the Strategic Air Command, lifted into the skies over Guam. After they passed into South Vietnamese air space, forty-eight of the huge planes peeled off from the rest of the mission and veered across the Cambodian border. Over the area suspected of containing COSVN they each dropped twenty-four tons of bombs. Then they skirted back over the border and returned to their island base.

Operation Breakfast did not destroy the shadowy COSVN, nor did it "neutralize" the Communists in the area. A U.S.-South Vietnamese reconnaissance team dropped there just after the raid was shot to pieces by Vietnamese. Nonetheless, Nixon and his military command were satisfied with the secret operation. In three weeks the Joint Chiefs recommended another strike, which was also approved. The number of raids grew as other areas along the border inside Cambodia were targeted. Each was designated by a similar name: Breakfast was followed by Lunch, Snack, Dinner, Dessert, and Supper. Taken together, the bombing raids were known as Operation Menu.

It is not known whether Sihanouk agreed to Operation Menu. Certainly he did not object in principle to measures that pressured the Vietnamese to leave his country, although his desire to stay out of the war precluded him from pressing them too hard. The stakes were too high for the Vietnamese: fully 80 percent of their supplies were now being shipped from Kompong Som to the base camps. He also knew that he had little chance of preventing the United States from doing anything it wanted in Cambodia. So, instead of revealing whatever he knew about the raids, he chose to remain silent.

Thanks to elaborate records falsification, Operation Menu continued for fourteen months in absolute secrecy from the American public. In that time the B-52s flew 3,630 sorties against targets in Cambodia, dropping over 100,000 tons of bombs. Their effect on the war in Vietnam was minimal: when the bombing began the Communists simply moved their sanctuaries deeper inside Cambodia. What suffered was the political situation in Cambodia, where the attacks tipped the precarious balance away from neutrality in the Vietnam War. And most affected, of course, were the Cambodians living and dying in areas blasted by tons of American bombs.

By mid-1969, Sihanouk was pressed from every corner. Cambodia's economy was in ruins. The 30,000-man army could field only about a third of its men, and the quality of its equipment had seriously deteriorated in the years since

the prince had cut off U.S. aid. His conservative allies wanted both to drive the Vietnamese out of Cambodia and crush the small Khmer Rouge insurgency, but Sihanouk was unwilling to provoke the Vietnamese. His strongest ally, China, was being run by Maoist radicals who had attempted to export their revolution to his country. And with Operation Menu, the United States was gradually expanding the war into Cambodia.

The prince had been edging closer to the United States for some time. In November 1967 Jacqueline Kennedy, widow of the slain U.S. president, had been escorted by Sihanouk on a tour of Angkor Wat in northwestern Cambodia. Three months later Chester Bowles, U.S. ambassador to India and a respected Washington figure, flew to Phnom Penh to confer with the Cambodian leader. Sihanouk told him that he was willing to restore relations if Washington would accept the inviolability of his nation's borders. Around this time, too, Sihanouk began to accept intelligence reports from the United States that detailed Vietcong and NVA activity inside Cambodia.

The architects of U.S. involvement in Cambodia, President Nixon and his national security assistant, Henry Kissinger, confer in the White House's Oval Office in February 1971.

In 1969 Sihanouk, under rightist pressure, moved closer to the United States. In July he announced that Cambodia and the United States would reopen diplomatic relations. Around the same time he quietly suspended shipments of arms from Cambodian ports to the Vietnamese Communist sanctuaries, a move that put him in direct confrontation with the Communists, who depended on the shipments. Then in August he announced the new right-wing Government of National Salvation, under Lon Nol. Lon Nol continued the rightward shift by insisting that Sihanouk's royal rival, Sisowath Sirik Matak, be included in the government. The prince again relented.

Given a mandate to save the economy, the Salvation Government soon began to dismantle Sihanouk's Buddhist socialism by vowing to return state-owned enterprises to the private sector. At the heart of this drive was Sirik Matak, who, with others, began to criticize not only Sihanouk's policies but also the tremendous corruption that had drained so much of the nation's wealth. The anticorruption attacks were aimed primarily at Sihanouk's family, especially his wife, Monique, and her venal relatives, who for years had sold positions, skimmed off profits from government monopolies, and profited from gambling and other wasteful enterprises.

Sihanouk was distressed, but his credit was almost at an end. When Lon Nol left the country for another medical visit to France, Sihanouk tried to assert his authority at a December 1969 session of the National Assembly. Without specifically mentioning Sirik Matak, he defended his Buddhist socialism against conservative critics. By the end of the session, though, it was clear that the majority of ministers stood with Sirik Matak against Sihanouk.

Disheartened, the prince announced that he would again travel to France, this time for treatment of "obesity, blood disease, and albuminuria." On January 6, 1970, he left Cambodia for France.

Sirik Matak and the conservatives wasted no time in implementing their own reforms. At the end of January 1970, Sirik Matak closed down a state casino run by Sihanouk's family. In February he loosened controls on foreign trade to allow private companies the right to import and export goods. His third move, directed specifically against the Vietnamese Communists, was the most profound: on February 24, the government announced that old 500-riel bank notes would be exchanged by the government for new notes; any significant amount of money was subject to government impoundment and inspection. This move was aimed at depriving the Communists of the cash they used to buy Cambodian rice.

The exchange scheme had an immediate and damaging effect. The Vietnamese Communists in the border regions tried to get rid of their old notes by forcing them on local Cambodian peasants. The government, suspecting the Communists might try to smuggle in dollars to buy new 500-riel notes, announced that it would reserve the right to inspect diplomatic pouches entering the country. By using economic pressure against the Communists, Sirik Matak and Lon Nol, who had by March returned to Cambodia, were forcing a confrontation with the Vietnamese.

Tensions rose. When the government moved against the Vietnamese, other Cambodians responded. The ancient hatreds between the two peoples, always just below the surface, began to flare. Led by the army, ethnic Khmer rioted against ethnic Vietnamese in eastern sections of Cambodia. Then the riots moved to Phnom Penh. On March 11, a mob of 10,000 students, monks, and soldiers sacked the embassies of the DRV and NLF. The government backed the disturbances, calling the rioters "worthy of praise" and noted that the riots were "an expression of the real sentiments of the Cambodian people exasperated by...the occupation of Cambodian territory." One day after the demonstration, March 12, the government made an impossible demand, summarily ordering the 40,000 Vietnamese Communists in the sanctuaries to leave Cambodia within three days.

Sihanouk remained in France, ignoring the entreaties of those still supporting him to return to Cambodia. His hubris, nurtured by thirty years at the head of his nation, caused him to underestimate the right wing's determination to force events. He assumed that, as in the past, he could return to power after the right wing had exhausted its supporters. Instead of flying to Phnom Penh, the prince denounced the rightists in a press conference, then left France on March 13 for a visit to Moscow.

In Cambodia, the anti-Vietnamese rioters killed native Vietnamese, destroyed their shops, desecrated their churches. At the same time, Sirik Matak and Lon Nol quietly moved against Sihanouk. On March 16 Oum Manorine, a Sihanouk relative and head of the national police, was hauled before the National Assembly and accused of corruption. Sensing the extent of danger, he attempted a coup against Lon Nol and Sirik Matak that night. It failed miserably; Lon Nol's troops detained Oum Manorine's police in their barracks and arrested him.

The next day the National Assembly met to debate the fate of Cambodia's leader. Sihanouk was denounced as corrupt, deceptive, debauched, and beholden to the Vietnamese. Shortly after noon the assembly passed, ninety-two to zero, a resolution: "The National Assembly and the Council of the Kingdom, meeting in joint session, have withdrawn on the 18th of March, 1970, at 1:00 P.M. their confidence in Prince Norodom Sihanouk in the functions of chief of state." After twenty-nine years at his nation's helm, Sihanouk was now an exile, a prince spurned by politicians and generals who were about to lead Cambodia into disaster.

Cambodian students protest outside the DRV/NLF embassy in Phnom Penh, mid-March 1970. They opposed the Vietnamese presence in eastern Cambodia.

Pawns of War

After the fall of Prince Sihanouk, Cambodia tumbled swiftly into the abyss of violence that the prince had skirted for so long.

All of the parties involved bore a share of the blame for the catastrophe that followed: the new Cambodian leadership, which marched naively into a war it did not have the means to win; Sihanouk himself, whose injured pride and thirst for revenge led him into a hasty alliance with Vietnamese and Khmer Communist forces he could not control; the Hanoi and Saigon governments, which both stepped up military operations on Cambodian territory; and the United States, which grasped for short-run tactical advantages in Cambodia while disregarding the grave longer-range risks of a widened war.

Neither the country's new leaders nor the ousted Sihanouk tried to preserve Cambodia's vulnerable neutrality. Instead, both quickly lined up with the opposing forces in the regional war. From Peking, five days after his overthrow, Sihanouk proclaimed the establishment of the National United Front of

Kampuchea and a liberation army that would fight in alliance with his former bitter enemies, the Khmer Rouge, and with the other Indochinese revolutionaries against Lon Nol.

In Phnom Penh, meanwhile, military commanders approached the U.S. Defense Attaché Office staff barely a week after the coup to request U.S. military aid. Following that initial approach, American and Cambodian officers met every day, sometimes more than once, to discuss Cambodian military needs and requests, which "shortly began to pour into DAO and the embassy" for U.S. air strikes on Communist positions in Cambodia.

Cambodia at war

The first major action by outside forces after Sihanouk's overthrow was a two-day incursion by South Vietnamese Rangers into Cambodia's Kandal Province on March 27 and 28. Then, on the twenty-ninth, the North Vietnamese launched widespread attacks against Cambodian military outposts in the border region—the start, as one Cambodian general later wrote, of "overt aggression against Cambodia."

The U.S. briefly halted its secret B-52 raids after the coup. A week later, however, the Joint Chiefs of Staff recommended to Defense Secretary Melvin Laird that the raids be resumed. When the bombs began falling again shortly afterward, they were aimed not only at Communist logistical bases but also in direct support of Cambodian troops in the field. JCS targeting memos indicated strikes in early April only three kilometers from the nearest "friendly" troops, so close that there must have been some liaison between American planners and Cambodian field commanders.

During April, military actions by all sides escalated. The North Vietnamese and Vietcong easily drove the poorly trained and inexperienced Cambodian army (now called FANK, for Forces Armées Nationales Khmères) out of all but a few isolated enclaves in eastern Cambodia. By mid-April, Communist units were ranging far to the west of the traditional sanctuary areas, ambushing road convoys and attacking isolated FANK outposts.

U.S. and Cambodian officials usually referred to the attacks as a "foreign invasion" aimed at conquering all of Cambodia. Intelligence assessments showed a more ambiguous picture, however, suggesting that the Vietnamese were mainly concerned with preserving their support and supply system along the border. Their attacks on FANK positions and lines of communication away from the border regions were not the opening battles of an all-out offensive, in this view, but an essentially defensive effort

to keep FANK off balance while the Communists prepared to meet an expected U.S. and South Vietnamese assault. The North Vietnamese may also have hoped that their pressure would force the Lon Nol government to renew Sihanouk's policies of accommodation.

Though their operations were widespread and inflicted substantial casualties on the Cambodians, the Vietnamese in fact fought rather economically, seldom committing major forces or risking heavy losses of their own. They also moved quickly to develop a Cambodian resistance movement, centered in the border region and under direct Vietnamese control, in contrast to the Khmer Rouge insurgents elsewhere in the country. The Vietnamese-sponsored resistance units would both legitimize the Vietnamese presence and help defend the sanctuary areas while conforming with Hanoi's doctrine that "the liberation and defense of each country is the work of its people."

The American and South Vietnamese involvement in Cambodia also deepened during April. Military cooperation between the new Cambodian leaders and the Saigon government was arranged in a series of secret conferences involving South Vietnam's vice president Nguyen Cao Ky, who made two unannounced nighttime flights to Phnom Penh, and Lon Nol's brother, Lon Non, who traveled several times to Saigon. Following those meetings South Vietnamese commanders received secret orders allowing "offensive operations against NVA bases, installations and storage points" up to fifty-eight kilometers inside Cambodia. Two major incursions followed, one on April 14 to 16 involving two regiment-sized task forces and a second on April 20 to 23 carried out by elements of the 9th ARVN Division. Though no American ground troops crossed the border, the U.S. gave fire and logistical support to the ARVN operations while also beginning clandestine assistance to the new Phnom Penh government.

While the U.S. and South Vietnam were thus consolidating their military relationship with the new Cambodian regime, Prince Sihanouk took the fateful step of consolidating his alliance with the Vietnamese Communists. At a "summit conference of the Indochinese peoples" held in southern China on April 24 and 25, Sihanouk, the Lao Communist leader Prince Souphanouvong, North Vietnam's prime minister Pham Van Dong, and leaders of the South Vietnamese National Liberation Front proclaimed a common struggle by the three Indochinese peoples against "the U.S. imperialist aggressors."

Even at that early stage, the historic enmities between the Cambodians and Vietnamese must have caused some tensions within the alliance. Pham Van Dong and the rest of the North Vietnamese delegates made a visible effort, one witness noted, not to appear as "imperialists, or even excessively forceful federators."

If the Vietnamese and Cambodians were uneasy allies, so were the hostile and mutually suspicious forces within the Cambodian resistance itself. A legacy of hatred and

---

Preceding page. Lon Nol, leader of the Khmer Republic in the early 1970s, appears for a press conference outside Phnom Penh's presidential palace in August 1973.

violence lay between Sihanouk and the Khmer Rouge revolutionaries, and both looked with mistrust on the Hanoi-trained Cambodian Communists, often called Khmer Vietminh. They had gone to North Vietnam with the Vietnamese Communists after the 1954 Geneva accords and were now returning to Cambodia after many years to help run the new Vietnamese-sponsored resistance forces. As Cambodia slid into the conflagration, the disparate insurgent factions were united only by their temporary dependence on North Vietnamese military force and their opposition to Lon Nol and the United States, not by any shared vision of Cambodia's future.

The origins and nature of the Cambodian resistance was the last thing on the minds of American military planners and policymakers in Saigon and Washington. American attention was fixed, instead, on the opportunity to do what U.S. commanders had urged for years: take the war into the Cambodian sanctuaries.

On the evening of April 26, President Nixon signed a directive authorizing an attack by U.S. forces into the area called the Fishhook, adjacent to South Vietnam's Tay Ninh Province—the area, U.S. intelligence believed, where COSVN was located. Meanwhile, ARVN units with U.S. support would attack into Cambodia's Svay Rieng Province, called the Parrot's Beak, which at its closest point lay only fifty-three kilometers west of Saigon.

Nixon withdrew his order for a day so that Secretary of State William Rogers could testify to the Senate Foreign Relations Committee that there was no decision to use American troops in Cambodia. Rogers, as well as Defense Secretary Laird, had reservations about the use of U.S. forces. But Nixon's mind was made up. On April 30, as the first of 32,000 U.S. troops rolled across the border, Nixon announced his decision to the nation in one of the most controversial speeches of his career, declaring that the United States would seem "a pitiful, helpless giant" if it did not act in Cambodia.

The announcement brought a torrent of protests, not just on college campuses (including Kent State University, where four students were killed by the Ohio National Guard) but in Congress and even from executive-branch officials. Three of Kissinger's senior aides resigned, and 50 foreign service officers, along with 200 other State Department employees, signed a statement opposing administration policy. In the furor, Nixon hastily announced (without military advice, according to General William C. Westmoreland) that the incursion would penetrate no deeper than thirty-four kilometers and would end by June 30.

Cambodians battle Vietcong troops in Prey Veng, April 1970. The war in eastern Cambodia escalated dramatically as Lon Nol's troops pushed against entrenched VC positions.

In a sense, that decision was even more significant than the decision to go into Cambodia in the first place. Limiting the U.S. operation in time and space meant that whatever successes it achieved could only be temporary. A CIA memorandum drafted several weeks before the incursion stated the issue clearly: Hanoi's strategy would suffer "a serious blow . . . perhaps a critical one" if it lost its Cambodian bases, the CIA's Office of National Estimates concluded. But it continued, "Cambodia has no chance of being able to accomplish this by itself; to deny base areas and sanctuaries in Cambodia would require heavy and sustained bombing and large numbers of foot soldiers which could only be supplied by the U.S. and South Vietnam."

That analysis was never forwarded to the White House, however. It was withheld by CIA director Richard Helms, possibly, as Senate investigators obliquely suggested six years later, out of reluctance to submit an assessment that was inconsistent with administration policy.

Halfway through the Cambodian campaign, President Nixon declared it "the most successful operation of this long and very difficult war." Similarly exuberant announcements followed the withdrawal of American forces at the end of June. The U.S. command claimed to have captured or destroyed enough weapons to equip seventy-four North Vietnamese infantry battalions, sufficient rice to feed the entire Communist army for four months, and vast quantities of ammunition.

As often happened, CIA analysts reached more conservative conclusions. The rice would be "easily" replaced from that year's bumper harvests in Cambodia and South Vietnam, a CIA estimate declared, and only about one-third of the captured weapons were types still being used by the Vietnamese Communist forces. The rest were obsolete arms that had apparently been stockpiled in the sanctuaries for some time. Besides, many of the weapons lost were being replaced from the huge quantities the Communists were capturing from the Cambodian army. As for COSVN, its main elements had "escaped essentially intact," the CIA analysts believed. "Despite some temporary disruption during the early weeks of the Cambodia campaign, the Communist command and control system was quickly restored to almost normal efficiency, and no lasting damage seems to have been inflicted."

Still, the incursion caused substantial if temporary damage to the Communists' war effort. Following the operation, Vietcong and North Vietnamese attacks in the southern regions of South Vietnam dropped off significantly, with a corresponding reduction of U.S. casualties. In that sense the operation was successful, from the perspective of American commanders in Vietnam.

Prince Souphanouvong and Prince Sihanouk pass beneath a banner proclaiming Lao and Khmer unity during a rally at a Pathet Lao headquarters in Sam Neua Province, early 1970s.

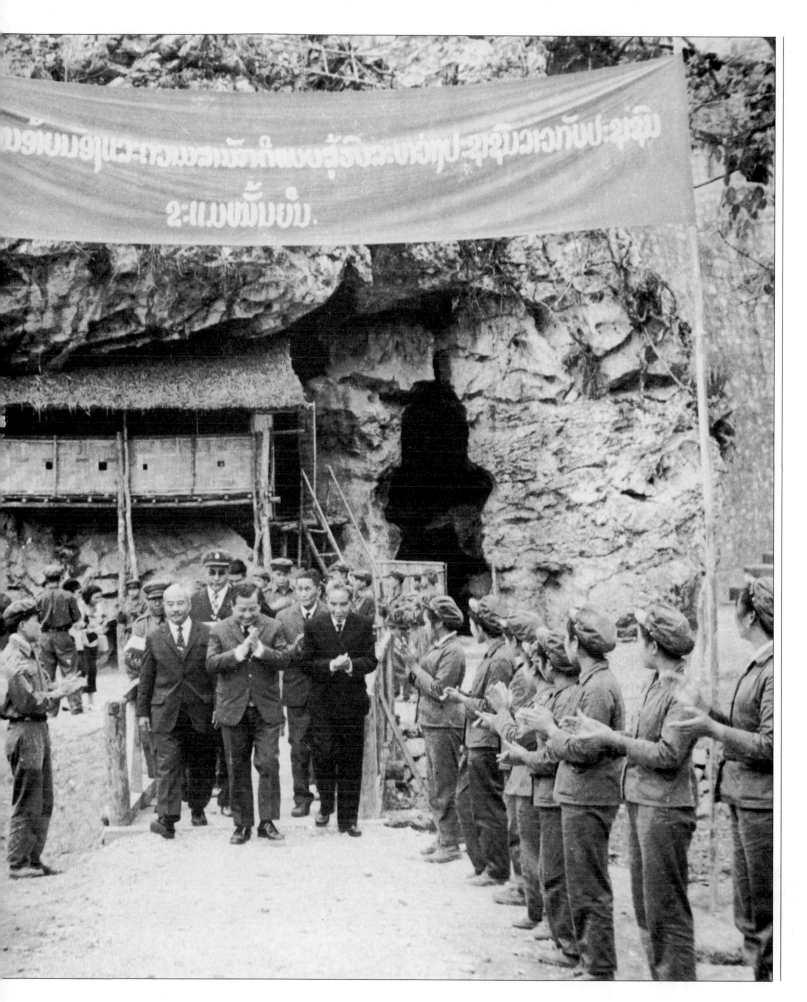

From Cambodia's viewpoint, however, the picture looked very different. "Within the framework of Vietnamization," the operation might be considered a success, a Cambodian general, Sak Sutsakhan, wrote after the war, but the incursion had other repercussions that "fell with all their weight" on the ill-prepared Cambodian forces:

To avoid massive bombings by U.S. and RVN of Vietnam forces, the enemy fell back deeper and deeper inside the Cambodian territory. These bombings and attacks by friendly forces also caused the complete evacuation of these areas by the civilian population, whereupon the enemy immediately moved in. The result of all this was that a sizable part of the Cambodian territory was lost to the enemy.

The withdrawal of American forces, General Sak concluded, resulted in "a void so great on the allied side" that neither the Cambodian nor the South Vietnamese armies were ever able to fill it.

Despite the disastrous reverses suffered by Cambodian forces in the first months of the war, it remained a popular crusade for much of the Cambodian public, particularly in the cities where opposition to Prince Sihanouk and resentment of the Vietnamese Communist encroachments had been strongest. University and high-school students in Phnom Penh flocked to recruiting stations, while civil servants turned out in the city's parks to learn marching, judo, and small-unit tactics. After only a few hours' training or none at all, soldiers were sent off to the battlefields gaily waving flags and rifles from the tops of overloaded civilian trucks or buses.

Some of those rifles were turned not on the armed Communist enemy but on Vietnamese civilians who had lived peacefully in Cambodia for many years. The massacres began at Prasaut, in the Parrot's Beak. In subsequent days more mass killings occurred in Takeo, south of Phnom Penh, and in villages along the Mekong, where the bloody, bound corpses of victims were thrown into the river by the hundreds, swelling gruesomely as they floated downstream in the sluggish brown water.

Terrorizing unarmed Vietnamese civilians was one thing. Facing North Vietnamese troops was another. In the first four months of the war, Pentagon analysts reported, a force of as few as 10,000 Communist troops "had overrun half of Cambodia, taken or threatened sixteen of its nineteen provincial capitals and interdicted—for varying periods—all road and rail links to the capital."

In late June, just before the deadline for withdrawal of American forces, U.S. helicopters and Air Force transports darted into Ba Kev and Labang Siek, two isolated outposts in Ratanakiri Province in far northeastern Cambodia, to help rescue about 7,500 FANK soldiers and dependents who were trapped there. Hardly any other government units in the northeast were saved, however. The remaining FANK garrisons were simply left to be overrun or, in some cases, to desert to the Communist side.

The pace of battle slowed somewhat in the final months of 1970. Early in the new year, however, the Cambodians were further demoralized by a spectacular attack on Phnom Penh's Pochentong airport. Before dawn on January 22, about 100 Communist sappers penetrated the airfield's defense perimeter and succeeded in blowing up practically the entire Cambodian air force, including all of its MiG fighters.

The end draws near

In the fall of 1971, the Cambodian army's offensive spirit was broken for good in a disastrous operation called Chenla II, after the name of one of the ancient Cambodian empires. Launched on August 20, the Chenla campaign was intended to reopen Highway 6 between Phnom Penh and Kompong Thom, about 140 kilometers to the north, which had been cut off for over a year. The strategy was the customary one: government forces simply lined up on the road and drove north in a long slender column, without flank security and with the usual total lack of intelligence on enemy dispositions.

The Communists initially offered little resistance, and on October 5, units driving up from the south linked up with troops from the besieged city. Lon Nol exulted in an order of the day: "You have overcome the enemy and destroyed his finest regiments. Your exploits have exceeded our hopes, and you have held high the flag of the Republic." Religious and military ceremonies were ordered to celebrate the victory. But three weeks later, the Communists fell on the vulnerable, stretched-out government forces and turned the triumph into a debacle. Whole battalions vanished, and survivors of the assault were permanently demoralized.

Despite that and similar though smaller disasters on other battlefields, Lon Nol proved unwilling to recognize the weaknesses of his own tactics and his subordinates' leadership. Instead, he constantly peppered the Americans with "numerous intemperate requests," as U.S. Ambassador Emory C. Swank once called them, for more aid. Meanwhile, much of the assistance that was supplied was squandered by inefficiency or corruption.

A U.S. Senate Appropriations Committee delegation, after visiting Cambodia, issued one of the most scathing reports in congressional memory, charging that through payroll padding and other forms of corruption, the Khmer government and military were "substantially subverting the intended purpose" of U.S. aid. "The situation which the delegation found is wholly unacceptable," the report added, demanding that the U.S. Embassy "immediately take whatever steps are necessary to ensure that United States assistance to the Khmer Republic is properly managed and accounted for."

American pressure for reform was unavailing, however. Lon Nol proved a remote, ineffective leader with an almost infinite ability to ignore bad news or unwelcome advice. After he suffered a severe stroke in early 1971, his leadership seemed even more inept and unfocused than ever. Nonetheless, after assuming the rank of marshal a few months after his stroke, Lon Nol then made himself president through an election in June 1972 that most observers believed was flagrantly rigged.

By that time, all of Lon Nol's principal collaborators in the 1970 coup against Sihanouk had long since left or been pushed out of the government, destroying the unity that had briefly flowered in the early months of the republic. Many American officials hoped openly for a change in leadership, but in Washington, President Nixon's chief adviser Henry Kissinger opposed all suggestions that the U.S. try to nudge Lon Nol out of office. In Kissinger's view that should be done only in return for concessions by the Communist side. Since no concessions were ever made, however, Kissinger's critics felt that U.S. policy actually helped serve the Communists' interests by keeping a weak and incompetent leader in power in Phnom Penh instead of encouraging a potentially more effective leadership.

Military defeats and political decay in the Khmer Republic were accompanied by social and economic disaster. School enrollment dropped by two-thirds in the first year of the war, reflecting the utter disruption of civilian life. More than half of the country's civilian public hospitals were destroyed, as were the railroad system and two-fifths of the road network. Cambodia's two chief commercial products, timber and rubber, fell to only one-fifth of prewar production. The rice harvest plunged from 3.8 million tons in 1969 and 1970 to 493,000 tons four years later. More than a million people were uprooted from their homes and flocked into Phnom Penh and the other towns, where the ruined economy provided next to no jobs. Inflation drove food prices beyond the reach of many poor families; in a land that had once been the best fed in Southeast Asia, hunger and malnutrition now began to affect a growing number of people.

By the third year of the conflict, popular support for the war and the government had utterly evaporated. In place of the naive enthusiasm of 1970, there was now only a devastating mood of hopelessness, sorrow, and fear.

For years, in the Vietnam peace negotiations, the United States had proposed an Indochina-wide cease-fire, including Laos and Cambodia as well as Vietnam. But when the long stalemate finally appeared to be ending in the fall of 1972, American negotiators dropped that demand, recognizing that neither Congress nor a war-weary American public would accept delaying a Vietnam agreement for the sake of Laos or Cambodia.

Henry Kissinger repeatedly sought assurances from North Vietnam's Le Duc Tho that Vietnam would arrange a Cambodian settlement, but Tho was cautious. It would be "illogical" for Hanoi to want the war to continue in Cambodia after the Vietnam War was settled, he told Kissinger,

A badly wounded Vietnamese villager sits with other survivors of the April 1970 massacre of hundreds of ethnic Vietnamese by Cambodian soldiers in Takeo.

but he could not make a commitment on behalf of the Cambodians. By the end of 1972 the Cambodian insurgents, who now fielded some 40,000 troops, had taken over most of the ground fighting against Lon Nol's army, and their leaders—still shadowy and mysterious to the rest of the world—were determined to pursue their own policies, not Hanoi's, on the issues of war and peace.

On January 28, 1973, the day the Vietnam agreement took effect, Lon Nol announced what U.S. officials called a "unilateral cease-fire," which, if the Communists had reciprocated, might have led to a de facto Cambodian truce. What the Cambodian leader actually proposed was, in effect, an enemy surrender: a total withdrawal of Vietnamese Communist forces and the reoccupation by government troops of all the territory lost since the start of the war. The proposal ignored the Cambodian insurgents, who immediately rejected his offer as "a deception engineered by the U.S. imperialists and their allies."

At 7:00 A.M. the next morning, the time Lon Nol had fixed for halting "offensive" operations, U.S. air strikes halted. On February 9, however, American bombers again began striking Cambodian targets. At first, under a policy authorizing strikes "only to avert actual loss of positions" by government units, only about two or three B-52 sorties and perhaps a dozen tactical strikes were flown each day. Early in March, however, the Joint Chiefs of Staff proposed a vastly expanded air campaign. On March 9, new orders were issued allowing "use of the full spectrum of U.S. air strike forces against targets posing a threat to friendly forces and population centers." The new policy also authorized bombing "VC/NVA supply routes, storage areas, and transshipment points" throughout the area code-named Freedom Deal—the eastern part of the country, where the North Vietnamese support and supply system operated.

From then on, until Congress ordered the bombing halted on August 15, sortie and tonnage rates rose astronomically. Altogether during the 1973 campaign, U.S. aircraft dropped over 250,000 tons of bombs in Cambodia, more than fell on Japan in all of World War II.

The dispirited government army continued to lose ground, however. The Khmer Communists "seized considerable territory" despite the heavy bombing, noted a U.S. Defense Department appraisal, while FANK's response "was grossly inadequate. FANK combat performance was characterized by poor leadership, low morale, and the refusal of units to advance against enemy resistance."

Late in April 1973, the insurgents were so close to Phnom Penh that U.S. helicopter units in Thailand were alerted to evacuate the American embassy staff; the evacuation was canceled only after F-111 bombers spent an entire night blasting Communist positions on the east bank of the Mekong just opposite the city. Though that threat was beaten back, the government's position continued to deteriorate in the following months. In Washington, meanwhile, Congress approved legislation forcing an unwilling Nixon administration to end the bombing on August 15. The cutoff came nine days too late to avoid a misdirected B-52 strike on August 6 that killed 137 people, most of them government soldiers or their dependents, in the town of Neak Luong.

The bombing lasted just long enough, however, in the opinion of American military commanders, to save Phnom Penh. In mid-July, the city appeared in grave danger of falling even while the bombing continued. Insurgent troops were dug in only a little more than six kilometers from Phnom Penh's Pochentong airport, while other Communist forces were approaching the suburb of Takhmau south of the capital and also briefly seized a stretch of Highway 1 less than three kilometers from the city itself.

For the remaining weeks before the cutoff, the full fury of the bombing campaign was concentrated around the threatened capital. Finally, "beginning about six days before the actual termination of the bombing," according to the 7th Air Force commander, General John W. Vogt, Jr., "the enemy began to fall back. He had suffered such heavy casualties in all areas, particularly in the southern front area, that he could no longer sustain the offensive."

If their casualties prevented the Khmer Rouge from winning the war in the summer of 1973, the mystery was why they had chosen to press their offensive with such fury instead of waiting a few more weeks for the bombs to stop falling. Their tactics left an impression of madness—"a lasting image," wrote the British author William Shawcross, "of peasant boys and girls, clad in black, moving slowly through the mud, half-crazed with terror, as fighter bombers tore down at them by day, and night after night whole seas of 750-pound bombs smashed all around."

On the morning of August 15, when the last bombers swooshed away to the west and the skies over Cambodia suddenly fell quiet, the overwhelming mood in Phnom Penh was a dazed relief at having survived the siege. But mingled with the relief was a frightening new perception of the enemy, who had been beaten back this time but whose suicidal fanaticism under the rain of bombs boded only more dark unknowable violence in Cambodia's future.

Laos: running out of mountains

"The most positive thing that can be said about Laos," a CIA study concluded early in 1970, "is that it still exists as a non-Communist state." U.S. support was still keeping the kingdom afloat as the war dragged on into the new decade. But American bombs and dollars could not remedy the essential weaknesses of the regime. The central government lacked authority over regional warlords; animosity persisted between lowland Lao and the hill tribes; Prime Minister Souvanna Phouma, though he remained the indispensable figure of Lao political life, was at age sixty-nine visibly losing his vigor and had no apparent successor.

The military situation was deteriorating as well. From 1969 on, the fighting in northern Laos, particularly around the Plain of Jars, reached levels of intensity unknown earlier in the war, as did U.S. bombing. On the ground, the seesaw pattern of earlier years continued, but the end of each cycle left the balance somewhat more favorable to the Pathet Lao and their North Vietnamese allies. The plain itself, after changing hands several times, fell firmly under Communist control by the end of 1971, while American bombing flattened virtually every habitable structure in the villages that had once dotted the area.

In southern Laos, meanwhile, North Vietnamese forces consolidated their grip on the Ho Chi Minh Trail region—always their chief strategic interest in Laos. In the spring of 1970, when the outbreak of war in Cambodia made their supply routes through Lao territory even more vital, the North Vietnamese easily seized the towns of Attopeu and Saravane, securing the trail's southern portion. Then, after

Right. *A Cambodian infant sleeps inside the bombed-out shell of a government building in Neak Luong. American B-52s accidentally attacked the government-held town in August 1973.*

South Vietnamese forces backed by U.S. air and artillery unsuccessfully attacked the trail region in Operation Lam Son 719 during February and March 1971 (to the "great surprise" of Lao government commanders, who were never consulted before or during the operation), the North Vietnamese promptly began expanding their corridor through the Lao panhandle in order to widen the buffer zone protecting the trail. Pushing Lao government troops farther westward toward the Mekong, they constructed a new network of trails west of the traditional route.

The regular Lao forces in the area, who had experienced little serious combat in the past, offered only token resistance to the Vietnamese. The reaction of senior Royal Lao Army commanders, as one Lao general recalled after the war, "was that this was a problem between the South Vietnamese, Americans and North Vietnamese. As a result of this attitude, RLA forces suffered little in the attacks, giving up ground in great chunks in exchange for relatively light casualties."

Elsewhere, too, the regular Lao armed forces, despite years of U.S. aid and training, continued to be ineffective. The CIA-controlled Hmong irregulars under Vang Pao, who had long carried the brunt of the war, were also beginning to weaken, chiefly because of high casualties. By 1970 the guerrillas could no longer replace their losses, and beginning that year the CIA began clandestinely reinforcing the Hmong with "volunteers" from Thailand.

According to Theodore Shackley, the CIA station chief in Laos in 1966 to 1968, each 550-man Thai battalion "was led by 50 officers from the Royal Thai Army, but the remaining 500 men were recruited from civilian life, primarily from among those Thais who had previous military service. Regular army personnel were required to resign before they joined their units. It was understood, however, that they would be reinstated without loss of benefits after they returned from Laos. The program," Shackley added, "developed a formidable combat force." By the end of 1971, 6,000 to 8,000 Thai soldiers were fighting in Laos. A year later, the number had risen to about 21,000. Like the Lao irregulars, the Thai troops were paid by the U.S.

Meanwhile, the devastation of the Hmong—both soldiers and civilians—accelerated. Military casualties in Vang Pao's units mounted to the point that, as one U.S. aid official noted in 1971, "It is not uncommon today to see boys ten to fourteen years of age in uniform and carrying decrepit M1s into battle." Another U.S. official admitted, "Their morale is shot." Of the civilians loyal to Vang Pao, nearly all had been forced to flee their traditional villages as more and more areas fell to the Pathet Lao and North Vietnamese. Some families had moved six times in the

South Vietnamese and American units ferry men and supplies to the Lao border on the eve of Operation Lam Son 719. ARVN troops, backed by U.S. air and artillery, began the cross-border attack on the Ho Chi Minh Trail on February 8, 1971.

course of a year—with each march bringing more casualties from illness and exhaustion.

By 1971 tens of thousands of uprooted Hmong were concentrated in the regions south and west of Vang Pao's headquarters at Long Cheng, kept alive by U.S. food supplies acknowledged to be barely enough to fend off starvation. Malnutrition lowered their resistance to malaria, dysentery, and other diseases, which took a gruesome toll of lives. Nor was there any apparent hope of an end to their ordeal, because there was simply no place left for the Hmong or other highland refugees to resume their traditional lives.

Just as no one had a solution for the Hmong, no one had a solution for Laos, either. "No one we met in Laos, American or Lao, seems to have a prescription for the future other than to continue to do what is being done now," wrote Senate investigators after visiting Laos in the spring of 1971. The South Vietnamese Lam Son 719 operation earlier that year, and the extensive use of Lao territory to resupply and reinforce North Vietnamese forces staging for the massive 1972 Easter offensive in the South, both underscored the reality that Laos's fate did not lie with the Lao on either side of the war but with the more powerful nations that were pursuing their own international strategies on Lao territory.

The last coalition

The process that would eventually lead to a Lao cease-fire agreement began, not coincidentally, exactly as North Vietnam's Le Duc Tho and America's Henry Kissinger were approaching their breakthrough in the Vietnam peace talks in Paris.

Following a series of exchanges during the summer of 1972, in which Prime Minister Souvanna Phouma accepted the Lao Patriotic Front's program as the "basis for discussion" between the two sides, the Pathet Lao agreed to a new negotiating effort. Their delegation, headed by Politburo member Phoun Sipraseuth, arrived in Vientiane on October 14, just as Kissinger and Tho had finished a crucial round of talks on a draft Vietnam peace agreement. Two weeks later, shortly after Kissinger's electrifying an-

North Vietnamese soldiers haul supplies from an ARVN fire support base, hastily abandoned during ARVN's hectic withdrawal from southern Laos at the end of Lam Son 719.

nouncement in Washington that peace was "at hand" in Vietnam, Phoumi Vongvichit, secretary general of the Lao Patriotic Front, arrived in Vientiane to join the Pathet Lao negotiators. Phoumi's title, "special adviser," was the same as that used by Le Duc Tho in the Vietnam negotiations.

By participating in a new round of peace talks, the Pathet Lao had tacitly dropped their long-standing insistence that U.S. bombing must stop before negotiations could begin. On the other hand, the very first of the five points in their program, which Souvanna had accepted as the basis for discussion, demanded that the U.S. must "completely cease the bombing of the Lao territory [and] withdraw from Laos all U.S. advisers and military personnel." The remaining points included "a foreign policy of peace and neutrality," election of a new national assembly, a provisional coalition government, and compensation and resettlement "in their native places" for all people who had been "forcibly" relocated. The last point appeared to mean that the Hmong and other tribal people who had cooperated with the U.S. clandestine guerrilla effort would be forced to return to Pathet Lao-controlled areas.

When the Vietnamese peace talks stalled in late October, so did the negotiations in Laos. For the next three months, the Lao negotiators continued to meet every Tuesday on the fourth floor of the Ministry of Education in Vientiane. But the sessions were taken up with desultory recitations of past proposals and arguments about such trivia as the placement of the Lao flag in the meeting room.

With the signing of the Vietnam cease-fire agreement on January 27, 1973, the Lao peace talks suddenly regained a sense of urgency. The military and political weaknesses of the Vientiane government, however, put Souvanna Phouma at a serious disadvantage. Having unsuccessfully appealed to the U.S. to include a Laos cease-fire in the Vietnam agreement, Souvanna now faced an unpromising choice: either sign an agreement on almost any terms or continue the war with virtually no prospect of success. If the U.S. was abandoning its role in Indochina, Souvanna reasoned, he had no choice except to settle as quickly as possible. "Each time an impasse occurred" in the negotiations, recalled Major General Oudone Sananikone, the Royal Lao Army chief of staff, "Souvanna Phouma ordered his delegation to concede." American embassy officials strongly supported Souvanna's policies, sometimes delaying military aid shipments or withholding payroll funds in order to keep the right-wing military commanders in line.

The Pathet Lao were under pressure too. Their North Vietnamese allies, who had promised Henry Kissinger that a Lao cease-fire would follow within fifteen days of the Vietnam agreement, wanted a settlement in Laos for powerful reasons of their own: it would end U.S. bombing and give them unimpeded use of the Ho Chi Minh Trail. The political interests of the Lao Communists, no doubt, were less important to Hanoi. Still, Souvanna's anxiety and the general political frailty of the Vientiane side gave the Pathet Lao the upper hand in the final stages of the talks.

In February, Souvanna took over the negotiating himself, settling the major outstanding issues in a round of private meetings with Phoumi Vongvichit. In those sessions, Souvanna yielded on point after point in order to get an agreement.

The fifteen-day deadline passed with no announcement, but the delay did not last long. On the morning of February 21, in a brief ceremony at Souvanna's villa on the outskirts of Vientiane, Phoumi and the chief government negotiator, public works minister Peng Phongsavan, signed the Agreement on the Restoration of Peace and Reconciliation in Laos.

In both style and substance, the agreement was even more favorable to the Pathet Lao than the worried rightists had feared. Even the terminology used for the two sides— "the Vientiane administration" and "the Patriotic Forces"— seemed to give the Communists an edge in stature and prestige. The main provisions of the agreement included:

A statement of "general principles" calling for the withdrawal of all foreign forces. The United States and Thailand were mentioned by name; North Vietnam was not.

A cease-fire and a halt to U.S. bombing, to take effect at noon, February 22. The terms of the cease-fire did not even assure that the Vientiane side could keep supplying its enclaves in Communist-held areas or receive U.S.-supplied replacements for worn-out or destroyed military materiel. Both those issues were left to be determined by a joint military commission that would operate "according to the principle of unanimity," meaning the Pathet Lao would have a legal veto over continued U.S. aid to the government army.

Formation of a new coalition government, headed by a prime minister and two other "qualified persons" agreed on by both sides. Of the remaining seats, half would go to the Vientiane side and half to the Pathet Lao. A parallel institution, the National Political Consultative Council (NPCC), would be formed to "support and assist" in carrying out the agreement and in arranging elections for a permanent government.

Withdrawal of foreign forces within sixty days after the new coalition was formed. As the dismayed rightists quickly pointed out, that meant the Pathet Lao's Vietnamese allies would remain in the country during the political negotiations, while the Vientiane side's principal military asset, U.S. bombing, would have ended with the cease-fire.

Neutralization of Vientiane and the royal capital, Luang Prabang, meaning the two cities would be patrolled by mixed government and Pathet Lao security forces and would not be considered part of the Vientiane government's zone of control.

As had also happened in Vietnam four weeks earlier, the Laos cease-fire agreement was preceded by intense combat as the Pathet Lao and North Vietnamese attempted to seize as much territory as they could before the truce took effect. American bombing ended at noon on February 22, as required by the agreement. But heavy fighting on numerous battlefields continued on past the cease-fire hour, leading an anguished Souvanna Phouma to declare, "We have been tricked." At Souvanna's request, on the night of February 23, nine U.S. B-52s returned to strike targets near the Communist-held town of Paksong, on the Bolovens Plateau in southern Laos.

The fighting died down relatively quickly, however. By March, government casualties were reported 75 percent below the pretruce level. Occasional flare-ups occurred, and one more round of American air strikes—the last of a bombing campaign that had lasted nearly nine years—hit targets south of the Plain of Jars on April 16 and 17. For the most part, though, only minor skirmishing marred the cease-fire.

As the fighting subsided, the political negotiations for a new government proceeded at a pace that was sluggish even by the traditionally leisurely standards of Laos. The agreement had called for the new coalition to be formed within thirty days after the cease-fire, but long after the deadline had passed, government and Pathet Lao negotiators were still sparring inconclusively over how the agreement would be carried out.

The Vientiane rightists, whose reaction to the peace agreement had been utter consternation ("This is the worst defeat we have suffered," said one senior official), were further demoralized by the outcome of a bizarre coup attempt on August 20 led by the former air force commander, Thao Ma. During the affair, the U.S. chargé d'affaires, John Gunther Dean, went to extraordinary lengths to demonstrate American support for Souvanna. Risking death or capture, Dean went to the rebel-held airport to confront the coup leaders and tell them in person that the U.S. opposed their attempt; several days later, Souvanna publicly thanked Dean for his efforts.

Dean's actions were a convincing demonstration to the rightists that they could not expect American support and thus had no realistic hope of resuming the war. From then on, although their fears remained unabated, active opposition to the peace agreement subsided.

On September 14, barely three weeks after Thao Ma's failed coup, government and Pathet Lao representatives signed a long protocol spelling out the distribution of cabinet seats and other arrangements for implementing both the political and military provisions of the February agreement. Six more months of desultory bickering passed before the coalition was actually established by a royal decree on April 5, 1974—more than a year behind the scheduled start of the new government.

As expected, Souvanna Phouma was named prime minister. Overshadowing Souvanna, however, was his charismatic half-brother, Prince Souphanouvong, whose dramatic arrival in Vientiane on April 3 was greeted by huge, wildly cheering crowds. Souphanouvong's popularity appeared to spring from an image of austerity, honesty, and sacrifice, contrasting sharply with the pleasure seeking and corruption associated with the Vientiane leaders. To the surprise of most observers, instead of accepting one of the two vice-premierships established in the new government, Souphanouvong chose to become president of the National Political Consultative Council, a platform he used with great effectiveness.

Despite their long isolation in one of the most remote regions of a poor and backward land, Souphanouvong and the other Pathet Lao leaders displayed remarkable political skills, while the rightist leaders seemed—even to their sympathizers—divided, unsure, politically inept, and defensive. During the short existence of Laos's third and last coalition, that painful contrast would remain the dominant factor in Lao political life.

The Khmer Rouge come to power

Awareness of a gathering violent madness in the Cambodian war grew almost imperceptibly, as if heard in a soft but insistent and menacing whisper in the night.

Even as late as the signing of the Vietnam peace agreement in January 1973, there was a commonly held view among both Khmers and foreign observers that the war was essentially a foreign conflict and had not created real hatreds in the Cambodian population. Before many more months had passed, however, that perception began to change. The ferocious tenacity displayed by the Khmer Rouge under U.S. bombing and their total rejection of peace talks began to suggest that their fanaticism and capacity for violence were deeper than anyone inside or outside the country had suspected.

Beginning in 1973, too, reports of inexplicably brutal policies started seeping out of the insurgent-held zone. Refugees told of the forced relocation of entire villages, for no apparent reason, and of the almost casual killing of civilians who resisted Khmer Rouge orders. The change coincided with the rather abrupt withdrawal of the Vietnamese Communists from the Cambodian battlefields—a change of major significance that was only gradually recognized in Phnom Penh and Washington. Preferring to see the war as a case of North Vietnamese aggression, not a Cambodian civil war, the Lon Nol government and the U.S. were both slow to acknowledge that the insurgency was no longer under Vietnamese control and that a solution, if there was one, would have to be arranged with their Cambodian opponents.

Those opponents were shadowy even by the standards of underground revolutionary movements. Ordinary Cambodian civilians often referred to the Khmer insurgents merely as the *peap prey* (forest army). Their real leaders and plans remained almost completely unknown outside their jungle bases. Equally hidden was the bitter antagonism that was rapidly replacing their former partnership with the Vietnamese Communists.

The Cambodian Communist leaders Saloth Sar, Ieng Sary, and their associates—the group who had gone into the jungles to launch the Khmer Rouge resistance in the 1960s—had long mistrusted the Vietnamese. But the final break between the two movements was precipitated by the Vietnam cease-fire agreement. To the Cambodians, the significance of the Vietnam cease-fire was that it released American air power for the unprecedented 1973 bombing campaign in Cambodia. In the twisted delusions of the Khmer Rouge leaders, that represented a deliberate Vietnamese plot to cripple Cambodia's revolution.

Shortly after the Vietnam agreement was signed, according to Prince Sihanouk, the Khmer Rouge leadership asked the Vietnamese to "dismantle their military and other bases in Kampuchea and purely and simply clear out of Cambodian territory." Though the Vietnamese did not give up their traditional sanctuary areas along the border with South Vietnam, they quickly withdrew their remaining combat forces and advisers from the Cambodian battlefields. As Sihanouk publicly complained at the time, they also stopped sending arms and munitions to the Cambodian insurgents.

The Vietnamese departure was a death warrant for most of the Hanoi-trained Cambodians who had returned to Cambodia in 1970 to help develop the Khmer resistance under Vietnamese direction. Following the withdrawal of Vietnamese forces, hundreds of the Vietnamese-trained Cambodians—now regarded as "Vietnamese in Khmer bodies"—were secretly executed and replaced by cadres loyal to Saloth Sar's Khmer Rouge faction.

At the same time, the Khmer Rouge also began eliminating Sihanouk loyalists from the insurgent ranks. For international consumption, they maintained the façade of their alliance with the prince, who remained the titular leader of the revolutionary movement. In the spring of 1973 the insurgent leadership even allowed the prince to spend a few weeks in rebel-held areas of the country—carefully keeping him away from any peasants, however. In fact, by that time Khmer Rouge cadres were telling peasants that the revolution did not need Sihanouk anymore. "In April of 1973 they stopped talking about Sihanouk," said one refugee after escaping from the Khmer Rouge zone. "If you still use his name and support Sihanouk, then you will be sent away and you will never return."

The prince was well aware that his future role would only be as a figurehead. When he was no longer useful to the Khmer Rouge, he predicted, "they'll spit me out like a cherry pit."

Thus, during 1973, the revolution slipped under the control of the most violent and fanatical of its various

Khmer Rouge troops dash past fallen FANK soldiers during an assault on a government position in Prey Veng Province in October 1973.

factions, driven by the idea, as one analyst wrote, "that Cambodia was to go through a total social revolution and everything that had preceded it was anathema and must be destroyed."

The Khmer Rouge movement itself passed through two crucial formative events in 1973. One was its betrayal, as the Khmer Rouge saw it, by the Vietnamese Communists. The other was its "victory" over the U.S. bombing campaign, which the Khmer Rouge achieved by a single-minded fury and an extraordinary disregard for their own casualties. That combination of experiences reinforced all the elements that shaped their lethal vision: an angry sense of isolation, a primitive xenophobia, and a dark belief in pure violence as the means to overcome more numerous and better-armed enemies.

While the revolutionaries spiraled downward into their mindless rage, America's ally continued to decay. Despite U.S. military aid that eventually totaled more than a billion dollars—over $4,000 for every government soldier, if the official strength figures could be believed—the Cambodian army was still a poor match for its opponents. One journalist wrote late in the war: "The army has no ration system worthy of the name. Soldiers are issued uncooked rice but nothing else. When they go into battle they must carry their own food and cook it themselves, and when it runs out, they usually have to retreat, if they can. Their pay is so low—about $10 a month for a private—that their families are often hungry. If a soldier is sick or wounded he often dies because of the severe shortage of medical supplies. The recruitment system has been a massive failure and there are few replacements for those killed, wounded or missing."

Corruption and flagrant incompetence were pervasive among senior officers, who built blocks of expensive villas in Phnom Penh with the profits from padded payrolls or black-marketeering. Their soldiers, meanwhile, had to pay bribes to have bandages changed or litters kept clean in military hospitals. "If a soldier has money he can get medicine," an infantryman said bitterly, "but if he has no money, he will die."

The civilian population, too, sank deeper into misery and hopelessness as the war dragged on. By late 1974 about half of the entire population in government-held territory had been uprooted from their homes, either as refugees or as military dependents who, because the army had no pay allotment system, had to follow soldiers from front to front in order not to starve.

Because so much of the farming and fishing land was a battle zone or occupied by the enemy, and because the ruined economy provided virtually no jobs, few displaced Cambodians could find the income necessary to meet soaring prices for food or other essentials. As a result, malnutrition and disease began to ravage the country. "The general level of health of almost the entire Cambodian population," said one U.S. government report early in 1975, "has deteriorated rapidly."

The international response to Cambodia's catastrophe was not one of which anyone—particularly Americans—could be proud. During the entire first three years of the war, U.S. assistance for refugee relief reached a total of

Citizens of Phnom Penh's southern suburb, Psar Deum Kor, flee a Khmer Rouge mortar barrage in January 1974. The capital itself was by then virtually in a state of siege.

$1.15 million, less than one dollar for every displaced person (and less than two-thirds of the cost of a single day's bombing). Until February 1974, only one junior officer on the 200-member American embassy staff was assigned to deal with refugee issues.

U.S. policy was somewhat less miserly in 1974 and 1975, when approximately $27 million, or about 5 percent of the economic aid program, was earmarked for humanitarian purposes. (The other 95 percent supported the Cambodian government budget.) Even then the relief effort was far from adequate. A month's ration of rice for refugee families usually lasted only a week or less, even when it was cooked in a watery gruel to make it stretch further. About three out of every four refugees received no rice or other assistance at all.

As late as February 1975, while 545 tons of rice a day were distributed through official channels, only 18 tons were available for free distribution through relief agencies. This was at a time when the U.S. was providing 80 percent of Cambodia's rice supply—and when more than half of Phnom Penh's population could not afford to buy enough food. There was enough food in the city to feed everyone, U.S. officials admitted. But high prices and Khmer and American policies meant that many, perhaps the majority, of the refugee-swollen and war-impoverished population went hungry.

By the fifth year of the war there was not even a pretense of returning refugees to self-sufficiency. In schools or pagodas or empty fields, huddling on straw mats or board pallets under flimsy thatch shelters or sheets of cheap blue plastic, Cambodia's uprooted waited in growing misery and despair for an end to the fighting. "We keep praying every day for the war to end," said one woman. "Whichever side wins, we don't care. We just want to live in peace."

The final Khmer Rouge offensive began an hour after midnight on the first day of 1975, when government positions on all sides of Phnom Penh came under heavy attack. During the following weeks, for the first time in the war, the Khmer Rouge also succeeded in cutting off ship traffic on the Mekong—for more than a year, the only supply route to the Cambodian capital. Communist mines and gunfire sank a dozen ships in January, more than had been lost in all of 1974. The last supply vessels reached Phnom Penh on January 30. By then, Khmer Rouge forces were permanently dug in at numerous riverbank choke points and had also cut off Neak Luong, the chief garrison town along the river between Phnom Penh and the Vietnamese border. More than 60,000 civilians, half of them refugees, were trapped there, under constant fire and with dwindling supplies of medicine and food.

With the Mekong blocked, the only remaining supply route to Phnom Penh was by air. Aircraft "lent" by the U.S. Air Force to a civilian charter airline flew ammunition and fuel into Phnom Penh from U Tapao air base in Thailand, while other charter planes flew rice from Saigon. By March the airlift was landing 1,000 to 1,500 tons of supplies every day at Phnom Penh's Pochentong airport, under sporadic but gradually intensifying attacks by Khmer Rouge rockets and artillery.

Late in January, President Ford asked Congress for an additional $222 million in military aid to help the Cambodians hold out until negotiations could be arranged. Outside the White House, however, few observers believed the Cambodian government could survive much longer, with or without more aid. In Phnom Penh, Ambassador John Gunther Dean, who had been transferred from Laos to Cambodia in March 1974, began speaking of a "controlled solution," which could not mean much more than a negotiated transfer of power to the Khmer Rouge.

Clearly, no such process could begin as long as Lon Nol remained in power. As early as February, Dean indirectly began trying to promote the marshal's resignation—only to be quickly reined in by Henry Kissinger, who still believed, apparently, that the Cambodian leader's departure was a potential bargaining chip and should be offered only after negotiations began. In fact, there was not a particle of evidence that the Khmer Rouge would negotiate under any circumstances. Two years earlier they had remained utterly intransigent under the fury of American bombs and the pressure of their Vietnamese allies. Now, with victory almost in their grasp, they had no apparent reason to pause and negotiate with an enemy who was, as the Khmer Rouge leader Khieu Samphan declared, "writhing in death-throes."

Late in March, at the urging of several Asian ambassadors, senior government and military leaders asked Lon Nol to leave the country temporarily, so that a cease-fire could be worked out. After stalling for several days, the president agreed to leave—after first asking the cabinet for funds to live on abroad. He was promised a half-million dollars, Ambassador Dean later testified in a congressional hearing, of which at least $200,000 was actually paid.

On April 1 the marshal left the country, declaring he would return when "our national problem requires my presence." Later that day, Neak Luong fell to the Khmer Rouge. Only 160 of the 4,500 government troops there ever made it back to government lines. In Washington, meanwhile, the Ford proposal for $222 million in additional military aid for Cambodia remained stuck in a skeptical Congress. In both the Senate and House, compromise formulas were drafted approving some new funds on condition that the administration arrange an "orderly solution" to the war by the end of June, after which all military assistance would be banned. The president refused to accept any deadline, however, and Congress recessed for Easter without breaking the impasse.

Two days after Lon Nol left, his successor, former Senate president Saukham Khoy, appealed for negotiations "to

save the nation from ruin" but received no response. The same day, FANK lost all of its remaining positions on Highway 1 leading toward the city. Ambassador Dean proposed evacuating the embassy staff on April 5, before Phnom Penh's defenses deteriorated any further, but was overruled by Kissinger, who was preparing one last approach to Prince Sihanouk.

On Kissinger's instructions, George Bush, then chief of the U.S. liaison office in Peking, delivered the U.S. proposal to Sihanouk on April 11, inviting him to return to Phnom Penh to take power. Sihanouk immediately and brusquely refused the offer—which came so late, and with so little apparent chance of success, that many wondered if Kissinger offered it seriously or only so the historical record would show an attempt to reach a negotiated solution.

At six minutes before nine o'clock the following morning, the first of thirty-six U.S. helicopters touched down on a soccer field known in evacuation plans as LZ Hotel. During the next two hours, Operation Eagle Pull, as the evacuation was called, flew eighty-two Americans, 159 Cambodians, and thirty-five persons of other nationalities to U.S. ships waiting off the coast in the Gulf of Thailand.

Ambassador Dean, before leaving, offered to fly out Prime Minister Long Boret and the other members of the Cambodian government who were under threat of execution by the Khmer Rouge. But only the acting president, Saukham Khoy, accepted the offer. Long Boret refused. So did Sirik Matak, who was also on the death list although his only post was "adviser" to the government.

Sirik Matak's reply to Dean's offer, delivered just as the first helicopters landed, expressed gratitude but said: "I cannot, alas, leave in such a cowardly fashion. You leave and my wish is that you and your country will find happiness under the sky. But mark it well that, if I shall die here on the spot and in my country that I love, it is too bad because we all are born and must die one day. I have only committed this mistake of believing in you, the Americans." Like the other Khmer leaders, Sirik Matak would be executed within days of the Khmer Rouge victory.

Shortly before the evacuation ended, Khmer Rouge rockets and mortar rounds began falling around the landing zone but without inflicting any American casualties or damaging any U.S. helicopters. Exactly two hours and twenty-three minutes after the operation began, the last helicopter lifted off the landing zone carrying fifteen passengers, including the Marine security force commander, several members of his staff, and Air Force communicators. The helicopter climbed sharply over the besieged city and then headed for the coast, leaving behind a country that was once claimed to embody an American policy

As the Khmer Rouge close in on Phnom Penh, government soldiers and their dependents board a U.S.-donated helicopter for evacuation to a safer area.

success—"the Nixon Doctrine in its purest form"—but had long since come to symbolize only endless defeat and agony.

Following the American departure, although the military situation appeared completely hopeless, no panic developed in Phnom Penh. Instead, the daily struggle for survival seemed to consume all available energy and attention.

A seven-member Supreme Committee, headed by the armed forces commander, Lieutenant General Sak Sutsakhan, assumed administrative authority in place of the departed Saukham Khoy. Prime Minister Long Boret was named vice chairman. On April 13, which was also the Cambodian new year, Long Boret proposed a cease-fire but only if the Khmer Rouge agreed to a plebiscite to decide on Cambodia's future government—a proposal that was, under the circumstances, sheer fantasy.

On all sides of the capital, government soldiers were falling back along roads that were also choked with streams of refugees. Huge smears of black smoke and dust hung on the horizon; the slamming sound of government artillery, firing out toward the perimeter from positions right in the center of the city, echoed over streets that swarmed with homeless civilians and lost, leaderless soldiers.

On the fifteenth, the Khmer Rouge captured Pochentong airport and the large suburb of Takhmau south of the city, and that night they poured artillery and rocket fire into the heart of Phnom Penh, setting huge fires. The next day, dropping the absurd idea of a plebiscite, the government transmitted a new proposal to Prince Sihanouk in Peking, offering to hand over power to the revolutionaries after a cease-fire and asking only that there be no reprisals against soldiers or officials of the Phnom Penh regime.

Early on the morning of the seventeenth, Sihanouk's answer came: The members of the Supreme Committee "should try and escape while they can," and the government army should lay down its arms, raise the white flag, and surrender. Shortly afterward, General Sak and Long Boret boarded helicopters at the Olympic Stadium to flee the city. Sak eventually reached safety in Thailand. But Long Boret's helicopter never left the ground. That afternoon he was arrested by the Khmer Rouge and later executed.

In a few places around the city, small government units prepared to fight the Khmer Rouge. But most soldiers simply waited to surrender. Army trucks with strips of white cloth tied to their radio antennas dashed through the streets, while white flags also fluttered from gunboats moored in the Mekong and Tonle Sap. Families hung pillowcases or bed sheets from windows and rooftops.

The atmosphere was one of celebration rather than despair. Sydney Schanberg of the *New York Times*, one of a handful of journalists who refused evacuation in order to cover Phnom Penh's fall (and whose story, with that of his

Cambodian friend and assistant, Dith Pran, was told in the movie *The Killing Fields*), wrote that Cambodians and foreigners alike "looked ahead with hopeful relief to the collapse of the city, for they felt that when the Communists came and the war finally ended, at least the suffering would largely be over. All of us were wrong."

The first "liberators" to appear in the city smilingly accepted the surrender of infantrymen and the crews of armored personnel carriers parked near the Hotel Le Phnom and then joined in joyously tearful embraces with onlookers. These turned out not to be Khmer Rouge troops at all, however, but a group of Phnom Penh students involved in a bizarre scheme to take over the city and then hand it over to the "elder brothers from outside."

When the real Khmer Rouge entered the city, the mood of elation disappeared as if blown away by a sudden chilling gust of wind. The "forest army" turned out to be an army of terrifying children: teen-aged boys and girls with unsmiling masklike faces and dark peasant skin who seemed, Schanberg wrote, "universally grim, robotlike, brutal. Weapons drip from them like fruit from trees—grenades, pistols, rifles, rockets."

To the cheers and waves from civilians who had come out to greet them, the young guerrillas in their black uniforms and sweat-stained checked scarves responded only with a contemptuous, impassive silence. Under the blazing midmorning sun columns of Khmer Rouge troops fanned out along the city's wide boulevards, rounding up groups of surrendering government soldiers and forcing them to disrobe in the streets.

As they took over the increasingly fearful city, the liberation troops kept mentioning a mysterious authority whose name hardly anyone in Phnom Penh had ever heard before: Angka Loeu, "Organization on High." No more than a couple of hours after the first Khmer Rouge soldiers arrived, guerrillas with loudspeakers began announcing an order from Angka that was as fantastic as it was frightening: The entire population of the city, immediately and with no absolutely exceptions, must leave Phnom Penh for the countryside.

By afternoon, great crowds of cowed, bewildered people were already flowing along the roads leading out of the capital in an exodus that symbolized their new rulers' vision of total and instantaneous revolution. To the Cambodian revolutionaries, April 17 was not just a day when a government or social order changed but a day when time itself would start again: the first day of "year zero" in a new world where a hated past would not only be left behind but would, quite literally, cease to exist.

Grim-faced Khmer Rouge soldiers—some of them mere boys—walk the streets of Phnom Penh as the capital's residents cautiously look on, April 1975.

FANK: Lon Nol's Army

The Khmer Republic army in the 1970s, known as FANK (Forces Armées Nationales Khmères), was a model of weakness and vice. Despite $1 billion in U.S. aid between 1970 and 1975 and the support of U.S. air power, it was a hapless force that could never match its opponents, the North Vietnamese Army or Khmer Rouge. Its steady physical and moral decay mirrored that of Cambodian society as a whole.

The army's problems began with the inexperience and inadequate training of its soldiers. In early 1970, Cambodian leader Lon Nol tripled the size of the army to 110,000 in the hopes of creating a grand force capable of expelling the Vietnamese Communists from their bases within Cambodia. Few of the recruits, however, met professional military standards; some, in fact, were children drafted to pad the army's numbers. All received cursory military training at best. Nevertheless, the ragtag army of students, laborers, and peasants was sent out to fight Lon Nol's war and was promptly routed by the Vietnamese. Between March and June 1970, FANK lost nearly all its outposts in the eastern half of Cambodia.

Just as soldiers were green, their officers, appointees of Lon Nol, were incompetent. Their basic tactics consisted of lining up troops and vehicles along a major route and ordering them to advance, usually without flank security or knowledge of the enemy's whereabouts. The Communists repeatedly isolated and cut down overextended FANK lines. In December 1971, FANK suffered its most crushing defeat, losing over 3,000 soldiers and enough equipment for twenty battalions when it became stranded along Highway 6 during Operation Chenla II. After that, the army stuck to defensive operations.

Perhaps worse than the officer corps's inept leadership, however, was its utter corruption. Officers regularly sold army equipment and ammunition on the black market. They delayed paying their troops and sometimes fed them nothing more than thin rice gruel, taking for themselves the troops' alloted food money. In the most common military scam, officers listed nonexistent soldiers on the military payrolls and then kept the pay. By 1973, the army contained between 40,000 and 80,000 "phantom" soldiers, which represented some $2 million per month pocketed by military leaders. With their graft, they built beautiful mansions in Phnom Penh and imported luxury cars.

For the average soldier, meanwhile, conditions grew execrable. Troops received inadequate equipment and clothing and frequently ran out of food and ammunition. Medical treatment was meager and drugs scarce. Survival often depended upon whether a soldier had money of his own, because under the pervasively corrupt system nothing came for free. Wounded soldiers sometimes even paid to have their dressings cleaned. What little they had left they gave to their families, who, because the army had no allotment system for them, were forced to trail along after their husbands, fathers, and brothers in the army.

By 1973, FANK was in complete disarray. Popular support for the war had long since dissipated, forcing the National Assembly to pass its first draft law. Morale was low among the troops, leading to desertions and severe discipline problems. In a number of cases, soldiers refused to advance into battle.

Despite U.S. air support, the dispirited army rapidly gave up ground to the seemingly invincible Khmer Rouge and withdrew toward the capital. By summer 1974, the battle lines had closed to within fifteen to thirty kilometers of Phnom Penh. When U.S. bombing ended in August, the destruction of the army and Khmer Republic seemed just a matter of time.

FANK reinforcements aboard a government troop carrier arrive at Kompong Som, formerly known as Sihanoukville, in May 1973. One soldier wears a white scarf with a charm wrapped inside for luck.

FANK troops retrieve the bodies of government soldiers killed in a Khmer Rouge ambush in August 1973. By that summer, the army was losing a 500-man battalion per week to injury, death, and desertion.

FANK troopers lift the charred body of a government soldier who was burned by the Khmer Rouge after they overran this FANK position along Highway 5 in late 1974. In the background are the remains of other dead soldiers and their families.

Government soldiers attack Khmer Rouge positions along Highway 4, southwest of Phnom Penh, in 1974. Early in the year, the Khmer Rouge made a major drive against the capital but FANK troops rallied, temporarily pushing the Communists away from the city's perimeter.

Only one month before the fall of Phnom Penh, crippled and wounded FANK soldiers attend a ceremony in the capital marking the fifth anniversary of the Lon Nol government.

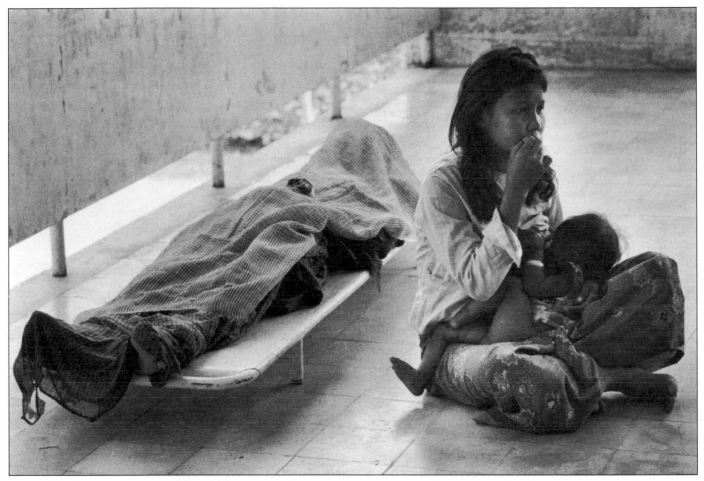

A Cambodian woman sits with her child near the body of her husband, a FANK soldier recently struck down by a Khmer Rouge bullet, inside a makeshift hospital in Phnom Penh, mid-March 1975.

Liberation

"Young soldiers aimed their guns at us, telling us to hurry. In our haste we left the house almost empty-handed, even forgetting to take any rice, pots and pans, or fish. After a few hundred yards we could go no farther. It was a stupefying sight, a human flood pouring out of the city, some people pushing their cars, others their overladen motorcycles or bicycles overflowing with bundles, and others behind little homemade carts. Most were on foot, like us, and heavily laden. "The sun was fierce but we were so dazed we hardly minded it. Children were crying, some were lost and searching vainly for their parents. The worst part of the whole march was the stopping and starting: there was such a crowd that we could never go forward more than a few yards at a time before we had to stop again. Sometimes the Khmer Rouge fired into the air to scare us and make us go faster. We nearly died of fright when there was a burst of machine-gun fire just beside us.

"By evening that day we had reached Kilometer 4, in Russey Keo, and slept in an abandoned house,

We begged a little rice because the children's stomachs and our own were crying famine. The people on the road with us were kind and helped each other out. The next morning at dawn shots were fired and we got back on the road in a hurry. The crowd was as dense as ever. When we got to Kilometer 5 we were very frightened by the sight of several corpses lying by the roadside. Their hands were tied behind their backs and nobody dared go near them."

Year zero

That account, given to the French priest François Ponchaud and reported in his book *Cambodia Year Zero*, is one survivor's story of the exodus from Phnom Penh, the act that began the Khmer Rouge regime. The orders putting nearly 3 million people onto the roads out of the Cambodian capital came only a few hours after the first teen-aged Communist soldiers marched into the city on the morning of April 17, 1975. Shouting their instructions angrily and firing in the air, the Khmer Rouge allowed no exceptions—not even for the many thousands of sick and wounded who lay in Phnom Penh's hospitals.

"From now on the Angka will attend to your injured," a black-clad soldier told Dr. Oum Nal after stopping him in a corridor of the Preah Ket Mealea Hospital, the largest civilian hospital in the city, where more than 2,000 patients had overflowed the wards and were now lying in hallways, storerooms, and any other available space. The Americans were going to bomb the city, the soldier explained, and therefore it would be necessary to leave immediately. "Useless to burden yourself with luggage," he added. "You will be back in a night or two."

More soldiers moved through the hospital roughly ordering patients and staff alike out into streets that were turning into a nightmarish spectacle of cruelty, fear, and suffering. One witness was Father Ponchaud, who had spent ten years living among Cambodia's poor and expected to welcome the revolutionaries' victory, but felt the city's elation turn to "sinking dread" in the early hours of the occupation. His own misgivings mounted as he watched sick and wounded from Preah Ket Mealea and the other hospitals begin their terrifying trek:

"The strongest dragged pitifully along, others were carried by friends, and some were lying on beds pushed by their families with their plasma and IV bumping alongside. I shall never forget one cripple who had neither hands nor feet, writhing along the ground like a severed worm, or a weeping father carrying his ten-year-old daughter in a sheet tied round his neck like a sling."

As the young, heavily armed Khmer Rouge soldiers marched through the streets ordering families out of their

homes, they usually gave the same explanation that had been given to Dr. Oum Nal: the Americans were going to bomb the city. Khmer Rouge leaders later claimed they ordered the evacuation because they could not provide enough food for the urban population—though that did not explain why hospital patients had to be turned out of their beds or the rest of the population evicted with such brutal haste.

The real reasons probably lay chiefly in the revolutionaries' paranoid fear that in the hated and unfamiliar environment of the cities, hidden enemies might cheat them of their victory. "Our strength is in the countryside; our weakness is in the cities," the Khmer Rouge leader Pol Pot commented nearly three years afterward, explaining that Phnom Penh had to be evacuated to foil plots "to overthrow our revolution."

In the deserted capital, after the population was expelled, the Khmer Rouge quickly began destroying symbols of the old society and particularly of Western influence. They blew up the National Bank and razed the French-built Catholic cathedral, later hauling away the piles of bricks where the cathedral had been so there was no sign it had ever stood there at all.

The Khmer Rouge also wasted no time in beginning the bloody work of eliminating their enemies—a blood bath that soon proved far worse than even the most pessimistic Cambodians had feared. Senior officials and military leaders of the Lon Nol government who surrendered on April 17 were executed within a few days. But the revolution's vengeance was not just directed at the top ranks of the old leadership. Virtually anyone who had been in the civil service or the army of the Khmer Republic or had been associated with foreigners or was a teacher or intellectual or belonged to the wealthy or educated classes was considered an actual or potential counterrevolutionary.

Among the many massacres in the immediate aftermath of the revolution's victory was the slaughter of hundreds of former officers in the Lon Nol army who surrendered to the Khmer Rouge in Battambang. Their captors ordered them to put on dress uniforms, telling them they were to be taken to Phnom Penh to greet the returning Prince Sihanouk. Instead, after being driven a short way down Highway 5 toward the capital, they were taken off the trucks and killed with rifles, grenades, and mortars. Several other large groups of officers from Battambang were murdered in similar fashion at various other places around the city.

In the villages, Khmer Rouge officials drew up lists identifying everyone's social background and status. Those classed as rich or privileged were automatically under the threat of death. Two weeks after occupying one village in Battambang Province, the Khmer Rouge executed four entire families, apparently because they had owned two ox carts or two plows. The abbot of the local Buddhist monastery was also executed.

Preceding page. *Youthful Khmer Rouge soldiers gather weapons surrendered by government soldiers after the Communists captured the city in April 1975.*

The countrywide massacres clearly reflected a deliberate policy of the revolutionary leadership. But they also seemed to spring from a vengeful hatred and envy burned into the youthful Khmer Rouge fighters themselves during their long and brutal war. When revolutionary troops occupied the Battambang airfield, they dismantled two T-28 aircraft with their bare hands, leaving one witness with the impression that "they would have eaten them if they could."

The revolutionary terror was inflicted on a country that had already suffered appalling loss of life. Approximately one-tenth of the entire population died from war-related causes from 1970 to 1975. The number of additional victims in the following three years would never be precisely known. But most historians eventually accepted a rough estimate that somewhere between 1 and 2 million Cambodians were murdered, or died from exhaustion or starvation or disease, as the result of Khmer Rouge policies—making their regime one of the bloodiest in history.

The authors of this scourge of violence were still known to the Cambodian people only as the faceless and nameless Angka Loeu (Organization on High). Unlike any other successful Communist movement in history, the Cambodian revolutionaries chose to keep disguising their own and their party's role even after their victory. For nearly a year, the revolutionary administration remained behind the mask of the wartime exile government nominally headed by Prince Sihanouk. The name Saloth Sar, who most foreign experts believed was the head of the Kampuchean Communist party, appeared on no list of government officials, and he remained as shadowy as ever.

Not until January 1976 was a new constitution promulgated, changing the country's official name to Democratic Kampuchea and calling for "direct and prompt general elections" to choose a new legislative body, to be called the People's Representative Assembly. On March 21, the members of the assembly were announced. Among the 250 persons on the list was a "representative of rubber plantation workers" who had never before been mentioned in any party statement. His name was Pol Pot.

Even after the government of Democratic Kampuchea was formally established on April 14, with the mysterious Pol Pot as premier and Khieu Samphan as president of the state presidium, the party's existence and ideology remained officially unmentioned for nearly another year and a half. Finally, in September 1977, the Kampuchean Communist party was revealed as the country's ruling party.

As Prince Sihanouk had often predicted, his usefulness to the Khmer Rouge ended with the establishment of Democratic Kampuchea. In September 1975, the prince had finally returned to his homeland from Pyongyang, North Korea, for a three-week visit. With his wife, Monique, and with Khieu Samphan, who was escorting him on the trip to Cambodia, Sihanouk stopped on the way to visit China's eighty-two-year-old Chairman Mao Tse-tung in Peking.

Mao, with only a year to live, was already feeble with Parkinson's disease and spoke so indistinctly that his listeners could barely understand him. But, as the writer Nayan Chanda reported, Mao did manage to tell Khieu Samphan and Khieu's wife, Ieng Thirith, "Please do not send Prince Sihanouk and his wife to the cooperative"—words that may have saved Sihanouk's life.

The prince and his escorts also visited Chou En-lai, the durable Chinese premier who was already hospitalized with his final illness. Recalling China's disastrous experience with its own attempt at instant revolution building at the end of the 1950s, Chou advised his visitors: "Don't follow the bad example of our 'great leap forward.' Take things slowly: that is the best way to guide Kampuchea and its people to growth, prosperity and happiness." In response, Sihanouk wrote later, "Khieu Samphan and Ieng Thirith just smiled an incredulous and superior smile."

The trip to the ravaged and deserted Phnom Penh, which the prince had not seen since January 1970, was a shock. After Sihanouk's party returned to Peking, some of his aides and relatives chose to move to France—with Sihanouk's permission—rather than return to revolutionary Cambodia.

The currency of the toppled Khmer Republic lies strewn inside the abandoned shell of the National Bank after triumphant Khmer Rouge soldiers destroyed the building.

Sihanouk himself, after spending several months traveling, went back to Phnom Penh on the last day of December. If he expected to keep playing a role in Cambodia's political life, however, he was quickly disillusioned. Less than a week after his return, he was called on to sign the new constitution, which replaced the royal government with the new state of Democratic Kampuchea. Three months later, in the only message he was ever allowed to broadcast to the country after his return, he announced his retirement, explaining that after the coup d'état of 1970, "I swore to myself and to the Cambodian people that after I had accompanied my countrymen to complete victory over U.S. imperialism and the traitorous clique, and after the opening of the new revolutionary era, I would retire completely and forever from the political scene, for my role would logically come to an end."

After his retirement, the prince was promptly placed under house arrest, sealed off from everyone except his immediate family and young Khmer Rouge guards who amused themselves, Sihanouk later recalled, by torturing animals. The chief guard and his men "took great pleasure in catching mice, shutting them in a cage, and setting fire to it," Sihanouk wrote. "They seemed to love watching the mice run around in circles, desperately and hopelessly looking for a way out, then die in the flames"—a gruesome reflection of the spirit of the regime itself.

Democratic Kampuchea would achieve its place in history, Khieu Samphan and Son Sen once explained to Prince Sihanouk, by becoming "the first nation to create a completely Communist society without wasting time on intermediate steps." In their increasingly fanatical pursuit of that aim, the Khmer Rouge tried to obliterate all traces of the old society. "Two thousand years of Cambodian history have virtually ended," Phnom Penh Radio boasted in 1976.

Buddhism was a particular target. Monks were ordered to shed their orange robes and work in the fields with everyone else. The Khmer Rouge smashed Buddha statues in the temples, burned religious books, and destroyed the temples themselves or turned them into animal pens or storehouses for manure.

The Khmer Rouge also savagely persecuted ethnic minorities. Large numbers of Chinese and Vietnamese were murdered, as were many in the Thai community in coastal Koh Kong Province. The Cham, a Muslim people thought to be descended from the ancient nation of Champa and who had for generations stubbornly resisted assimilating into the Khmer majority, suffered particularly harsh treatment. The Khmer Rouge prohibited their language, their distinctive dress, and their religious practices, while routinely executing their religious leaders and sometimes entire communities.

Downtown Phnom Penh remains a ghost town four years after the Khmer Rouge ordered the capital's 3 million inhabitants to evacuate in 1975.

"At the beginning of 1976 they asked all the Cham in my area of Kompong Cham province to assemble at Coc Pho," a blacksmith named Sen Mat told the writer Wilfred Burchett after escaping to Vietnam. "They said they wanted to consult with us about various problems. Everyone had to pass by a table and give his name and hamlet. I was one of the last and saw that 1,116 had been listed before me. Then the table was taken away, and troops hidden among the trees opened up with mortars and heavy machine guns. When the firing was over, there were just eight of us left. We pretended to be dead and escaped at night."

Many Cham villages rose up in hopeless revolts, which were suppressed with enormous brutality. Altogether, the writer Elizabeth Becker estimated in her history of the Khmer Rouge movement, *When the War Was Over,* up to half of the entire Cham community in Cambodia may have died during the Khmer Rouge years.

While thus "purifying" Cambodia, the Khmer Rouge imposed a draconian system of agricultural cooperatives, turning the country into a huge slave-labor camp, guarded by teen-aged soldiers possessed by a primitive violence and an utter contempt for weakness. Their authority was enforced by pure terror. People could be executed for not working hard enough, for leaving their work sites without permission, for stealing food to keep from starving, for complaining—even for weeping in the dark at night, which was considered criticism of the regime.

Though ostensibly carrying out a Marxist revolution, the regime actually seemed motivated less by Marxism than by a fierce national and racial chauvinism, a violent hunger for revenge against the formerly privileged and powerful, and a paranoid fear of hidden enemies in their own ranks. Under Pol Pot, reported the Australian left-wing scholar Ben Kiernan, "not a single text of Marxist-Leninist proletarian ideology was translated into Khmer and made available for study. The only complete work from the Communist world to be translated was *Who's Who in the C.I.A.;* its list of names was used for interrogation purposes in the regime's central political prison."

Convinced that they had won the greatest revolutionary victory in history ("never before had there been such an event in the annals of the world's revolutionary wars," Pol Pot declared a few months after liberation), the Khmer Rouge leaders in their empty capital were equally grandiose in their plans to transform Cambodia virtually overnight into a "developed industrial country with great strength for national defense."

Their economic goals would have been far beyond Cambodia's abilities even in favorable circumstances. With the economy and rural infrastructure already devastated by five years of war and the population traumatized by violence, exhaustion, and disease, the regime's plans were sheer fantasy. But when they failed, Pol Pot and his associates did not look for flaws in their own policies. Instead they blamed unseen but ubiquitous "class ene-mies" and traitors in their own ranks who had to be found and, in the sinister vernacular adopted by the regime's security apparatus, "crushed to bits."

Thus the violence they had originally aimed at their wartime enemies increasingly began to turn on the Khmer Rouge themselves. As early as August 1975, one prominent Khmer Rouge leader, Interior Minister Hou Yuon, disappeared—reportedly executed for protesting the evacuation of Phnom Penh. From then on, the party devoured itself in an almost uninterrupted succession of purges and factional disputes, including one mysterious affair, still not fully explained more than a decade later, in which Pol Pot himself temporarily gave up the premiership for "health reasons." In the purges, hundreds of high-ranking officials and thousands of their followers were killed, usually after they were tortured into making fantastic "confessions" of their crimes.

Outside Cambodia, little was known about the bloody purges that wracked the party. But the world did learn about the horrors inflicted on the general population. Refugees' accounts of mass executions and slave-labor camps prompted frequent comparisons to the Nazis' slaughter of European Jews during World War II. For a generation, Western statesmen had declared that such a crime must never be allowed to happen again. Yet during Pol Pot's rule in Cambodia, no Western nation took any action to stop the slaughter. When the Khmer Rouge were overthrown, it was not because their crimes horrified the world into action but because their leaders' fears, megalomania, and twisted national pride led them into war with their totalitarian neighbor and former partner: Vietnam.

The first shots in Cambodia's new war were fired almost as soon as the old war ended. On May 4, 1975, only two and a half weeks after the Cambodian revolutionaries marched into Phnom Penh (and less than a week after the Vietnamese Communists won their long war against the U.S.-backed Saigon government), Khmer Rouge troops assaulted Vietnam's Phu Quoc Island in the Gulf of Thailand—territory long claimed by Cambodia. Six days later, the Cambodians occupied another disputed island, Poulo Panjang, burning homes and taking away 515 Vietnamese civilians, who were never seen again.

The Vietnamese recaptured Poulo Panjang on May 26 and eleven days later seized the Cambodian island of Poulo Wai, 100 kilometers from the mainland, where a Khmer Rouge gunboat had seized the American freighter *Mayaguez* a few weeks earlier. U.S. air strikes in response to that event destroyed seventeen Cambodian aircraft, heavily damaged the Ream air base near Kompong Som, damaged port facilities, and sank a number of Cambodian

Pol Pot, the architect of Cambodia's horrific Communist revolution, poses for a picture during a rare meeting with Western journalists at the former French governor's palace in Phnom Penh, December 1978.

Two Who Survived

"If you entered, you were dead."

Before the Khmer Rouge victory, Heng Nath was a village artist, painting portraits and scenes and selling them to his neighbors. In December 1977, for reasons he never discovered, he was arrested by the Khmer Rouge and eventually became one of the few known survivors of the notorious Tuol Sleng prison. After the Vietnamese occupation of Phnom Penh, Heng told his story to David Hawk, the director of the Cambodian Documentation Commission.

When Heng Nath was arrested, the only explanation he was given by his Khmer Rouge jailers was framed in the twisted logic of totalitarianism. "They said the organization has never been insane, but only takes into custody those who have done wrong."

He assumed his offense must be political, however, simply because he was taken to prison instead of the killing fields. His reasoning was a chilling comment on life in Pol Pot's Cambodia: "Those who were imprisoned for political reasons were kept for a long time so they could interrogate them," he said. "For minor matters, there was not so much of this kind of thing. For such minor things people would be killed right away."

Heng's first prison was on the grounds of a temple in Battambang. There his captors blindfolded him, handcuffed his wrists behind his back, and trussed his upper arms while interrogating him under electric-shock torture. They demanded that he confess his acts of treason and describe his "network," Heng recalled, "but I had none. I had no answers to give."

After a week of interrogation in the Battambang prison, he was taken by truck with thirty-one other prisoners, shackled together in groups of five or six, to Tuol Sleng, the former Phnom Penh school that served as the headquarters of the Khmer Rouge security police. Arriving there at three in the morning, Heng was photographed, ordered to write a short biography, and then put into a cell with about sixty other prisoners on the second floor of Building D. Written on a blackboard were the prison regulations, which, among other things, prohibited prisoners from talking to one another. Prisoners were forbidden to sit down in their cells; if they were not standing, they had to lie on the floor.

The prison diet consisted of two or three spoonfuls of rice gruel served at eight o'clock each morning and again at eight o'clock at night. Prisoners were blindfolded when they were taken from their cells for interrogation and torture. But the terror pursued them into their cells as well. "Screams were heard at all times," Heng remembered. "There was one kind of scream, the scream of fear, there was another kind of scream, the scream of terror, there was another kind of scream of asphyxiation near death."

For Heng, Tuol Sleng was like experiencing death itself: "I felt that as soon as one took one's first step into Tuol Sleng, one had no hope [of] ever seeing the light of life again. I felt that one's life would certainly end at Tuol Sleng. It was merely a matter of not knowing which day it might end. Tuol Sleng was a place that one could enter but could never leave. If you entered, you were dead."

After a month of starvation and torture, Heng was so exhausted and thin he could no longer walk and expected to die. "They wouldn't have to kill me," he remembered thinking. But then one day he heard guards going from cell to cell, calling out his name. When they got to his cell door, Heng identified himself. This time he was not interrogated about his supposed crimes. Instead, he was asked if he could still draw. Then he was taken downstairs, for the first time without a blindfold, to meet the commander of the prison himself, Kong Kech Eav (known by his revolutionary name, Comrade Duch).

Angka wanted a portrait of "Brother Number One"—Pol Pot—Duch explained. Could Heng draw one? Fearing he would be too weak, Heng recalled, "I did not yet dare to guarantee that I could do it...they said that I should first rest for three days, and that when my energy came back, when my strength came back, I should begin work."

For the next six months, working from a photograph, Heng drew six portraits and also helped make a mold for statues that, he was told, were to be displayed at the party's anniversary celebration.

At eleven o'clock on the morning of January 7, 1979, a little over a year after he was first arrested in Battambang, Heng and his fellow prisoners heard gunfire outside the prison. An hour and a half later, with a few other prisoners who had been spared to work as artists or mechanics, he was led out of Tuol Sleng under the rifles of the prison guards. All of the other surviving prisoners, Heng believed, were killed and their cells left closed and locked.

Heng's group, under orders to remain in perfect file or be shot immediately, marched out to the southern outskirts of Phnom Penh, where they spent a sleepless night still under Khmer Rouge guard. The next morning, however, along the road leading to Pochentong airport, the prisoners and guards suddenly found themselves in the middle of a firefight between Khmer Rouge and Vietnamese troops. In the confusion, Heng managed to break away from his guards and climb aboard a rebel truck, which eventually drove him back into the city.

Under the Vietnamese occupation, Heng helped the new authorities prepare Tuol Sleng as a museum of Khmer Rouge crimes. As he had realized while still in prison, leaving Tuol Sleng alive was nothing less than miraculous. Records left behind by the prison authorities showed that approximately 20,000 people were tortured and murdered there under the Khmer Rouge. The total number of known survivors, including Heng, was seven.

Inside Tuol Sleng, the Khmer Rouge's notorious interrogation center that became a museum under the Vietnamese.

Footsteps

Under the Lon Nol government, Kassie Neou was a translator for the official Phnom Penh radio station. As part of his job, he translated children's stories broadcast in English by the British Broadcasting Corporation. Evacuated from the capital along with all its other residents in April 1975, Kassie concealed his background, assuming several false names and identities as he was moved from one collective to another. A year and a half after the Khmer Rouge victory, however, someone overheard him say a few words in English. As a result he was arrested and imprisoned for six months on suspicion of working for the U.S. Central Intelligence Agency. Following the Vietnamese invasion, Kassie escaped to Thailand and eventually settled in the U.S. He was interviewed by David Hawk of the Cambodian Documentation Commission in 1983. Kassie's story also appears in To Bear Any Burden, *a 1985 book of oral histories collected by Al Santoli.*

Following his careless slip into English, Kassie Neou was ordered by the Khmer Rouge authorities in his village to go to the military post a kilometer away to get some gasoline. When he got there, however, he was met by three soldiers who bound his arms, then tied a rope around his neck. The other end was tied to a bicycle, which one of the soldiers rode down the highway while Kassie trotted behind. "I fell down many times on the paved road," he remembered. While he struggled awkwardly to get up, the soldiers "would stop and laugh; I was not allowed to say a word."

In this fashion Kassie arrived at an interrogation center where he was savagely beaten. He knew a little English because he had driven a taxi in Phnom Penh, Kassie kept saying, but his interrogators insisted he was an agent for the CIA. The interrogation ended when his torturers hooded him with a plastic cloth that they tightened over his face until he lost consciousness. He came to in the local prison, a crude thatched shed with no walls where the prisoners lay on the ground in neck chains and ankle irons with rice sacks for bedding.

Most of the other prisoners, Kassie learned, had been arrested for traveling without permission from the Khmer Rouge authorities. Those who were found to have committed no other offense were ordinarily released after three or four months. But those identified as former Lon Nol soldiers, or who were suspected of some other crime, were executed. "Mostly in the evening," Kassie said, "you would hear footsteps as they would call a name. I was terrified whenever I heard footsteps."

During his imprisonment Kassie passed the time by telling stories—the same ones he had translated for Phnom Penh Radio from BBC broadcasts—to some of the younger guards, including the eleven-year-old son of the prison chief. Though he did not know it, the pastime would save his life.

One night Kassie and thirty-six other prisoners were lined up and roped together, each one's neck joined to the wrists of the prisoner ahead. They were to be killed, evidently for no other reason than to make room for some newly arrived prisoners. But Kassie heard the prison chief's son tell some of the other teen-aged guards, "I need him."

Then, Kassie told the oral historian Al Santoli, "two other guards, thirteen and fourteen years old, snuck in and pulled me out. They hid me in a little pond used by buffaloes. It was full of mud. And leeches. Oh! Hundreds of leeches. The guards told me, 'Stay here. Don't move.' So I stayed the whole night. You can't imagine how many leeches were on me."

Early in the morning, from his hiding place, Kassie heard a truck arrive and then listened to the soldiers calling out numbers as they counted the arriving prisoners, seventy-two of them. When the count reached seventy-one, one of the young guards who had saved him the night before came dashing over to Kassie's pond, pulled him out of the mud, and thrust him into the line, shouting "Seventy-two."

The real number seventy-two, meanwhile, was just getting off the truck—a sickly young man, Kassie remembered, who looked "a little bit Chinese, and a little bit insane." To make the numbers come out right, the prison chief's son and the other teen-aged guard took the new arrival out to the back field and killed him. "Thirty-seven executed. Seventy-two alive in the jail," Kassie said—exactly according to the plan.

Finally, by repairing a motorbike for one of the soldiers, Kassie convinced his captors that he really had been a taxi driver after all. After six months and eighteen days in prison, he was freed. When the Vietnamese army reached Battambang in January 1979, Kassie was forced to evacuate and spent another four months with the Khmer Rouge before escaping. He reached Thailand but with some 40,000 other refugees was forced back over the border at Preah Vihear in June 1979. The following year, Kassie escaped to Thailand again. On March 20, 1981, he arrived in the United States.

gunboats. Washington, while claiming "victory" for having recovered the ship and its thirty-nine crewmen (at the cost of forty-one U.S. Marines and airmen killed during the rescue operation), may thus have inadvertently aided Vietnam by seriously weakening Cambodia's military capability in the coastal region.

Despite their skirmishes, neither Vietnam nor Cambodia was ready for an open confrontation. Both had just emerged from a long and extremely destructive war; for the moment, at least, the new governments in Phnom Penh and Hanoi were both more concerned with consolidating the power they had just won than with their quarrels with each other.

The Vietnamese, having made their show of military strength (and having received expressions of regret from Pol Pot, who paid an unannounced visit to Hanoi in mid-June), returned Poulo Wai to the Cambodians in August, also promising to return some 600 Cambodian prisoners. Later in the year, in a gruesomely cynical gesture of good will, the Vietnamese authorities forcibly returned several thousand Khmer and Chinese refugees who had fled from the Khmer Rouge blood bath into Vietnam's An Giang Province and who almost certainly faced execution after being handed back.

The two sides reached no permanent settlement on their various territorial disputes, however. In December, by Hanoi's later account, Cambodian forces encroached on Vietnamese territory in two provinces in the central highlands, while Cambodia complained that Vietnamese troops remained in some of the wartime sanctuary areas along the border, particularly in remote Ratanakiri Province. Meanwhile, tensions grew over other issues as well, among them Cambodia's expulsion of about 200,000 ethnic Vietnamese during the first months of Khmer Rouge rule and the growing friendship between Cambodia and China, which the Vietnamese observed with increasing suspicion and hostility.

In public, both sides continued to proclaim fealty to their wartime alliance. Just beneath the surface, however, simmered a hostility of which the border disputes were only a symptom, not a cause. Vietnam and Cambodia were divided by ancient hatreds, ideological differences, and rival alliances reflecting the Soviet-Chinese struggle for regional advantage. From those forces would come the next chapter in Indochina's long story of violence.

Revolution in Laos

A revolution "must be able to accept a compromise," the Lao Communist general secretary Kaysone Phomvihan once wrote, but must also be ready to renounce it "when the compromise becomes a hindrance to the revolution, especially when the struggle has reached the highest degree of intensity, conditions are ripe for an explosion and an immediate revolutionary situation has arisen."

In Laos, where events had always been determined chiefly by outside forces, the revolutionary moment ripened with the sudden and unexpected success of the Vietnamese Communists in the spring of 1975. While the world's attention was riveted on the tragic rout of the South Vietnamese army and on the death throes of the Khmer Republic, the precarious Lao coalition also began to totter.

The last stage of the Lao Communists' march to power began in late April, when Pathet Lao forces assaulted government positions around Sala Phou Khoun, an important crossroads on the main highway between Vientiane and Luang Prabang. General Vang Pao, the regional commander, had thrown back previous attacks with the help of air strikes by Lao air force T-28s. This time, however, after a week of confused fighting during which the road junction and nearby airfield changed hands several times, Prime Minister Souvanna Phouma refused to authorize further air strikes—feeling, apparently, that avoiding military action might help save the coalition while the rest of Indochina fell under Communist control.

In the following days, while the victorious North Vietnamese Army marched into Saigon, Vang Pao's discouraged and embittered troops fell back from Sala Phou Khoun southward along the highway or slipped away into the jagged mountains to the east. Behind them, Pathet Lao infantry accompanied by a handful of tanks advanced slowly through the descending mountain passes in the direction of Vientiane, where thousands of dispirited officials, businessmen, and others associated with the traditional Lao elite were already beginning to flee the country.

The pursuing Communist forces made little effort to overtake and engage the retreating government troops; nor did they need to. From early May on, the "liberation" of Laos would unfold with almost no fighting but through a sort of ritual dance of defeat in which the Vientiane political and military leaders and their rightist supporters acquiesced, step by step, to adroitly orchestrated pressure from the Pathet Lao.

Souvanna's despairing decision not to oppose the Pathet Lao attacks reflected not only the impact of the Communist victories in Vietnam and Cambodia but also a political balance that had shifted sharply since the coalition government was formed in 1974.

The year since Prince Souphanouvong's triumphal return to Vientiane had seen growing defeatism and political deterioration on the rightist side, while the often-underestimated Pathet Lao leadership scored a series of political successes. The rightists, united only by a common belief that they were doomed without U.S. support, had been demoralized ever since the 1973 cease-fire agreement. In the coalition, their representatives proved unable to form a common front against the Pathet Lao or to respond to public hopes for political and economic reforms. Instead, they squandered time, energy, and popular support in endless petty squabbles over position and power.

The Pathet Lao, meanwhile, shrewdly capitalized on the war-weariness and political discontent in the Lao public. By contrast with the intrigue-ridden Vientiane leadership, widely seen as bumbling and corrupt, the Pathet Lao appeared honest and dynamic. As was widely acknowledged even by Vientiane-side officials, they soon won a surprising popularity among ordinary Lao citizens.

Souphanouvong's base was the presidency of the National Political Consultative Council, which was established under the Lao cease-fire agreement with vaguely defined responsibilities to "support and assist" the provisional coalition government. In May 1974, the NPCC adopted an eighteen-point program that became the vehicle for Pathet Lao proselytizing. The document consisted largely of platitudinous calls for a "peaceful, independent, neutral, democratic, unified and prosperous Kingdom of Laos." Buried in the boilerplate, however, were key elements of Pathet Lao policy, including a demand that the U.S. contribute to "healing the wounds of the war" and a declaration of support for "the struggle of the peoples in the various countries in Indochina."

Less than two months later, the Pathet Lao succeeded in turning an embarrassment into another political victory. The issue was the withdrawal of foreign military forces and advisers from Laos, which was supposed to be com-

pleted on June 4, sixty days after the formation of the coalition government. The U.S. and Thailand complied, with the removal of the last of some 20,000 Thai troops and of the U.S. "attachés" and CIA case officers who had controlled the Hmong and other irregular forces. However, an estimated 50,000 to 60,000 North Vietnamese troops, whose presence had never been acknowledged by the Pathet Lao, remained in the country.

To protest the continued Vietnamese presence, several right-wing members of the Lao National Assembly announced in early July that they would collect petition signatures calling for the withdrawal of all Vietnamese forces from Lao territory. Their appeal drew large crowds to the assembly building to sign the petitions. At the insistence of embarrassed Pathet Lao officials, guards prevented the potential petitioners from entering the building. The next day, following a stormy cabinet meeting, Souvanna announced the closing of the assembly, declaring amid some skepticism that the "two sides" in the coalition had both requested him to take such a step. Suspending the assembly left the NPCC, dominated by

Prince Souphanouvong (in front with tie) and other Laotians are received in Hanoi by Acting Premier Le Thanh Nghi (to the prince's left) in April 1974.

Souphanouvong, as the principal forum for public treatment of political issues.

A day after the assembly was suspended, the seventy-two-year-old Souvanna suffered a severe heart attack and was incapacitated for several months. During his illness, though both sides carefully avoided an open split that would destroy the coalition, the Pathet Lao orchestrated an unprecedented wave of strikes and demonstrations against Vientiane-side officials and in support of the NPCC's eighteen-point program. Even more alarming to the rightists was a mutiny in December involving seven guerrilla battalions in Ban Houei Sai, in the far northwest of the country. The mutinous troops issued demands coinciding exactly with Pathet Lao policies, calling for implementation of the eighteen points, neutralization of Ban Houei Sai, and the formal dissolution of the suspended National Assembly so new elections could be held.

Prime Minister Souvanna, resuming his duties as the new year began, announced a ban on demonstrations, but he also made concessions to Pathet Lao political demands. The NPCC eighteen-point program was adopted, with a few modifications, as official government policy, and in April, just as the final crisis was about to begin, Souvanna and King Savang Vatthana finally agreed on the formal dissolution of the assembly. In addition, the king accepted an invitation to visit the "liberated zone," further heightening the prestige of the Pathet Lao. The royal visit took place between April 28 and May 4, coinciding precisely with the events that would lead to the end not only of the coalition government but of the monarchy itself.

On May 1, 1975, the day after the fall of Saigon and while Vang Pao's forces were retreating from Sala Phou Khoun, demonstrations in Vientiane called for the ouster of Defense Minister Sisouk na Champassak and other leading rightists in the cabinet. Barely a week later, Sisouk and four colleagues resigned and shortly afterward left the country. By then many wealthy private citizens were also fleeing, along with most of Vientiane's Chinese and Vietnamese merchants, whose shops stood shuttered and locked in the city's business district.

Flights out of the country from Wattay airport were booked full, and long lines of cars waited at the Vientiane ferry for passage across the Mekong to Thailand. The less prosperous, without cars, crowded onto flat-bottomed boats that left every few minutes "loaded with passengers," one journalist wrote, "and bulging suitcases and boxes." Soldiers in various military units, meanwhile, including the cadets at the Vientiane Military School, announced they would no longer obey their commanders but instead considered themselves directly under the prime minister's command.

By now, as one observer noted, Souvanna "apparently saw his role as a bridge between the old and new orders." On May 11, he appointed General Khamouane Boupha, the Pathet Lao officer who had served as deputy defense minister in the coalition cabinet, to "take charge of the national armed forces throughout the kingdom." Promptly, Khamouane issued orders grounding the Lao air force and stopping all troop movements. At Vang Pao's headquarters in Long Cheng, an airlift was already under way, evacuating several thousand of the Hmong general's followers to Thailand over the course of three days. Another 40,000 set out on foot, following their leaders into exile—the start of a diaspora that would eventually see one-third or more of the entire Hmong tribe driven out of Laos.

Vang Pao himself, who had resigned his command by angrily tearing off his general's stars and flinging them down on the prime minister's desk a week earlier, flew to Thailand on May 14, joining other prominent rightist generals who had already fled the country. Other Vientiane-side officers who remained with their units quickly sent messages accepting the change of command and promising to obey orders of the new military leadership.

With the army effectively neutralized and their principal opponents removed from the coalition cabinet, Pathet Lao people's revolutionary committees began taking over local and province administration, in most cases through demonstrations followed by the unopposed entry of Pathet Lao forces. Pathet Lao cadres were also organizing protests directed at another target: the U.S. presence in Laos. Demonstrations at the American embassy had begun as early as May 1, and on May 20, a large crowd of students and Lao employees of the U.S. Agency for International Development seized the AID compound in Vientiane. They occupied it for the next eight days, leaving only after Christian Chapman, the U.S. chargé d'affaires, reached agreement with the Pathet Lao authorities that the AID mission would close and all aid programs would end on June 30. When the ensuing exodus was completed, the embassy's American staff consisted of exactly twenty-two persons—the last remnant of a huge official American presence in Indochina that had often dominated its allies without ever finding the way to make them effective instruments of U.S. policy.

The final stage of the Pathet Lao's seizure of power began at the end of July, when a cowed coalition cabinet agreed to dissolve the mixed police and military units in Luang Prabang and Vientiane, leaving law enforcement and military authority in the hands of the Pathet Lao contingent alone. Following that step, a revolutionary committee took over the administration in Luang Prabang on August 18. Five days later, the Pathet Lao took control in Vientiane as well. Though Souvanna Phouma and the coalition government nominally remained in office, the Pathet Lao were now the effective rulers of the country.

Throughout the war, the Lao Communists had professed loyalty to the monarchy. The Lao Patriotic Front specifically pledged at its 1964 national congress "to respect and defend the Throne"—a promise repeated at its next congress four years later. But once the Pathet Lao took power, the kingdom of Lan Chang had only a few more months remaining of its 600-year history.

The monarchy and the coalition government were formally abolished by an All-Laos Congress of People's Representatives convened in Vientiane on December 1 and 2, 1975. The coalition "was no longer compatible with the changed situation in the country," Prince Souphanouvong declared in a speech to the opening session, and was therefore dissolved. The congress then accepted Souvanna's resignation as prime minister and an abdication message from King Savang Vatthana—fulfilling his prediction years earlier that he was "doomed to be the last king of Laos." "I now leave it to the people of Laos to shape the destiny of the country," the king's message concluded. "This once again affirms the right of the people throughout the country to be their own masters. Now, as an ordinary citizen of Laos, I wish unity, independence, happiness and prosperity to the whole of my beloved Lao people."

In place of the monarchy, the congress established a Lao People's Democratic Republic, with Souphanouvong as president. Kaysone Phomvihan, the fifty-five-year-old general secretary of the Lao People's Revolutionary party—a leader who was still almost entirely unknown to the Lao public, despite having led the party for more than two decades—was named prime minister.

By comparison with the Communist victories in Vietnam and Cambodia, the completion of the Lao revolution had been a relatively peaceful affair. The losers still paid a

harsh price, however, particularly the soldiers and officials of the former regime who were sent to labor camps in remote regions for "reeducation." Up to 40,000 people, it was estimated, underwent an ordeal that came to be referred to, with misleading mildness, as "seminar." Many were still confined more than a decade after the Pathet Lao came to power. One estimate in the mid-1980s, by the human-rights organization Amnesty International, put the number of prisoners at between 5,000 and 6,000.

Conditions in the camps were brutal. "We were loaded into trucks and taken to a dense forest in the mountainous area on the Laos-Vietnam border," recalled Prasith Sayaphon, a former Lao air force lieutenant who escaped after five years in reeducation. "There were no houses or shelters. The Pathet Lao made us build everything from scratch with bamboo and grass roofs." After building the camp, Prasith and his fellow prisoners—"civil servants, district chiefs, and military officers"—were put to work cutting logs and building roads.

"It was very dangerous to clear the wooded area," he remembered, "because there were many unexploded bombs sunk part way into the ground. The Pathet Lao guards forced us to dismantle the bombs by hand. Some exploded, killing many prisoners. The only food we re-

---

A group of Vang Pao's Hmong soldiers, along with several Thai mercenaries, are led to a detention camp following their surrender to advancing Pathet Lao troops, spring 1975.

ceived was old stale rice that the Pathet Lao had left over from the war. Some of it was up to ten years old. And only a little more than half a handful each day. To survive, we had to search for food in the forests, such as bamboo shoots. Because of the lack of nutrition and the type of food we ate, there was much disease. Dysentery was very common. I became very skinny and my skin turned pale yellow."

As usual, the Hmong suffered disproportionately. Almost the first reeducation prisoners were those officers of Vang Pao's Hmong army who had remained with their units instead of joining the general in exile. In May 1975, on the same day that Vang Pao fled the country, a Pathet Lao colonel, Kham Ai, arrived in Long Cheng to take over as commander of the 2d Military Region. Two weeks later, he ordered all of Vang Pao's former officers to report to his headquarters and give up their weapons.

Beginning in June, they were sent to labor camps where, according to the Australian-educated Hmong scholar Gary Yia Lee, "anyone above the rank of lieutenant was considered a major war criminal, and manual work was deemed an excellent means of atoning for one's sins and cleansing one's mind of capitalist ideas." The Hmong officers were told, Lee added, "that 'seminars' could last thirty days or thirty years, depending on the participant's level of cooperation with Vang Pao and the number of crimes he had committed against the Patriotic Forces and their Vietnamese 'brothers.' Each officer had to list the dates of armed attacks in which he had taken part, the number of PL or Vietnamese soldiers 'murdered' on each occasion, the cattle and livestock killed or stolen, and property damages suffered by civilians. If the PL officer-in-charge was not satisfied with the officers' 'confessions,' he would reduce their food ration to 300 grammes of rice a day per person and one can of meat for each ten people. As one survivor recounts, after 'six months of seminar we became mere skeletons without strength.' "

Very few if any of the imprisoned Hmong officers had been released by the time Lee's study was published seven years after "liberation." Except for a handful who managed to escape from the camps, Lee wrote, the majority of the prisoners "either died from physical exertion and malnutrition, or continue to be imprisoned."

Besides the secret army veterans in prison camps and those who were refugees in Thailand, other bands of former Vang Pao troops and their families neither surrendered nor fled but made their way to the slopes of Phou Bia, Laos's highest mountain, deep in the interior of Xieng Khouang Province south of the Plain of Jars. From bases among the jagged ridges and steep valleys of the Phou Bia Massif, the guerrillas maintained an active resistance

Pathet Lao soldiers aboard a PT76 tank lead a victorious train of troops and trucks into Savannakhet in May 1975 as jubilant citizens celebrate the end of hostilities.

movement for several years, attacking government supply convoys and burning crops and stealing livestock in pro-Pathet Lao villages.

How many were in the resistance was unclear; one estimate, by two American Quaker representatives in Vientiane, was that somewhere between 10,000 and 30,000 Hmong were living in the rebel bases, with up to 5,000 actively engaged in combat. The resistance bands became known as Chao Fa (King of Heaven) soldiers, reportedly because of their belief that Chao Fa would provide weapons and other supplies from the sky just as the CIA had, in fact, supplied the Hmong army for many years.

In 1977 and 1978, Pathet Lao and Vietnamese forces launched a major offensive against the resistance, and by October 1978 most of the bases around Phou Bia had been wiped out. The Vietnamese used air strikes, artillery, and chemical weapons, according to numerous refugee reports. A typical account from a resistance leader who reached Thailand early in 1979 said that his village "was bombed with a yellowish gas that made [him] nauseous and dizzy for about twenty-four hours." The U.S. government later officially accused the Vietnamese of using toxic gas against the Hmong resistance. Aside from refugee reports, however, the only available physical evidence was fragmentary and disputed by many scientists, and it seemed unlikely the issue would ever be conclusively settled.

The assault on the Phou Bia region, which drove tens of thousands more Hmong over steep, hazardous jungle trails to refuge in Thailand, did not completely end armed resistance to Pathet Lao rule. Following the open break between China and Vietnam, the Chinese were reported to have set up training camps in China's Yunnan Province for 1,000 to 3,000 resistance fighters drawn largely from the Hmong, Yao, and other Lao hill tribes. Right-wing Lao exiles, meanwhile, announced in September 1980 the formation of a new resistance group called the Lao People's National Liberation Front.

None of these groups, however, appeared able to mount more than a minor threat to the Pathet Lao and their Vietnamese protectors. Entering its second decade under Communist rule, Laos remained in the grip of a drab, alien totalitarianism whose spirit was harshly at odds with the traditions of tolerance, gentleness, and pacifism in Lao life. Because they felt pressed to consolidate their political and administrative control as quickly as possible and because they took as their model the Vietnamese Communists' wartime methods of mobilizing the population, the Pathet Lao imposed radical policies of social and economic transformation. The results were disastrous, partly because the government's programs conflicted with traditional Lao values but also because it had so few officials with the training, competence, or technical knowledge to run a managed economy. Even Prince Souphanouvong himself was reported to have remarked in late 1975 that the party had achieved power "five years too soon."

Most unpopular, perhaps, was the attempt to promote "collective mastery" of agriculture through a system of farming cooperatives, often established through the forced relocation of hill-tribe groups to unfamiliar valleys where they were supposed to practice new and more intensive methods of farming. Not surprisingly, far from improving production, the new programs led to serious food shortages, forcing many peasants to sell their few personal possessions in order to survive.

Impoverishment and heavy-handed party control in the cooperatives also disrupted the traditions and rituals of rural life: sacrifices to the spirits, gifts to monks, and the cycle of festivals that gave sequence, stability, and symbolic meaning to the peasant's year. Beginning in 1980, the Lao leadership liberalized its policies somewhat, mirroring similar policy relaxations in Vietnam. But outside of the regime and its ideological sympathizers, few disputed that for the peasants, who made up four-fifths of Laos's population, "liberation" had meant chiefly hardship, poverty, hunger, and the loss of cherished traditions.

The revolution's impact on Vientiane was no less bleak. The Lao capital, "with its growing fleet of bicycles and occasional automobiles, its mildewed buildings gradually decaying, its struggling shops and occasional antiques for sale, and its dreary Soviet-stocked bookstore and cinema," as one account pictured it, gave the impression—like Vietnam itself—of another failed Socialist vision.

In one sense, that impression was not entirely fair. Pre-1975 Laos had been so utterly dependent on U.S. aid, and its economy had been so distorted in the years of American involvement, that no regime, Socialist or otherwise, could have avoided a severe drop in living standards once that outside assistance stopped. The bleakness of life in Laos, however, was more than just a matter of economics. It also reflected an alien regimentation, imposed from outside, threatening to smother Laos's national identity as well as the essential spirit and character of Lao society. In the 1980s, Laos's status as a poor, submissive, and obscure vassal state of Vietnam seemed both inescapable and permanent: a sad future for a country and a people that had seemed to deserve a gentler destiny.

Brotherly enemies

On the night of April 30, 1977, while officially sponsored celebrations throughout Vietnam marked the second anniversary of the Communists' final victory over the Saigon regime, Cambodian artillery and mortar shells whined out of the darkness into villages and military posts in the border region of An Giang Province in the western delta. Ground attacks by two brigades and two independent battalions accompanied the shelling, according to Vietnamese accounts. The Cambodians attacked thirteen of the fourteen villages adjacent to the border, as well as nearly every army and police installation in the area. The fighting in An Giang lasted three weeks, during which the Vietnamese claimed more than 200 civilians were killed.

The outbreak of fighting in 1977 followed a period of relative peace on the border. Though talks between Vietnamese and Cambodian officials in May 1976 failed to produce a new border agreement, the negotiators did agree to try to reduce tensions and settle conflicts "in a spirit of solidarity, friendship and mutual respect" through a system of local liaison committees. Armed clashes diminished noticeably in the following months.

The apparent easing of tension was an illusion, however. Within the Khmer Rouge leadership, anti-Vietnamese virulence was not fading but gaining force. Their cautious policy in 1976 did not reflect peaceful intentions or even a realistic appreciation of Vietnamese military superiority. Instead, it masked yet another violent internal convulsion, as Pol Pot and his allies explicitly sought to eliminate any remaining Vietnamese influence, real or imagined, in the Cambodian regime.

The purge opened with the arrest of the veteran Communist Keo Meas, whose crime was having written a 1972 party history declaring that the Cambodian Communist party was founded in 1951, during the French Indochina War. Because the Cambodian Communists at that time still formed a section of the Vietnamese party, that date was no longer acceptable to Pol Pot and his associates. Instead, in a "rearranged" version, the party's founding date was declared to be the 1960 "founding congress," the clandestine meeting of Cambodian Communists in empty railroad cars at the Phnom Penh train station.

Pol Pot was not content just to rewrite the history of the party's establishment but also set out to prove that the 1972 history was the concoction of a pro-Vietnamese plot to subvert and take over the Cambodian movement. Thus the abstruse issue of when the party was founded became the basis for the torture and killing of hundreds of people.

Under torture at the Tuol Sleng Prison—a Phnom Penh school that was taken over as the headquarters of the secret police agency known as "S.21"—Keo Meas admitted the "conspiracy." He was then executed. With his confession in hand, Pol Pot could now proceed to eliminate other supposed Hanoi agents or sympathizers from the party. For many months, the regime's secret police tortured prisoners to develop more evidence of the Vietnamese "plot"—a perfect example of how the Khmer Rouge leaders invented enemies out of their own deranged fears and then used the most brutal violence to manufacture proof that their paranoid fantasies were real.

While thus intensifying the revolution and tightening their grip on the party, the Cambodian leaders avoided military actions on the disputed borders. Their caution may also have reflected the political upheavals in China, Democratic Kampuchea's only ally, where Mao Tse-tung's death in September 1976 was quickly followed by the arrest of his widow, Jiang Qing, and the rest of the ultra-

Maoist faction known as the Gang of Four. The dominant figure in the new leadership was Deng Xiaoping, known to represent the moderate forces within China's Communist leadership. Before launching new attacks on their Vietnamese enemies, the Cambodians wanted to make sure that Peking's foreign policy remained unchanged.

By early 1977, Pol Pot and his associates apparently were confident enough both about Chinese backing and about their grip on their own party to renew their harassment of Vietnamese border areas. Beginning in January, according to Hanoi's later account, the Cambodians gradually cut off all contacts between the liaison committees that were supposed to resolve local disputes. In March, minor clashes began, followed by the large-scale attacks in An Giang on April 30.

Neither side was ready yet to publicize the fighting. Instead, on June 7, the Vietnamese privately proposed to the Cambodian authorities that a high-level meeting be held "to rapidly settle the border question and to put an end to bloody incidents detrimental to the militant solidarity and fraternal friendship between Vietnam and Kampu-

Carrying toy guns, a Lao girl and her younger sister ride a tricycle on the streets of Vientiane a few days after the Communists assumed control in December 1975.

chea." The Cambodians replied eleven days later, declining to meet "until the situation returns to normal and some time [elapses] without further border clashes."

Instead, fighting continued. Both sides, meanwhile, made diplomatic moves that reinforced their enemies' worst suspicions. In July, Vietnam and Laos signed a Treaty of Friendship and Cooperation legitimizing the presence of Vietnamese troops on Lao territory and affirming a special relationship that the Cambodians, not entirely without reason, interpreted as a code word for Vietnamese domination. To the Cambodians, the treaty was a clear and alarming reminder of Vietnam's expansionist nature. "We don't want to become another Laos," a Cambodian diplomat told the writer Nayan Chanda.

In late September, shortly after Cambodian forces launched one of the most violent attacks of the undeclared border war against Vietnam's Tay Ninh Province, Pol Pot—who had at last removed the mask of the Angka and publicly declared the existence of the Kampuchean Communist party—paid a state visit to China. In a banquet speech the night of his arrival, the Cambodian leader pointedly declared that Cambodia had "clearly distinguished between friends and enemies of our country" and would "defend our existing frontiers and see to it that they will never be lost."

His hosts, in welcoming speeches and in a message congratulating the Cambodians on their party's anniversary (the seventeenth, as had just been decreed, rather than the twenty-fifth), assured the Cambodians of China's "profound revolutionary friendship," congratulated them for "smashing sabotage and subversion by enemies both at home and abroad," and praised Cambodia's policies of "unity with the genuine Marxist-Leninist parties" and opposing "hegemonism," the Chinese code word for Soviet expansion.

The outside world, which still had no more than veiled hints of the fighting on the Vietnamese-Cambodian border, could only guess at the full significance of the exchanges in Peking. But to Hanoi, their meaning was all too clear: China, Vietnam's most dangerous adversary, was backing and perhaps even encouraging the Cambodians in their aggressive policy on the borders.

In the closing months of 1977, both sides hurtled toward the breaking point. Shortly after Pol Pot's visit, China agreed to step up military shipments to Cambodia. The Vietnamese, meanwhile, had been mending fences for several months with their major ally and arms supplier, the Soviet Union. A visit by a high-level Soviet military delegation in July led to a substantial increase in Soviet aid and the arrival of additional Soviet advisers to train the Vietnamese in the use of new weapons and aircraft.

Cambodians build dikes by passing mud from person to person at one of the "model villages" shown to journalists by the Khmer Rouge in 1977.

The bodies of dead Vietnamese line a rice field in An Dinh village. They were among 200 civilian victims of the Khmer Rouge foray into An Giang Province in late April 1977.

In September, the Vietnamese—after replacing local militia units on the border with regular infantry divisions—conducted operations as far as sixteen kilometers inside Cambodia at numerous points along the border. Then, in late December, Hanoi sharply escalated hostilities, sending some 60,000 troops supported by tanks, artillery, and helicopter gunships deep into Cambodia. One prong of the attack reached the outskirts of the Svay Rieng Province capital; another approached Kompong Cham on the Mekong, only about eighty kilometers northeast of Phnom Penh.

On the last day of the year, Cambodian leaders abruptly removed the screen of secrecy that had shielded the growing conflict from foreign eyes. In a broadcast over the official Phnom Penh Radio, they announced that relations with Vietnam were being severed "until the aggressor forces withdraw from the sacred territory of Democratic Kampuchea." An accompanying statement charged that Vietnam, "according to its nature of annexationist and swallower of territory," was seeking to incorporate Cambodia in a Vietnamese-dominated Indochina federation. The Vietnamese angrily rejected Cambodian charges but

also proposed negotiations "as early as possible, at whatever level, so as to together solve the border issue between the two countries in a spirit of brotherly friendship."

On January 6, 1978, the Vietnamese began pulling their troops back—of their own accord, most Western analysts believed. The Cambodians, however, "blinded by pride and self-conceit," as Prince Sihanouk later wrote, issued an official decree declaring the date of the Vietnamese withdrawal an even more important victory than the liberation of Phnom Penh in 1975. Perhaps genuinely believing that their enemies were beaten, the Cambodian leaders ignored Hanoi's proposal for negotiations.

Both in their initial statements and in subsequent propaganda diatribes, the two sides accused each other of barbarous atrocities against civilians. Cambodia charged that Vietnamese troops had machine-gunned "young and old people," burned houses, stolen poultry and cattle, and "raped women and killed them." The Vietnamese responded that the Cambodians had burned temples and hospitals and "perpetrated utterly inhuman crimes, raping, tearing fetuses from mothers' wombs, disembowelling adults, burning children alive."

The violence was not just along the border or between the Vietnamese and Cambodians, however. Within Cambodia, as the self-destructive megalomania of the Khmer Rouge reached its final stage, the last and worst of its internal bloodlettings was beginning to destroy the very force that was supposed to defend the regime against the Vietnamese—the Eastern Zone army. In spite of having proclaimed the "historic victory" of January 6, the Cambodian leaders nonetheless appeared obsessed with the thought that the Eastern Zone party secretary, So Phim, and other cadres were secretly in collusion with Vietnam.

In the first few months of 1978, some 400 Eastern Zone party cadres were imprisoned in Tuol Sleng. Then, in May, hundreds of military leaders in the region were called to "meetings" where they too were arrested. After So Phim himself refused a similar summons, troops under the command of the central party authorities attacked Eastern Zone units. Trapped by central troops, So Phim shot himself before he could be captured; reportedly, his wife and children were massacred as they tried to bury his body.

In the paranoid view of Pol Pot and his associates, the entire population of the Eastern Zone had to be punished for the supposed treason of its troops and leaders. The region "erupted with waves and waves of butchery," wrote Elizabeth Becker in *When the War Was Over*. "Whole villages of people were moved to nearby fields and clubbed to death. The thick whacking sound of ax handles bludgeoning people at the neck was heard over and over again. The entire Eastern Zone had to be 'cleansed' of the 'Khmer bodies with Vietnamese minds.'" By July, Becker's study estimated, more than 100,000 people had died.

In the turmoil, a number of senior Eastern Zone commanders—among them the zone's deputy commander,

Heng Samrin—managed to evade the central troops. Together with several thousand soldiers, they took refuge in the jungle and eventually went over to the Vietnamese. Thus, as Elizabeth Becker noted, the real result of the Eastern Zone purge was to hand the Vietnamese a valuable prize: the nucleus of an anti-Pol Pot resistance, headed by experienced Cambodian Communist leaders. It was, in effect, the closing of a circle of madness. The imaginary traitors conjured up by the Khmer Rouge leaders' fears had now, as the result of their own savage violence, become real.

Hanoi's fears centered on China. In Vietnamese eyes, the Cambodians were no more than Chinese proxies; China remained the chief threat to Vietnam's independence—as it had been for centuries. As the confrontation deepened, and having had no success in their efforts to reach a reconciliation with the United States, the Vietnamese had only one place to turn. In early November, Vietnam's prime minister Pham Van Dong and the Communist party general secretary, Le Duan, flew to Moscow.

After two days of talks, the Vietnamese and their hosts signed a twenty-five-year friendship treaty pledging, among other things, to oppose both imperialism and "reactionary forces"—Hanoi's usual code word for the Chinese—and to consult on "appropriate and effective measures" if one party was attacked or threatened with attack. The Chinese response was swift and uncompromising. At a press conference in Bangkok on November 8, Deng Xiaoping declared that the Soviet-Vietnamese treaty endangered peace in Asia and the entire world. Calling Vietnam an "Asian Cuba," Deng added ominously: "We are waiting to see how far they advance into Cambodia before deciding on countermeasures."

Only one element of Vietnamese strategy remained to be put into place: an anti-Khmer Rouge resistance front that could serve, under Hanoi's direction, as an instrument of Vietnamese policy. That step came, less than a month after Pham Van Dong and his colleagues returned from Moscow, in a clearing among the rubber groves near the border town of Snuol in Cambodia's Kratie Province. Vietnamese troops had occupied the area for several weeks. On the morning of December 2, several thousand Khmer soldiers and civilians—most of them having been trucked in from refugee camps a few kilometers away on the Vietnamese side of the border—gathered in what was now declared to be a "liberated zone" to attend the founding ceremonies of the Kampuchean National United Front for National Salvation.

With Vietnamese Politburo member Le Duc Tho looking on, Heng Samrin, named as the front's chairman, announced its purpose: to overthrow "the Pol Pot and Ieng Sary clique" that had, in the words of the KNUFNS program, "usurped" the Cambodian revolution. The next day the front broadcast a long declaration denouncing the Pol Pot "gang" and its Chinese sponsors and calling on Cam-

bodians to overthrow the "dictatorial, militarist and genocidal regime." The statement proclaimed an eleven-point program that included the restoration of religious worship, personal freedoms, and family life; the reestablishment of private property, currency, and markets; punishment of those who had committed "bloody crimes"; and—not surprisingly—settling the conflict with Vietnam through peaceful negotiations and with respect for each side's independence, sovereignty, and territory.

Conceivably, at that point Hanoi still envisaged a gradual, drawn-out liberation war in Cambodia, of the type consistent with Vietnam's past experience, traditions, and doctrine. But the Vietnamese may have remembered, as well, the advice offered to Defense Minister Vo Nguyen Giap by a Soviet general nearly a year earlier, reflecting the quite different Russian tradition in such matters. As a Vietnamese official told the writer Nayan Chanda years later, the Russian visitor recalled the powerful Soviet invasion that crushed the liberal Dubcek regime in Prague in 1968 and then observed that Vietnam should solve its problem the same way. The way to deal with Cambodia, he told Giap tersely, was: "Do a Czechoslovakia."

A Vietnamese soldier escorts a column of Cambodian prisoners away from the border in An Giang Province, the site of continuing clashes between the two countries, January 1978.

Life in Hell

For over three-and-one-half years the Khmer Rouge regime governed Cambodia in a reign of terror of unprecedented misery and destruction. The Kampuchean Communist party, led by Pol Pot, attempted to transform the country overnight into a self-sufficient Communist state. Instead, it shattered Cambodian society and culture. As the revolution faltered, the paranoid party turned against the people and then its own cadres in a massive display of bloodletting. Before the horror ended, some 2 million Cambodians had died.

In the pursuit of self-reliance, the Khmer Rouge made Cambodia a virtual slave-labor camp. The party's soldiers emptied the country's cities and towns and herded the citizens to cooperatives in the countryside. Every able body was put to work in the fields planting rice or building dams, dikes, and canals. Cambodians toiled endlessly in response to the irrational economic policies of the party. They were allowed no entertainment, books, or education. In political meetings, they were admonished to work harder. Former city dwellers, called "new people" by the Khmer Rouge, received the harshest treatment, and many, unaccustomed to grueling outdoor work, became malnourished and diseased.

The Khmer Rouge imposed their harsh ideology on the population and tried to destroy the identities of the Cambodian people. They denied the rights and feelings of individuals and outlawed any show of "individualism." They banned private ownership, confiscating vegetable plots, livestock, and tools. They then attacked the fundamental relationship of Cambodian society, the family.

The party abolished the use of family names and limited families to parents and their children under six. Older youths were expected to work in the fields and become the vanguard of the new order. Pol Pot replaced the traditional family meal with unpopular communal eating. Unmarried men and women could marry only with the consent of the party. The party sometimes ordered forced marriages and often prevented new couples from living together, allowing them privacy only a few times per month.

The Khmer Rouge regime also tried to eliminate what it considered the impure cultural and religious practices of the Cambodian people. The party banned the Buddhist religion, and Khmer Rouge soldiers murdered thousands of monks, disrobing the survivors and sending them to work in the fields. The Communists desecrated Buddhist relics, statuary, and schools and converted pagodas to stables, granaries, and prisons.

As the revolution stumbled, Khmer Rouge brutality touched more and more people. Pol Pot ordered the elimination of ethnic and religious minorities, and the party's call for class warfare made any Cambodian with a bourgeois background vulnerable. Eventually, the party attacked "traitorous" Khmer Rouge cadres and zone leaders. Torture, murder, pogroms, and purges all became part of the Pol Pot reign.

With any show of resistance or even minor mistakes, a peasant might disappear, never to be seen again. Cambodians learned to shudder at the phrase that preceded condemnation: "If you keep this man there is no profit, if he goes there is no loss." To survive, Cambodians disguised their backgrounds and invented humble peasant origins. They learned never to protest and to ignore the overwhelming misery around them.

With the Vietnamese invasion of Cambodia in late 1978, hundreds of thousands of Cambodians fled to refugee camps in neighboring Thailand. At the behest of relief workers, some made paintings and drawings depicting their experiences under the Khmer Rouge. Following are samples of those done by refugees at Khao I Dang camp. The first two were painted by adults, the last three drawn by children. All express in a way words cannot the terror of life under the Khmer Rouge.

Khmer Rouge soldiers brutalize Cambodian civilians. The Cambodian Communists subjected men, women, and children alike to whippings, electric shocks, and dunkings in water. They designed special punishments for women. They slashed their breasts, burned them with hot pokers, and forced them to watch their children being tortured.

146

Cambodians are massacred by Khmer Rouge. In the background, two soldiers are poised to destroy the Buddha, symbolizing the regime's dismantling of Cambodian culture and society. The Soviet hammer and sickle flag hanging left of the Buddha is mistakenly used to represent Khmer Rouge-style communism; the Khmer Rouge's principal ally was Communist China, not the USSR.

Buddhist monks are led away by a Khmer Rouge soldier. Only 1,000 of Cambodia's previous population of 40,000 to 60,000 Buddhist monks survived the Khmer Rouge period.

Emaciated Cambodians work in the rice fields. Cambodians were pushed to exhaustion so cooperatives could meet the party's demand for larger rice harvests. The rice was usually shipped away, while workers tried to survive on starvation diets of 250 grams of rice per day.

Khmer Rouge soldiers butcher Cambodians and dump their bodies into a blood-filled well. The Khmer Rouge saved ammunition by killing the condemned with pickaxes, clubs, and other primitive instruments. After the invasion of Cambodia, Vietnamese soldiers discovered a number of wells containing the shattered skeletons of Khmer Rouge victims.

The Disinherited

In early 1979, tens of thousands of Cambodian men, women, and children began a mass exodus from their country. Pushed by the Vietnamese invasion of their already ravaged land, they staggered toward neighboring Thailand in search of a new life. By autumn, over 155,000 Cambodians had crossed the border and were living in temporary refugee camps. Many more were just inside Cambodia.

The refugees arrived at the camps exhausted and famished. Many were so weak they simply collapsed. Most suffered from diseases such as malaria, tuberculosis, and dysentery. Worse yet, they soon became prey for various guerrilla groups, especially the Khmer Rouge, who wanted control of the camps and their limited food supplies. Their condition was pathetic, the border camps squalid.

Images from the border shook the world's conscience. Under international pressure, Thailand agreed to the establishment of refugee holding centers farther inside its border, and the United Nations High Commission for Refugees (UNHCR) and other humanitarian organizations acted to bring relief. The UNHCR built the first center at Sa Kaeo, forty miles from Cambodia, in October 1979. Refugees were bused in from border camps, and volunteers from around the world arrived to help dispense food and medicine. It marked the beginning of a massive effort to relieve a tragic situation.

Cambodian children chase a food truck outside the Khmer Rouge-dominated refugee camp at Ta Prik in October 1979.

A Thai vendor sells noodles to Cambodian refugees at Sa Kaeo camp, the first official holding center in Thailand. The U.N.-controlled center was an improvement upon the border camps such as Ta Prik, where blackmarketeers, Thai soldiers, and the Khmer Rouge preyed upon the refugees.

A medical volunteer hurriedly sets up an intravenous unit of quinine solution for a Cambodian woman suffering from cerebral malaria, one of the worst strains of malaria found among the refugees. The treatment for this woman came too late; she died moments later.

Recently arrived refugees mill around makeshift tents and huts at Sa Kaeo camp during the center's second day of operation in October 1979.

Cambodian refugees fill their buckets at a primitive well in Sa Kaeo camp. There was no water available in the holding center when it opened in October 1979, so the UNHCR field officer had to hire eight trucks to transport water from a site six kilometers away.

A Cambodian youth washes an emaciated child at Sa Kaeo. For the first few weeks, living conditions at the camp were deplorable: There was little drinkable water, no proper drainage, and no privacy. Frequent rainstorms turned the ground to muck and caused flooding in the trenches that served as latrines.

Above. *Cambodian refugees walk toward the buses that will carry them from Ta Prik to the holding center at Sa Kaeo.*

Left. *Empty milk and diet supplement cans litter what remains of a refugee encampment near Ta Prik along the Cambodian border. In October 1979 the camp's refugees were moved to the holding center at Sa Kaeo. The abandoned huts and tents were burned to protect the local population from disease.*

The Third Indochina War

Beginning on December 25, 1978, Vietnamese attacks exploded along the length of the Cambodian
border like a string of new year firecrackers. From
Pleiku in Vietnam's central highlands, armor and
infantry units crossed the border into Cambodia's
Ratanakiri Province, heading toward the province
capital, Stung Treng. Another major Vietnamese
force headed west from Ban Me Thuot, where, almost four years before, Hanoi's troops had won the
first victory of their final offensive against the Saigon
government.

Farther to the south, the Vietnamese attacked
along the same routes U.S. forces had taken in the
invasion of 1970, into the areas the Americans called
the Fishhook and the Parrot's Beak. Other units from
the Mekong Delta struck into southern Cambodia,
some heading for the seaport of Kompong Som while
others turned away from the coast toward Phnom
Penh. Ahead of the advancing Vietnamese, fighter-
bombers streaked down to bomb and strafe Khmer
Rouge positions. The Vietnamese pilots faced little

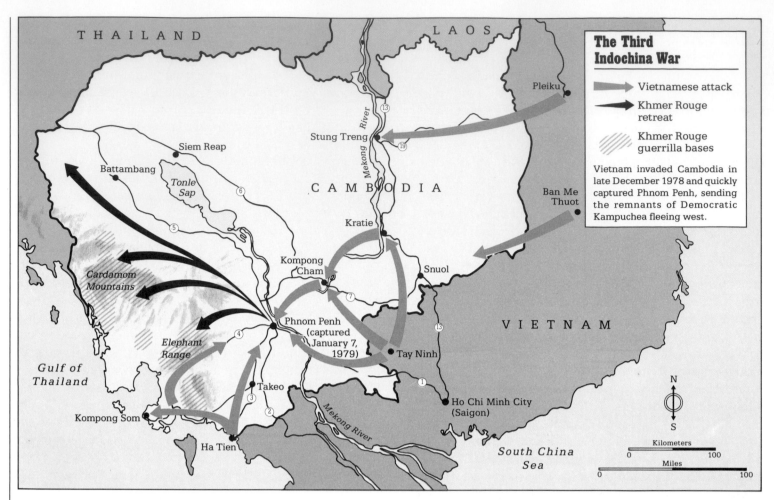

opposition; the Chinese advisers and technicians whose supervision was still needed by the untrained Khmer air force and antiaircraft units were instead being hastily evacuated, either by ship from Kompong Som or by truck overland toward Battambang and the Thai border.

Without Chinese support, the Cambodians had almost no ability to challenge the Vietnamese in the air. At Phnom Penh's Pochentong airport, rows of Chinese-supplied MiG fighters sat helplessly on the ground in neat lines when the Vietnamese arrived.

Altogether, about 100,000 Vietnamese troops made up the invasion force, along with 20,000 or so Cambodians hastily organized under the flag of the three-week-old Kampuchean National United Front for National Salvation. In Hanoi's propaganda broadcasts, the Cambodians were referred to as the Revolutionary Armed Forces of Kampuchea. To preserve the fiction that the fighting was a Cambodian uprising against the Khmer Rouge, Vietnamese forces were not mentioned at all.

On December 30, the Vietnamese captured Kratie, on the Mekong River 260 kilometers north of Phnom Penh. Two days later, on New Year's Day, other Vietnamese units crossed the Mekong 110 kilometers farther down river and surrounded Kompong Cham. The same day in Peking, China's leader, Deng Xiaoping, and U.S. representative Leonard Woodcock toasted the official resumption of diplomatic relations between the U.S. and China. In their lapels, both Woodcock and Deng wore buttons with crossed Chinese and American flags. The emblem symbolized what would soon become, in the context of Southeast Asian events, a de facto alliance against the Vietnamese, rooted in strategic and ideological considerations that for both Peking and Washington outweighed the embarrassment of an association with the murderous Pol Pot regime.

On January 2, as Cambodia's President Khieu Samphan charged in a broadcast speech that a "massive invasion" was under way, convoys of trucks, buses, and cars carried hundreds of Chinese advisers and most of Phnom Penh's small corps of foreign diplomats out of the capital on Highway 5 to the northwest, heading for Thailand.

The same day before dawn, a small detachment of Vietnamese infiltrators reached the bank of the Tonle Sap River directly opposite the royal palace in Phnom Penh. Their mission was to kidnap (or "liberate," depending on one's viewpoint) Prince Sihanouk, whom the Vietnamese apparently hoped would agree to head the anti-Pol Pot forces. The commandos came close to their objective but not quite close enough. Their dinghies were spotted crossing the river, and Khmer Rouge guards on the Phnom Penh

---

Preceding page. *After Vietnam's 1979 takeover of Cambodia, a Vietnamese soldier inspects one of the Khmer Rouge's gruesome legacies—a mass burial ground in Kandal Province.*

side opened fire, killing nearly all the Vietnamese. None reached the house where the prince and his wife, Monique, were confined.

By January 5, the invaders were rapidly closing in on Phnom Penh from three directions. That evening, a soft-spoken and remarkably deferential Pol Pot—who earlier that day had proclaimed that the "life-and-death struggle" against the Vietnamese would "go on for eternity, if necessary"—asked Sihanouk to represent Democratic Kampuchea's cause at the United Nations and to condemn the Vietnamese invasion. Sihanouk agreed, and the next morning, with his wife and other members of his entourage, he was driven to Pochentong airport to await a Chinese aircraft that would take him to Peking.

By then artillery fire was so close to the airport that no one knew if the Chinese pilots would land or not. For that reason, Sihanouk later told the writer Nayan Chanda, he had come to the airport with two very different sorts of luggage: a suitcase with business suits for New York and a backpack stuffed with canned food, peasant pajamas and scarves, and Ho Chi Minh sandals to wear in the jungle.

The canned food and rubber sandals turned out to be unneeded. At noon, the plane from Peking, a Boeing 707 with the five-starred, red-and-gold Chinese flag painted on its tail, landed at Pochentong. The prince and his party climbed aboard, listening anxiously to the gunfire a few kilometers away. Then the big jet hurtled back into the bright sky. As it climbed away from the threatened Cambodian capital, Sihanouk was weeping—partly in relief at being freed at last from his Khmer Rouge jailers, partly in sadness at the thought that the price of freedom was another flight into exile.

In Phnom Penh, meanwhile, the grip of Khmer Rouge rule was loosening. Most of the troops in the capital were retreating over the same route taken a few days earlier by their Chinese advisers. Those soldiers who remained milled about in the streets with no apparent purpose or destination or tore along the wide boulevards in speeding trucks. Panicky crowds gathered at the railroad station, where cadres and their families surged toward the last few trains leaving for Battambang. Outside the city's only hospital, hundreds of wounded soldiers lay in their bloody dressings, some screaming in pain and others suffering stoically, while great clouds of flies swarmed over them.

In the growing chaos, the Khmer Rouge failed to destroy the incriminating archives at the Tuol Sleng Prison. Some 10,000 dossiers and other documents and photographs detailing the torture and execution of thousands of prisoners were left intact to fall into the hands of the Vietnamese. In the confusion, the prison commander, Comrade Duch, missed the evacuation of Khmer Rouge leaders and cadres and had to slip out of Phnom Penh later, after it was already occupied by the Vietnamese.

The prison's gruesome work continued until almost the moment of Phnom Penh's fall. Confessions found there were dated as late as January 5, and pools of blood showing where the last prisoners were killed had not even dried when the Vietnamese occupied the complex. Later, when the prison was turned into a museum of horrors displaying Pol Pot's crimes, the last fourteen victims, killed on the very day of the "liberation," were buried in a garden in front of the prison, their graves marked by a row of white tombstones.

Despite Pol Pot's defiant broadcast, there was, in the end, no bloody battle for Phnom Penh. By the morning of January 7, Pol Pot and Democratic Kampuchea's other top leaders had escaped, and the Vietnamese entering the city met almost no resistance. Quickly and with hardly any fighting, they occupied government buildings and military posts. By shortly after midday, the city was in their hands—as was the port of Kompong Som, which was occupied the same day.

In Phnom Penh, the invaders found only a strange, desolate emptiness. Years later, Politburo member Le Duc Tho, one of the first senior Vietnamese leaders to arrive in Phnom Penh after its capture, vividly described the ghost-like silence of the Cambodian capital. "The first day I came to Phnom Penh," Tho recalled in a conversation with the American writer Robert Shaplen in 1984, "I could see no one, the city was deserted. There was no barking of dogs, no cackling of poultry. Then, slowly, there were long lines of people, returning. They were all in black pajamas and thin, like a line of ghosts."

On January 8, the Cambodians announced the formation of a Kampuchean People's Revolutionary Council, with Heng Samrin as chairman, to act as the new government of what was now to be called the People's Republic of Kampuchea.

Meanwhile, in Peking, an emotional Prince Sihanouk held an extraordinary, rambling six-hour press conference at which he denounced Pol Pot and his associates for the "terrible policy" they had imposed—but said he would support the ousted Democratic Kampuchea government because it still embodied the cause of Cambodian independence. "They are courageous fighters, I cannot say for freedom but for national independence," he said of the Khmer Rouge. "Unless he changes his national independence policy, I will speak out for Pol Pot."

Cambodia's new rulers, however, quickly began trying to discredit the Khmer Rouge both inside and outside the country by publicizing their brutality. The official Vietnam News Agency distributed gruesome photographs showing mass graves and the Tuol Sleng torture rooms. In the countryside, Vietnamese troops distributed medicine, food, and cooking pots in occupied villages, telling families they could once again cook and eat together.

Not surprisingly, many Cambodians were grateful for their rescue from the hardships and cruelty of the former regime. Yet the Khmer Rouge showed remarkable resilience. Sizable Khmer Rouge units withdrew in good order

from threatened positions and remained intact. Far from being overwhelmed or demoralized by the quick Vietnamese successes of the invasion's first weeks, the Democratic Kampuchea forces were able to maintain what one journalist called "continuous, widespread and often fierce harassment" behind Vietnamese lines and even briefly recaptured Kompong Som, Takeo, and several other towns. By the end of January the principal towns were once again in Vietnamese hands, but the Khmer Rouge had demonstrated that they could maintain discipline in their military units and effective authority over the civilian population remaining under their control.

Why this was so, after the savagery of their rule, was something of a mystery, but it probably reflected both an ineradicable fear of the Khmer Rouge cadres and deeply ingrained anti-Vietnamese feelings. Even among Cambodians who fervently welcomed the end of Khmer Rouge rule, there was an anguished ambiguity about their rescuers. As one émigré wrote a few days after Phnom Penh's fall, "The collapse of Pol Pot's Khmer Rouge regime, which brought suffering, death and summary executions to Cambodia for nearly four years, is cause neither for mourning nor celebration, for it is tied to Vietnamese annexationism and imperialism." It was, he added, as if an outbreak of bubonic plague had ended, "only to be replaced by the scourge of cholera."

If the Khmer Rouge had expected direct military support from their Chinese ally, they were disappointed. Traditionally reluctant to send their armed forces outside their own borders, the Chinese leaders also feared, not unrealistically, that direct intervention would only lead to another inconclusive attrition war in Indochina, with the same disastrous consequences for Chinese prestige that the Americans had suffered from their own intervention there.

The Chinese did, however, maintain diplomatic support for Pol Pot and also moved quickly to set up a clandestine supply route for the Khmer Rouge resistance. Their policy was cold-bloodedly calculated not so much to restore Pol Pot to power as to bleed away Vietnam's military power and regional ambitions. The longer the war in Cambodia lasted, Chinese Politburo member Geng Biao wrote in an analysis for his party colleagues, "the greater will be the consumption of the national strength of Vietnam."

Only a week after Phnom Penh's fall, at a secret meeting between two senior Chinese leaders and Thai military leaders at U Tapao air base in Thailand—from where American B-52 bombers had flown during the U.S. war—arrangements were quickly made for Chinese arms shipments to reach the Khmer Rouge through Thai territory. The agreement reflected Thailand's extreme apprehension at the presence of Vietnamese forces on its borders. To the

Cambodians mill about Phnom Penh in January 1984. The populace drifted back to the city after the Vietnamese invasion, slowly bringing the moribund capital back to life.

Thai leaders, the Cambodian resistance represented a buffer between themselves and the Vietnamese threat, and any policy that would help keep the resistance alive was welcome. Thus they were willing not only to allow the Chinese supply effort but also to let Khmer Rouge guerrillas pass through Thailand, if necessary, when they were being pressed by the Vietnamese.

The United States, while continuing to condemn the Khmer Rouge regime's human rights record, nonetheless insisted that the Vietnamese invasion could not be excused by the crimes of the Cambodian regime. "As a matter of principle," a State Department spokesman explained, "we do not feel that a unilateral intervention against that regime by a third power is justified." Sharing the basic Chinese perception of Vietnam as an instrument of Soviet policy and committed to what amounted to a strategic alliance with China against the Soviet Union, the U.S. willingly shaped its own policies toward Cambodia to suit Peking's preferences.

Washington's logic ended any pursuit of ties with Vietnam. It would also lead to the anomaly of Washington's backing Democratic Kampuchea's claim to Cambodia's seat in the United Nations, despite the moral qualms of many American diplomats.

Three weeks after Phnom Penh fell, the Carter administration welcomed Cambodia's most prominent ally, China's leader, Deng Xiaoping, in Washington. Only three weeks after that—so soon that the Vietnamese inevitably believed the U.S. and the Chinese were acting in collusion—the first of 85,000 Chinese troops plunged across Vietnam's northern border to administer the "lesson" Deng had publicly threatened during his Washington visit.

The sixteen days of fighting in the border region cost thousands of casualties on both sides and left four Vietnamese province capitals in ruins. But there was no evidence that China's muscle flexing could force the Vietnamese leaders to change their policies. Even at the height of the fighting on the Chinese border, the Vietnamese continued to extend their control across western Cambodia. On March 5, journalists at a place called Klong Luek on the Thai side of the Cambodian border looked across the invisible line into Cambodia and watched as Vietnamese soldiers in green uniforms and Cambodian troops in black pajamas raised the flag of the new Heng Samrin government. From a truck-mounted loudspeaker, the words of an unseen official floated across the boundary: "With this success, we have liberated Cambodia."

The main force of the Khmer Rouge army was still intact, however, establishing its new base in the mountainous wilderness of the Cardamom Range in the south-

Chinese soldiers maneuver in trenches near Cao Bang in northern Vietnam on February 17, 1979. China's limited attack was meant to punish Vietnam for its invasion of China's ally, Democratic Kampuchea.

western part of the country. And even where the Vietnamese had established their control, it was also true, as one observer wrote, that they had "occupied a wasteland."

The Cambodian wasteland

Cambodia's rural economy was all but totally destroyed, and millions of people were on the move in long, ragged columns across the starving land. Far from being able to reduce their troop strength and turn civil and security affairs over to their Cambodian clients, the Vietnamese found themselves saddled with almost the entire burden of administering the country while also facing an unexpectedly formidable guerrilla threat and the prospect of an indefinite military occupation.

From Hanoi's viewpoint, the diplomatic landscape was equally bleak. The "temporary" presence of Vietnamese troops—to help Cambodia "deal with the Chinese threat," as the Hanoi and Phnom Penh governments subsequently explained—was formalized under a twenty-five-year Treaty of Peace, Friendship and Cooperation signed on February 18 at a summit meeting between the Vietnamese leaders and their Cambodian clients in Phnom Penh. Not surprisingly, in their joint statement on the meeting, the two sides reported "a perfect identity of views on the problems discussed."

But the new Cambodian regime was recognized by almost no governments outside the Soviet bloc, while the Vietnamese, having failed to present the world with a fait accompli by quickly and decisively destroying the Khmer Rouge resistance, ended up even more isolated than they had been before plunging into the Cambodian morass. The invasion left Hanoi facing an intensified confrontation with China, increased wariness and suspicion in the non-Communist countries of Southeast Asia, and the loss of its hopes for a new relationship with the United States.

The Vietnamese did not even get—or deserve—much credit for ending the Khmer Rouge reign of terror. In August 1979, after an elaborately staged proceeding reminding some observers of earlier show trials in the Soviet Union, a "revolutionary tribunal" in Phnom Penh condemned Pol Pot and Ieng Sary to death for "genocidal crimes . . . bringing Kampuchean people the danger of extermination." But because so many former Khmer Rouge officials were now occupying positions of authority in the new government, investigating any further into the massacres would have been too embarrassing. After the initial trial, almost no one else was ever charged with any offense. In their propaganda, the Cambodian authorities and their Vietnamese sponsors ceaselessly put the blame for the massacres exclusively on the two top leaders alone and on the Chinese, as if no one else had carried out their murderous policies.

The sham could not have been lost on the Cambodians themselves, who saw their former torturers go unpunished even while the killings were being endlessly denounced. The hypocrisy surrounding the issue could be breathtaking, as the writer Elizabeth Becker reported: "Few official gatherings," she wrote after visiting Vietnamese-occupied Cambodia in 1983, "are complete without a speaker who details how he or she saw children, parents and friends murdered by Pol Pot's henchmen, and other atrocities. It is not unusual for some of the people who carried out such orders to be seated in the audience or even on the podium with the victim recounting the story."

If the Vietnamese and their Cambodian clients appeared cynical in harboring former officials of the Khmer Rouge, they seemed equally cynical, in the eyes of many observers, in responding to international efforts to help the stricken civilian population.

Because the Vietnamese invasion had come in the middle of the winter rice harvest, much of the year's crop was destroyed or abandoned in the fighting. Also disrupted was the dry-season planting, which would provide seed for the main crop to be planted later in the spring. Thus the immediate shortage of food was compounded by the prospect that the following crop would also be sharply diminished. Unless outside food aid could be supplied, experts warned, millions of Cambodians would face starvation before the end of the year.

Yet months passed with no response from the new Cambodian leaders or their Vietnamese masters to repeated offers of assistance from international relief agencies. In July, representatives of UNICEF and the International Committee of the Red Cross were finally allowed into Phnom Penh to assess the situation there, while Cambodia's foreign minister Hun Sen appealed for an emergency shipment of 108,000 tons of rice or wheat flour; 8,100 tons of vegetable oil; and 15,000 tons of sugar—the first Cambodian request for assistance from the West.

In the following months, under the auspices of the UN and various private relief organizations, a modest flow of food and other emergency supplies began arriving in Cambodia. But the authorities there continued to offer only the most grudging cooperation to relief agency officials, holding up barges of perishable food, for example, while demanding exorbitant "haulage fees."

The most cynical Vietnamese policy, in the view of many Western diplomats and relief officials, was the effort to keep food from reaching areas still controlled by the Khmer Rouge guerrillas. When plans were announced in September for food shipments into the Thai-Cambodian border region for the refugees stranded there, the Phnom Penh government quickly denounced it as a "trick" of Vietnam's enemies to supply the Pol Pot resistance forces in the area. The Cambodian foreign ministry, in a typewritten note pushed under the ICRC representative's hotel room door, demanded that all aid supplies should be turned over to the Cambodian government for distribution and that none should go to "the Pol Pot-Ieng Sary clique."

That callous policy would have denied aid to hundreds of thousands of innocent civilians. But the Cambodian leaders and their Vietnamese sponsors were not wholly incorrect in their view of the border relief program. The aid effort was in fact feeding the Khmer Rouge resistance as well as the civilian refugees—and was deliberately arranged by the Thai authorities to do so, with the acquiescence of the donor nations.

The expressed policy of the relief agencies was to assure that aid supplies did not help the military effort of either side. But in the Cambodian context that policy was unenforceable. As Richard Holbrooke, the Carter administration's assistant secretary of state for East Asian and Pacific affairs, wrote later, "The armies on both sides were strengthened by the relief efforts. The effort to save the Cambodian people unavoidably also helped the people who had nearly destroyed Cambodia." This was not "the deliberate objective of U.S. policy," Holbrooke added, "but an undesired and unavoidable result."

Food from the relief agencies was not merely an incidental benefit to the Khmer Rouge resistance; it almost certainly represented the difference between survival and extinction. To that extent, at the same time the relief organizations and their donors were saving the lives of starving civilians, they were also keeping alive the anti-Vietnamese guerrillas and thus sustaining a war that was taking other lives and would do so for years to come.

While the Vietnamese objected to the border relief program because it aided their enemies, the Khmer Rouge, who still held Cambodia's seat at the United Nations, were equally vehement—for the identical reason—in protesting aid shipments to the Phnom Penh government. Such aid, Democratic Kampuchea's UN representative declared in one official complaint, constituted "implicit recognition of the regime installed by Vietnamese aggression."

The unhappy truth was that all sides sought to use the international relief program to serve their own political aims. The distribution system, meanwhile, was abused in both the Vietnamese-controlled and Khmer Rouge zones. Less than half of the food supplied to Cambodia through the international relief agencies, one expert estimated, actually reached the civilian refugees for whom it was intended, while the rest was siphoned off to soldiers or officials or sold off for the personal profit of corrupt leaders.

While millions of Cambodians tried to survive the hunger and disruptions of the new war, the political and ideological conflicts that had brought it about were quickly hardening into a new and intractable stalemate. Arms from China and discreet military cooperation from Thailand enabled the Khmer Rouge to keep harassing the Vietnamese but not to dislodge them from the major towns and communications routes, meaning that until one side or the other changed its policy, the war could continue indefinitely. But neither side showed the slightest willingness to compromise. The Khmer Rouge and their Chinese spon-

A Khmer Rouge soldier retreats to the countryside with Cambodian villagers in 1979. Although driven from power, the Khmer Rouge survived as a formidable guerrilla force.

sors continued to insist that a solution was possible only if Vietnam withdrew its forces. But Hanoi's statements were unbending. "The situation in Kampuchea," Nguyen Co Thach, Vietnam's minister of state for foreign affairs, declared in August, "is irreversible."

The uprooted

"Your Nation, sir, and other free world nations have land and economies sufficient to support the Hmong refugees of Laos who desire to begin a new life. If you, sir, and your Government are not going to accept all the Hmong refugees, would you kindly completely drive out all the North Vietnamese from the land of Laos, so that the Laotian people will not have to be concerned with or involved with America in this refugee problem."

In January 1979, four representatives of the nearly 40,000 Hmong in Thai refugee camps addressed that appeal to a visiting American congressman, Joel Pritchard of Washington. Most of the Hmong refugees were housed in a camp called Ban Vinai, in Loei Province in northern Thailand, where another U.S. congressional team later that year reported finding "wretchedly poor camp facilities" and thousands of recent arrivals in "extremely poor physical condition."

The Hmong were part of a larger exodus in which 310,000 refugees—more than 10 percent of the total population of Laos, including perhaps one-third of all the Hmong who survived the war—fled to Thailand in the decade following the start of Communist rule. About 150,000 of them, including nearly 60,000 Hmong, were accepted for resettlement in the United States. Another 60,000 had settled in other countries, mainly France, Australia, and Canada, by 1986. But about 100,000 Lao, including 55,000 Hmong, were still in Thai camps.

The world's doors, meanwhile, seemed to be closing. Among the new arrivals, fewer and fewer were found qualified for resettlement abroad, arousing Thailand's chronic fear of admitting refugees who might never be able to leave. Yet more kept coming, usually crossing the Mekong at night in small boats or clinging to crude floats made of banana stalks or bamboo trees lashed together.

After several years of trying to discourage refugees by what was officially called "humane deterrence"—meaning that conditions in the camps were deliberately kept as grim as international opinion would permit—the Thai authorities in early 1985 began forcibly returning refugees to Laos, frequently sending them back across the river in the same flimsy craft in which they had arrived. In some cases, Thai border patrols fired on refugees, reportedly killing a number of them. There were also occasional suicides by refugees who killed themselves rather than returning to Laos.

After protests by the American embassy, the forced repatriations stopped. However, only about 40 percent of the Lao refugees subsequently arriving in Thailand were granted temporary asylum. Because the Lao government refused to take anyone back, those denied admission to Thailand were detained in "holding centers" along the border—prisons, in effect, whose inmates were serving indefinite sentences imposed not for any crime but simply by the harsh Thai refugee policy and the unconcern of the rest of the world.

The future of the 100,000 Lao stranded in Thailand remained uncertain. "An increasingly large percentage" of the Lao in Thailand "are being found ineligible for the U.S. refugee program," a State Department panel reported in 1986. This was not only true of the Lao; increasingly, in the view of American immigration officials, people fleeing all three Indochinese countries were doing so primarily for economic reasons or to avoid personal hardship rather than to escape political oppression and thus did not qualify as "refugees" under U.S. immigration laws. The State Department report called for "a renewed effort to identify other solutions" for those failing to qualify for resettlement in the U.S., "including voluntary repatriation, possible settlement in place, and a sharing out of any remaining population among resettlement nations."

None of those alternatives seemed realistic, however—least of all for the Hmong. With their rural, nomadic tradition, their long cultural isolation, and their lack of literacy, the Hmong were perhaps the least suited of all the Indochinese refugees for life in the industrialized world. Yet their past role in the CIA-led Vang Pao army meant many of them would risk terrible persecution if they returned to Laos.

In theory, the best available solution might have been for the Hmong to be settled in the hills of northern Thailand, in relatively familiar terrain and where there were already a number of long-established Hmong villages with a total population of about 50,000. Because of the resentment it would cause among Thailand's own people, however, giving land to refugees was a policy no Thai government could seriously consider.

It was far from certain, in fact, that even the Hmongs' fellow tribesmen in Thailand—who like other minority people throughout Asia were themselves being pushed out of some of their traditional land by the expanding majority population—would welcome settlers from Laos. When journalist Marc Kaufman traveled to a Thai Hmong village called Ban Lu in 1984, hoping to discover what the Hmongs' traditional peacetime life had been like, he found the

Lao Refugees

In the decade after the Communist takeover, nearly 350,000 people fled Laos. Most crossed the Mekong into northeastern Thailand, wending their way to refugee camps, which quickly grew to rival the largest communities in Laos.

The refugees came from all sections of Lao society, having left their home country for a variety of reasons. Some feared political repression; others were angered by Communist controls; and a number simply wanted to escape Laos's deteriorating economy. Not a few Lao were attracted to the refugee camps themselves, where they could receive medical attention and where the monthly food allotment had the value of three months' work in Laos.

Vue Ker, a twenty-five-year-old Lao soldier, and Yang Xing (with guitar), a former student in Laos, pose at Nong Khai refugee camp in Thailand in 1979.

people there concerned and sympathetic about the plight of the Hmong from Laos. But when the village leader was asked if any of them should be allowed to come to Ban Lu, Kaufman wrote, he was silent for some time and then began talking about how much land was already being lost to the Thais from the lowlands who were moving into the area. "That is a very hard question," said this son of a disappearing soil. "I really don't know if there is room. I think maybe not."

In fact, it grew increasingly difficult to think of a satisfactory solution for the Hmongs' diaspora or for the other Lao languishing in the refugee camps. An unwelcome but insistent comparison began to loom in the minds of relief agency officials: the refugees in Thailand, it was whispered, were going to become the Palestinians of Asia.

While reluctantly sheltering the Lao refugees, from 1979 on Thailand was an even more unwilling host to hundreds of thousands of Cambodians fleeing the violence and famine that followed Vietnam's invasion. Before 1979, about 33,000 refugees reached Thailand from Pol Pot's Cambodia. Nearly all were accepted for resettlement in other countries, chiefly the U.S., France, Australia, and Canada. Though not negligible, that was at least a manageable flow, from the Thai point of view. After the Vietnamese invasion, however, the refugee problem quickly became all but uncontrollable—seeming even more so because it coincided with the height of the boat people exodus from Vietnam. Within a few months of the inva-

sion, nearly 100,000 Cambodians had fled across the border, many of them exhausted, sick, and near starvation after their flight across their own ravaged land. Another half-million, it was estimated, were camped just on the Cambodian side of the border. By the end of the year, the figure was believed to be closer to a million.

The Thai government's first reaction was to try to seal the border and to expel those who were already on Thai territory. The most horrifying mass expulsion occurred in June, at Preah Vihear, the ancient Cambodian temple site located in the remote mountainous region almost at the eastern end of the Thai-Cambodian border. More than 40,000 Cambodians, rounded up from various holding centers along the border, were taken to Preah Vihear in hundreds of buses. Once there, Thai soldiers forced the refugees at gunpoint onto a trail that descended down a steep, thickly jungled mountainside back into Cambodia.

Most of the refugees started on the trek without water or food. Hundreds were killed or wounded on the way down by mines that had been sown on both sides of the trail; in the dense, jostling crowds, especially at night, it was almost impossible to avoid stumbling off the trail into the minefields. One of those forced down the cliffs at Preah Vihear was Kassie Neou, who made the terrible trek with his two children and his mother. "I walked over many dead bodies," he later told the oral historian Al Santoli. "In one spot, a whole family. Father, mother, grandmom, uncle, and babies, just piled together. All dead. But most of the

Most refugees that entered Thailand hoped to resettle in a third country, and many got their wish, moving to the United States, France, Australia, and Canada. A few thousand refugees, however, returned to Laos under a modest repatriation program; a small number of others probably returned home secretly.

Nevertheless in 1987, 100,000 Lao refugees remained in Thai camps, and their future seemed bleak. The U.S. and other nations began to turn their backs on the refugee problem, and the Thai government hardened its position. Many refugees were kept in harsh holding centers with little chance of returning home or living permanently in Thailand.

A mother and daughter, refugees of the war in Laos, prepare a meal at Nam Yao camp in Thailand in 1979. The woman is sifting rice while her daughter cleans fish.

bodies belonged to the first group, who had been unloaded on the evening of June 8. I was in the third group, and not as many of us were killed because we saw that terrible scene and were very careful. We stepped on each other's footprints. So you can imagine, thousands of people walking in a single line. It took three days." Nor was the ordeal over when the refugees reached the bottom of the cliffs. Instead, they were kept for weeks in the dry fields, hungry and desperately thirsty, while the Vietnamese commanders in the area tried to decide what to do about them.

The Preah Vihear tragedy, which caused an international outcry, was not repeated. But Thailand's dilemma was real. If it refused asylum to the hundreds of thousands of Cambodians and Lao flooding its borders, it risked being accused of heartlessness. But if it let them in, it risked becoming permanently responsible for them. The country was being "drowned" in refugees, Prime Minister Kriangsak told a visiting U.S. congressional delegation in August; on another occasion, he remarked to the British writer William Shawcross that the Cambodian refugees "were conceived by U.S. policies during the 1970-75 war, and were delivered by Vietnam. Why should they be left on our doorstep?"

The Thais nonetheless relaxed their policies, and in October, after visiting the border area and personally viewing conditions there, Kriangsak authorized the United Nations high commissioner for refugees to establish holding centers inside Thailand. Within a few months, the UNHCR camps housed about 160,000 Cambodians. The largest, Khao I Dang, had a population of 120,000, making it, as an American embassy officer pointed out, "the largest Cambodian city in the world."

Though still considered illegal immigrants or displaced persons, not refugees in the legal sense of the word, the Cambodians admitted to the UNHCR centers were at least a safe distance away from the border; they could begin the process of applying for resettlement abroad. Because they were formally under UN protection they had at least limited assurance that they would not be sent back to Cambodia as long as conditions there remained dangerous.

Within a few months, however, the door that Thailand had opened began to swing shut again. Alarmed at the continuing influx, and skeptical—with reason—that the rest of the world was really going to take all the refugees off its hands, the Thai government refused to allow any more Cambodians into Khao I Dang or the other holding centers. Instead, all those arriving after February 1980 were supposed to remain in the border camps—without the protection of legal asylum from the Thai authorities or the jurisdiction of the UN high commissioner. The number of people caught in this legal no-man's land fluctuated around the quarter-million mark.

Conditions on the border were chaotic, violent, and heartbreaking. A "battle zone," one journalist called it, where a bewildering assortment of armed factions preyed on the helpless, traumatized refugees. "In 1979 and 1980 the 200,000 or more people living in this area were repeatedly harassed by remnants of the Khmer Rouge, resistance fighters of the Free Khmer non-Communist, anti-Vietnamese group, Vietnamese troops of the Phnom Penh government, or soldiers of several other factions representing every shade of the political spectrum," said a report by one U.S. refugee agency—a list that could also have included Thai soldiers and black marketeers.

Though the Cambodian groups invariably claimed to be resistance forces opposing the Vietnamese, in fact they mainly fought each other, competing for control of refugee camps that in turn meant control of the food being supplied by international relief organizations along the border. Much of the food was then resold, either to the refugees themselves or farther inside Cambodia, for the personal profit of camp leaders.

After 1980, though the food crisis abated and conditions in the border camps slowly became somewhat less chaotic, the Cambodians there still regularly had to flee from Vietnamese attacks. The assaults came late every year when the dry season made the land passable for Vietnamese tanks, trucks, and mobile artillery.

Unlike the refugees admitted to the UNHCR-supervised centers before entry was shut off in 1980, the Cambodians on the border were generally prevented by Thai policy from applying for resettlement abroad. Instead, the official Thai view was that they would return to Cambodia when conditions there permitted. The refugees, meanwhile, remained in legal limbo. And as the military stalemate between the Vietnamese and the Cambodian resistance drew on into the ninth year of war, the plight of the border refugees—still numbering about a quarter million, by UN estimates—also began to appear permanent.

There was one change, however. In 1979 and 1980, the Cambodian refugees were at the center of world attention, filling television screens and the pages of newspapers and magazines. Seven years later, they were all but forgotten.

As early as 1982, one report on the Cambodians commented that "the problem appears to seem stale to all but the refugees themselves." The diminishing interest of other nations did not escape the notice of the Thais, who had been so frequently lectured about the refugees. "We in Thailand," a Thai military officer remarked in 1983, "cannot uphold the humanitarian rule much longer while the rest of the world has begun to lose faith in it."

In the United States, policymakers counted three-quarters of a million Indochinese refugees admitted since 1975 and concluded that Americans had more than met their obligations. "We have kept our promises," Wyoming's senator Alan K. Simpson, the leading Senate sponsor

Thai soldiers move the last refugees, most of them severely ill, from Ban Klong Kaithuen camp, where they were vulnerable to attack, to a site farther inside Thailand.

of immigration reform legislation, declared in a 1985 article calling for the winding down of the U.S. Indochinese refugee program. Only a few all-but-unheard voices pointed out that the problem was not "winding down" for a quarter-million Cambodian human beings in their ramshackle camps. As had been the pattern for more than a decade and a half, the world had no solution to offer for the continuing tragedy of violence in Cambodia; as was also a well-established pattern, Cambodian civilians were left to pay the price, in pain and despair, for the mistakes and cynical strategies from which the tragedy had grown.

Quagmire

Far from being "one of the shortest wars in modern history," as an American television commentator called it the day after the Vietnamese marched into Phnom Penh, the conflict between the Vietnamese occupiers and the Cambodian resistance would last longer than the entire American war in Indochina—and was even harder to resolve.

By the end of 1979, the phrase "Vietnam's Vietnam" was already becoming a cliché. And, in fact, the Vietnamese position in Cambodia was at least superficially analogous to that of the United States in Vietnam a decade earlier. Like the Americans, the Vietnamese appeared to be stuck fast in a war against a lightly armed and numerically weak but elusive and determined enemy. Also like the U.S., Vietnam found itself saddled with an unsatisfactory and ineffective client government. The analogy was sharpest, however, in that the Vietnamese in Cambodia, like the Americans in Vietnam, had to carry the heavy political burden of being intruders in a foreign land, resented even by those whom their presence was protecting.

In the occupied zones, that resentment intensified as Vietnamese occupation policies grew increasingly heavy-handed. In a land still scarred by the memory of hunger, the Vietnamese appropriated a substantial share of the rice harvest to help meet their own domestic food shortages. Meanwhile, more and more Vietnamese arrived to take up residence, apparently permanent, on Cambodian land, particularly in the rich regions around the great inland lake, Tonle Sap. Estimates of the number of settlers ranged from 250,000 to nearly 750,000 people, including farmers, fishermen, merchants, technicians, mechanics, and others. The Vietnamese authorities maintained the newcomers were in fact former residents returning to homes they had been driven from years before, as some perhaps were. But the Cambodians feared Vietnam was following a policy of outright colonization, continuing its centuries-old effort to swallow the Khmer people.

The same impression was forcefully conveyed in the government ministries of the nominally sovereign People's Republic of Kampuchea. Ubiquitous Vietnamese "advisers" treated their Cambodian colleagues with condescension or barely concealed contempt, hardly bothering to hide the fact that all important decisions were made by the Vietnamese. By the mid-1980s, though Hanoi's representatives were keeping a somewhat lower profile than in the PRK's first days, there were reported to be about 12,000 Vietnamese advisers and technicians in the country, including some 600 high-level administrators assigned to an advisory mission headquarters in Phnom Penh and additional cadres assigned to government offices at the province, district, and subdistrict level.

The weaknesses of the Heng Samrin regime were hardly surprising, under the circumstances. The Pol Pot terror had left the country appallingly short of people with administrative or technical skills. And the ranks of the new government contained a mix of mutually distrustful groups: Cambodians who had been associated for decades with the Vietnamese Communist party; the more recent defectors (such as Heng Samrin himself) from Pol Pot's regime; some supporters of Sihanouk; and non-Communist survivors of the Khmer Rouge era. The veteran pro-Hanoi cadres were those most trusted by the Vietnamese, but for precisely the same reason their loyalty and patriotism were suspect to other Cambodians.

As the Vietnamese occupation dragged on, more and more Cambodians became disillusioned with their "liberators." "Most Kampucheans see the Vietnamese as symbols of foreign domination whose political and economic programs have failed to produce an acceptable new order," wrote Cambodia expert Stephen R. Heder after interviewing hundreds of refugees in 1979 and 1980. "Hence, many 'good' people who originally welcomed the Vietnamese are no longer willing to work with them dependably or effectively. As time goes by, the Vietnamese are finding it increasingly difficult to replace supporters they have lost. This is true from the highest levels down to the villages, though especially at the latter level, where the people have the most autonomy."

Without the continued presence of Vietnamese troops, whose strength was estimated at 140,000 in early 1987, most observers agreed the Phnom Penh government would have almost no chance of survival. Weak, disunited, and ineffective at home, the Heng Samrin government remained diplomatically isolated as well, recognized by almost no foreign nations except Vietnam and its Soviet-bloc allies. Following the Vietnamese invasion, the ousted Democratic Kampuchea regime, even though still headed by the murderous Pol Pot, continued to be treated by most of the world as Cambodia's legitimate government, as evidenced by the seventy-one-to-thirty-five General Assembly vote in September 1979 by which it retained the Cambodian seat in the United Nations. The margin increased in following years, until the Vietnamese tired of repeated humiliation and stopped trying to unseat the Democratic Kampuchea delegation.

Vietnam's once-heroic international image had now turned, in many formerly admiring countries, to that of an

Veteran Khmer Rouge leader Khieu Samphan discusses plans for the resistance movement in July 1980 at a Khmer Rouge-controlled camp along the northern Cambodian border.

aggressor and colonial occupier, a change that was accompanied by a curious forgetfulness about the history and nature of the Khmer Rouge. From 1979 on, as the writer William Shawcross noted, most of the world's non-Communist governments chose "to see the Khmer Rouge first as the defenders of national sovereignty rather than as the perpetrators of massive crimes against man."

The resistance

Supplied by China, with the cooperation of Thai authorities and the tacit approval of the United States, the Khmer Rouge managed to grow from an estimated 20,000 immediately after the invasion to perhaps twice that many relatively effective guerrillas in early 1987. Among the smaller armed groups that had sprung up among the hundreds of thousands of Cambodians gathered along the Thai-Cambodian border, the most significant of these was the Khmer People's National Liberation Front, founded in March 1979 by the sixty-seven-year-old Son Sann, a veteran Cambodian politician who had served as prime minister and had held other high posts under Sihanouk during the 1960s before retiring in 1968.

In the following months, as competing groups fought for control of the border, Son Sann's movement received the evident blessing of the Thai military authorities. His officials were allowed to recruit new soldiers in the Thai-administered refugee holding centers on Thailand's side of the border, and local Thai commanders helped his troops in their battles with other guerrilla factions for control of the camps. With Thai help, the KPNLF became by mid-1980 the strongest group, except for the Khmer Rouge, in the border region.

For three years, Son Sann resolutely refused to ally his movement with the Khmer Rouge, whom the KPNLF had denounced as "bloodthirsty, savage hordes" responsible for "days and nights of genocide, holocaust, famine, destruction, ruin, and decadence without parallel." Ironically, it was pressure from his anti-Communist international supporters that forced him to change his policy. The Association of Southeast Asian Nations (ASEAN), supported by the United States, was the midwife to what eventually became a coalition of rival resistance groups against the Vietnamese.

ASEAN's motives were to some extent contradictory: its members (Thailand, Malaysia, Singapore, Indonesia, and

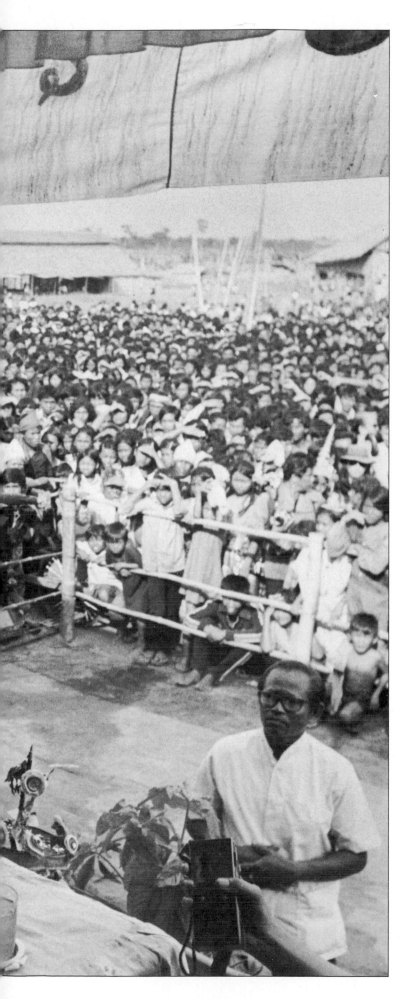

the Philippines) wanted to support the resistance but were reluctant to give aid to Pol Pot's Democratic Kampuchea forces—in part because of their brutal record but also in part because of their subservience to Peking. They wanted to strengthen the non-Communist resistance groups so that, if negotiations ever took place, there would be another alternative Cambodian force besides the Khmer Rouge and the Vietnamese-dominated Phnom Penh government. But aiding the non-Communist groups alone was not considered an acceptable option, because the military strength of the Khmer Rouge was also essential to keep pressure on the Vietnamese.

The solution, as the ASEAN nations (and particularly the two most involved members, Thailand and Singapore) grew to see it, was to form a coalition of the Khmer Rouge, Son Sann's KPNLF, and a smaller guerrilla force loyal to Prince Sihanouk, who could give the resistance the international respectability that would never be accorded to the Khmer Rouge alone.

The pro-Sihanouk guerrillas, known as "Moulinaka," a shortened form of the French name Mouvement de Liberation Nationale du Kampuchea, had been operating since August 1979 from bases not far from the border refugee settlement at Nong Chan. In mid-1981, Moulinaka merged with two smaller pro-Sihanouk guerrilla groups to form what became known as the National Sihanoukist Army. Sihanouk also formed, in 1981, a political organization cumbersomely called the United Front for an Independent, Neutral, Peaceful and Cooperative Cambodia.

Creating the alliance, however, took many months of tortuous negotiations—not just among the Cambodian parties but between ASEAN representatives and the Chinese, who tenaciously protected the interests of their Khmer Rouge allies. From the beginning, the proposed marriage was a reluctant one. Not only were both Son Sann and the disillusioned Sihanouk reluctant to join forces with Cambodia's former torturers, but the Khmer Rouge and their Chinese sponsors saw no advantage in sharing leadership with partners who had little to contribute on the battlefield. To accept a coalition, Chinese officials in Peking were reported to have told Thailand's foreign minister in May 1982, would be disastrous to Khmer Rouge morale; Son Sann, and Sihanouk, the Chinese added, just wanted to steal power from the Khmer Rouge, and China would not allow them to do so.

In the face of Chinese and Khmer Rouge intransigence, and without much bargaining power of their own, Sihanouk, Son Sann, and their ASEAN sponsors eventually dropped most of the conditions by which they had hoped to limit the role of the Khmer Rouge leaders in the new

Prince Norodom Sihanouk addresses Cambodian refugees at Khao I Dang camp in Thailand in July 1982, a few weeks after joining the coalition opposing the Vietnamese-installed Heng Samrin government.

coalition. On June 22, 1982, in a seven-minute ceremony in the Malaysian capital, Kuala Lumpur, Son Sann, Sihanouk, and the Khmer Rouge leader Khieu Samphan signed a formal agreement establishing what would become the Coalition Government of Democratic Kampuchea. Sihanouk was named president of the coalition and Son Sann prime minister. When the terms of the agreement were disclosed, however, it became apparent that if the two non-Communist leaders had been given the prestigious titles, the Khmer Rouge had prevailed on most of the previously disputed issues.

One key clause left the three partners in independent control of their own political and military organizations, while each could also independently receive and dispose of aid from international sources. That meant the Khmer Rouge would keep sole command of its guerrilla units while also retaining control of Chinese arms shipments—the main source of weaponry for the resistance—and thus would remain the coalition's dominant member. (At the same time, though, the aid provision also meant the KPNLF and Sihanouk's forces could seek assistance from donors who might refuse to contribute at all if the Khmer Rouge had access to their supplies.) The Khmer Rouge also secured a clause stating that if the coalition broke up, the government of Democratic Kampuchea under Khieu Samphan would be reconstituted as "the sole legal and legitimate state of Kampuchea."

The specific terms, though, were of less significance than the simple fact of the agreement. "What matters is not so much the content of this document," an ASEAN official was reported to have said privately after the signing ceremony. "We needed a legal base for the nationalists. This is it. Now it is up to us—and to them—to make the best of it."

In Washington, the State Department issued a statement welcoming the coalition as "a positive step forward in providing the framework for leadership and for ultimate self-determination for the Khmer." Sihanouk, as usual, was more candid. Joining forces with the Khmer Rouge for the second time in his career, he said, was "the lesser evil" compared to the loss of Cambodian independence.

The character of the new coalition was outlandish even by Cambodian political standards, as was vividly demonstrated several weeks later at a ceremonial meeting between Sihanouk and his new associates in "liberated" Cambodia. The site was a place called Phum Thmey, or "New Village," a collection of thatched huts housing about 2,000 people on the Cambodian side of a narrow stream marking the Thai-Cambodian border.

Signs welcoming Sihanouk greeted him at the Khmer end of a narrow footbridge when the prince arrived in a convoy of chauffeur-driven Mercedes limousines supplied by the Thai government. The entire Khmer Rouge leadership was on hand to meet him—except Pol Pot, who since 1980 had been deemed unsuited to the moderate image the

movement was now seeking to convey and thus kept away from foreign visitors, though he remained the military commander of the Democratic Kampuchea forces inside Cambodia.

Barry Wain of the *Asian Wall Street Journal*, an eyewitness to Sihanouk's visit, described the bizarre scene that followed the prince's arrival:

Like a politician on the comeback trail, Prince Sihanouk plunges into the crowd lining the narrow path between the huts. He takes the hands of elderly women and whoops with joy when he recognizes former members of his Peking badminton team of the 1970-75 exile. The sight of babies leaves him moist-eyed. "It appears that the Kampuchean nation cannot be wiped out," he says. To the sound of beating drums and rhythmic clapping, Prince Sihanouk passes through a guard of honor—two columns of green-clad, sunburned Khmer Rouge guerrillas cradling AK-47 assault rifles. . . . Prince Sihanouk seems enthralled by folk dances performed beneath the trees by young men and women in colorful, traditional costumes. Before the Khmer Rouge's change of political heart, these women would have been killed, after two warnings, for using the cosmetics they now wear.

The highlight of the occasion, Wain wrote, was the luncheon served "at a long table in a small, open-sided bamboo hall," while a seven-piece Khmer band played traditional music in the background. The dishes listed on a typed menu included "spring rolls in a clearing," "grilled brandy chicken," "curry with crispy eggplants," "skewer of beef in a kitchen garden," and rice, washed down with fresh fruit drinks and bottle after bottle of Möet et Chandon champagne. The meal concluded, Sihanouk turned to his onetime captors and told them graciously, "You always did have very good cooks."

Not all prominent Cambodian émigrés accepted the coalition's argument that Son Sann and Sihanouk "legitimized" the resistance to Vietnamese rule. Instead, critics argued, by joining the Khmer Rouge, the non-Communist leaders fatally compromised the cause of Cambodian freedom. The coalition was "suicidal for free Cambodians," former information minister Chhang Song, a leading spokesman for the Khmer community in the U.S., wrote in his magazine *Cambodia Today*. "The world has now in fact eliminated all alternatives for the Cambodians and has instead forced these long-suffering people to make a choice between two Communist regimes: one in Phnom Penh which would guarantee the Vietnamese domination, and the other, the 'coalition,' which would guarantee death."

Rather than legitimizing the resistance, Chhang Song argued, the coalition would "legitimize instead the Vietnamese occupation," since Cambodians would continue to fear a return of the Khmer Rouge. And he warned against depending on pledges by the ASEAN countries and others to prevent Pol Pot's restoration if the Vietnamese withdrew. A "naive belief" in similar promises led Cambodia into the war in the first place, Chhang Song recalled, and after its

U.S. Aid to the Cambodian Rebels

In the spring of 1985, ten years after the United States withdrew from Indochina, U.S. policy toward Cambodia again became a major topic in Washington. The provocation was Representative Stephen J. Solarz's (D-NY) proposal that the United States provide, for the first time, overt economic and military aid to Cambodia's two non-Communist resistance groups fighting Vietnamese occupation—the Khmer People's National Liberation Front and the National Sihanoukist Army.

The proposal touched off an emotional debate in Congress colored as much by the Vietnam War as by Vietnam's occupation of Cambodia. While supporters of the proposal, led by Solarz, saw the aid as a legitimate way to strengthen Cambodia's non-Communist "freedom fighters," critics viewed it as an ominous return of U.S. activity in Indochina. Representative Jim Leach (R-IA) cautioned that the United States should have already learned "the liabilities of involvement in land wars in Asia."

The White House too had doubts about the aid proposal, having rejected all previous appeals from rebel leaders Son Sann and Prince Sihanouk for overt military assistance. Although it provided some covert assistance, the administration argued that direct support from the United States would hinder regional negotiations and taint the rebels in the eyes of other countries.

Despite these apprehensions, the aid proposal worked its way through Congress, and the Reagan administration reluctantly dropped its opposition. In its final form, hidden within an omnibus spending bill, the aid provision called for the administration to provide the non-Communist rebels with between $1.5 and $5 million in economic or military aid annually in 1986 and 1987, to be distributed by Thailand. By law, none of the aid could reach the murderous Khmer Rouge.

While the proposal was politically and diplomatically sensitive, raising as it did the specter of U.S. involvement in Indochina, the actual amount of aid that reached the rebels in 1986 was meager. The administration allocated $3.5 million for the guerrillas, which the budget-balancing mandates of the Gramm-Rudman-Hollings deficit bill reduced to $3.35 million. Believing that other countries gave the rebels a sufficient supply of arms and ammunition, the administration chose to provide only nonlethal help such as short-wave radios, medical supplies, and paramedical training. Disputes within the two non-Communist camps then delayed the distribution of the U.S.–supplied materiel for much of 1986.

This modest amount of aid was not nearly enough to affect appreciably the struggle in Cambodia and was minuscule in comparison to the money spent by the major actors in Cambodia—China, Vietnam, and the Soviet Union. Representative Solarz admitted that even with the aid, "I don't for a moment believe that the non-Communist resistance can force the Vietnamese out of Cambodia." While almost insignificant militarily, the American aid at least gave the rebels a sorely needed boost in morale. "It's not very important as aid," said Prince Sihanouk, "but it is a great symbol of solidarity."

For many, however, the fundamental question remained whether American aid to the rebels represented a token response to their precarious position or early installments of a long-term commitment. The rebels clearly hope for the latter. "The tap is open," Son Sann said in March 1985, "and even if in the end only a drip comes out, I will be happy. Perhaps later we will receive water."

---

defeat, "the world did nothing to prevent the Cambodian genocide. It has instead allowed the crime to continue unprosecuted."

Establishment of the coalition did nothing to break the military and diplomatic deadlock over Cambodia, however. In essence, the next five years saw little significant change either on the battlefields or in the policies of the conflicting Cambodian sides and their international allies.

The three coalition members were still only nominal partners, whose relationship was marked by continuing distrust and hostility and not infrequent armed clashes between their rival armies. Within each faction, moreover, there were constant intrigues and disputes.

By 1984, the two non-Communist groups claimed a total strength of over 20,000 guerrillas, of whom about 16,000 belonged to Son Sann's KPNLF and about 5,000 to the National Sihanoukist Army. But these forces were still far less effective than the 35,000 to 40,000 Khmer Rouge troops, who remained, as one ASEAN diplomat acknowledged, "the largest, best equipped, and best trained" of the resistance groups.

Of the three armies, only the Khmer Rouge regularly operated outside the narrow strip of resistance-occupied Cambodian territory along the Thai border, where a string of base camps housed some 250,000 civilians as well as the guerrilla headquarters. Son Sann's and Sihanouk's troops spent nearly all of their time in the border camps. The KPNLF commanders, in particular, who were mostly former Lon Nol officers, had little knowledge or experience of guerrilla tactics and often seemed to prefer, as one journalist noted, a settled life in the relative comfort of the base camps to the dangers and hardships of guerrilla war.

The rationale for supporting the resistance was not that they could expel the Vietnamese, which no one expected. "The main purpose of the resistance," a Singaporean diplomat wrote in late 1983, "has been to deprive the Vietnamese of any legitimacy for their stay in Kampuchea, to act as a focus of Kampuchean nationalism and to increase the costs to Vietnam for its occupation. If the resistance continues to grow in effectiveness, it would increase incentives for Vietnam to agree to a compromise settlement."

Offensive and aftermath

Instead, however, in November 1984, the Vietnamese launched their heaviest offensive of the war against the border base areas. For political as much as for military reasons, the KPNLF camps were the first targets. By mid-January, in battles that glaringly revealed the inexperience of Son Sann's forces, Vietnamese tanks and infantry had overrun all of the KPNLF base camps. Most of the defending troops and nearly all of the 150,000 civilians who had been living under front control fled into Thai territory.

The offensive brought familiar images back to TV screens and magazine covers in the West—images of ragged, retreating soldiers, burning villages, and frightened, exhausted refugees huddling under flimsy blue plastic tents in dusty Thai fields. The attacks on the camps also brought a renewed torrent of international criticism of Hanoi's policies. But the Vietnamese were undeterred. A month after routing the KPNLF, they also captured all the major Khmer Rouge bases along a sixty-four–kilometer stretch of the border, including the showcase village of Phum Thmey, where Sihanouk had lunched with his new Khmer Rouge partners after the coalition was formed. Last to be attacked were the Sihanoukist troops, who abandoned their main border base on March 11.

The loss of the border camps did not mean the destruction of the resistance forces. Military casualties were fairly light, in fact, with almost all the guerrillas reaching sanctuary in Thailand. The coalition's international supporters tried to put the best possible face on events. "This has not been a military victory for the Vietnamese," U.S. assistant secretary of state Paul Wolfowitz insisted. "It was never the plan for Cambodian guerrillas to hold fixed positions against Vietnamese tanks." But the KPNLF, particularly, had suffered a severe psychological setback. Its tactics, morale, and discipline had been proven inadequate, and its leaders admitted they had to learn to fight a guerrilla war away from the security of the base camps—derisively described by one ASEAN diplomat as "black-market and rest-and-recreation areas."

Whether the front's military commanders had the capacity to change their entire strategy and way of life was another question. "We recognize that this is needed," said one front official, "but it is one thing to say and another to do." In the end, the official insisted, "we will succeed," but the months following the offensive saw little improvement in the KPNLF's effectiveness. In October, ten months after it was driven from its base camps, the front's military strength had declined from an estimated 16,000 before the Vietnamese offensive to between 13,000 and 14,000 troops, of whom only 1,000 were operating inside Cambodia.

A KPNLF guerrilla fires his rocket launcher blindly at Vietnamese tanks advancing against the Cambodian resistance camp at Ampil, January 1985.

Heng Samrin stands in salute alongside Soviet general secretary Leonid Brezhnev after arriving at Moscow airport to begin an official visit in February 1980.

The weaknesses exposed by the Vietnamese offensive undercut a key argument of the coalition's international supporters: that the non-Communist resistance groups must be maintained to guarantee against a Khmer Rouge return to power. Even Sihanouk, in August 1985, commented gloomily: "The day the Vietnamese go home, the Khmer Rouge will wipe out our nationalist forces and there will be no reason for them to step down."

For their part, the Khmer Rouge announced, unconvincingly, that they had abandoned their former policies. As early as the end of 1979, they had suspended the constitution under which they ruled Democratic Kampuchea; in December 1981 they announced that the Kampuchean Communist party itself had been dissolved, so that "all patriots" could participate in political affairs. In order to unite all Cambodians and to attract support from abroad, the Khmer Rouge radio declared in a series of broadcasts in July 1985, they now espoused a "liberal capitalist regime, economically, and a parliamentary regime, politically." In September they announced the "retirement" of Pol Pot—an announcement that was also greeted skeptically. "In my official capacity I must believe them," Prince Sihanouk commented. "But if you ask me for my personal opinion, I would say that it is better not to believe what they say."

In the aftermath of the offensive, the U.S. Congress—at the urging of a liberal Democratic representative, Stephen J. Solarz of New York—appropriated a token $5 million grant for military assistance to the KPNLF and Sihanouk's forces. Solarz's argument was exactly the same as ASEAN's: strengthening the non-Communist factions would help keep the Khmer Rouge from regaining power after a Vietnamese withdrawal and in the meantime could "substantially raise the pressure on Vietnam, thereby increasing the possibility of a political settlement."

Critics of his proposal recalled that exactly the same formula—applying military pressure to "raise the price of aggression" and make Hanoi change its policies—had been unsuccessful during all the years of America's war against the Vietnamese Communists. Some even argued that the best way for the United States to help resolve the Cambodia problem would be to resume the normalization negotiations with Vietnam that had been aborted in 1978. Washington could then seek concessions in return for the political and economic relations with the U.S. that Hanoi clearly wanted.

That argument may have been theoretically plausible. But there was no realistic possibility that any American administration would resume relations with Vietnam against the desires of both China and the ASEAN nations or while the Vietnamese were still occupying Cambodia. Trying to establish American influence through diplomatic ties with Hanoi was a lost opportunity, perhaps, but hardly an available policy. In fact, despite the token aid appropriation and expressions of support for the non-Communist resistance, the United States had no significant impact on Indochinese events. In the context of the Third Indochina War, Washington remained hardly more than a concerned but passive spectator.

With Thai cooperation and continuing aid from China and the ASEAN group, the coalition survived the 1984-1985 fighting. The non-Communist forces gradually resumed operations in the border region. Khmer Rouge guerrillas continued to harass the Vietnamese occupiers in many regions of the country, though in late 1986 reports began circulating of a violent power struggle within their ranks between followers of Son Sen, the former defense minister of Democratic Kampuchea, and Ta Mok, one of the Khmer Rouge regime's most notorious executioners. The mystery of Pol Pot, whose "retirement" had been announced more than a year earlier, continued to deepen: he was now said to have been evacuated to Peking, gravely ill, in the fall of 1986.

Although plenty of evidence suggested that the Vietnamese leaders were weary of the Cambodian impasse, there was no sign of an end to the stalemate. In Vietnamese eyes, Cambodia was not a marginal issue but a vital one, because of the potential threat that Chinese influence might reappear with a restored Khmer Rouge government. "When we look at Cambodia," a Vietnamese official told the American writer Stanley Karnow, "we see China, China, China."

In 1986, one new factor entered the picture: a slender hope that the Soviet Union, under its new leader Mikhail Gorbachev, might help promote a Cambodian settlement as part of Gorbachev's broader attempt to ease Soviet-Chinese tensions. It was far from clear, however, whether Moscow would really press its Vietnamese allies to retreat from their Cambodian venture. Nor was it clear that the Vietnamese would respond to Soviet pressure even if it were applied. Historically, Hanoi had always maintained a bristling independence on matters of fundamental national policy, and its determination to preserve a subservient regime in Cambodia and to prevent China from regaining a role there appeared absolute. Once again, it appeared, Vietnam's enemies had underestimated the price its leaders could and would pay for what they saw as essential national purposes, which meant that just as in the early 1970s, Cambodians were condemned to an unending and unwinnable war made permanent not by Cambodian needs or circumstances but by the calculations and strategies of Vietnam and its enemies.

"If ASEAN's concern is simply to make Hanoi's involvement in Cambodia economically and politically costly for Vietnam, then its policies have been successful," wrote one scholar early in 1986. "If ASEAN's interest lies in integrating Vietnam into a peaceful Southeast Asian re-gional order, then alternative policies must be considered." But more than halfway through Cambodia's second decade of violent conflict, neither the contending Cambodian factions nor their foreign sponsors seemed to know—or care—how such alternative policies might be found.

A new Indochinese federation?

The idea that a special relationship linked the revolutionaries in Vietnam, Cambodia, and Laos could be traced back almost as far as the Indochinese Communist movement itself. In 1932, Ho Chi Minh's fledgling Indochinese Communist party listed "fraternal union of all nationalities of Indochina" as one of the ten "fundamental tasks of the revolution." Nearly two decades later, at the height of the war against the French, the party's most famous military leader, Vo Nguyen Giap, called the three countries of Indochina "a single strategic unit, a single battlefield." Vietnam, Giap wrote in a 1950 article, could not be considered independent if Cambodia and Laos were "under imperialist domination."

In the 1970s, Vietnamese officials spoke of the special relationship almost as a blood debt owed by the Lao and Cambodians in return for Vietnamese sacrifices in their countries during the anti-U.S. war. The issue was not Hanoi's domination, the Vietnamese claimed. The party's 1932 call for "fraternal union" also specifically declared that "Cambodians, Laotians and other nationalities of Indochina have the right to freely decide for themselves." Instead it was a matter of a natural bond arising from shared struggle against common enemies.

Still, there was no doubt that the Vietnamese regarded themselves as the senior partner in the alliance, by virtue of their population, military strength, and historical leadership of the revolutionary movement. Twelve years after capturing Saigon, and eight years after driving their former Cambodian partners out of Phnom Penh, the Vietnamese Communists had in effect turned the "special relationship" into virtual colonial power over their two weaker neighbors. Vietnam strenuously denied its opponents' long-standing charge that it sought an "Indochinese Federation" in which the two smaller countries would be incorporated into a federated state under Vietnamese domination. In all but that literal, legal sense, however, a Hanoi-controlled federation did seem to have become the reality of Indochina: "a Vietnamese empire," as one writer called it in 1985, "in which the Lao and Khmer will be nothing but ethnic minorities—as the Tibetans and Mongols are within the Chinese Communist empire."

Laos's status as a virtual Vietnamese protectorate was symbolized in subtle but striking fashion at the very birth of the Lao People's Democratic Republic in December 1975. The name used by the founding assembly—the Congress of People's Representatives—was identical with that used at the founding of Ho Chi Minh's Democratic Republic of

Vietnam three decades before. Further, King Savang Vatthana's abdication message was worded, surely not by accident, to echo the 1945 abdication of Vietnam's emperor Bao Dai in favor of the Vietminh. After renouncing the throne, Bao Dai was named "supreme adviser" to the revolutionary government; thirty years later, Savang Vatthana was named an adviser to the new Lao president, Prince Souphanouvong.

Vietnam kept a substantial military force in Laos, fluctuating from 30,000 to more than 50,000 troops. There were also reported to be about 6,000 Vietnamese civilian advisers, of whom about 1,000 were assigned to government ministries in Vientiane. The Vietnamese also deemed, apparently, that the Lao internal security apparatus needed their assistance as well. Some 800 Vietnamese security police, under the control of the interior ministry in Hanoi, were assigned to track down dissidents in the Lao army and administration and to keep tabs on foreigners in the country. Presumably, the police shared responsibility for the fate of the 20,000 to 40,000 Lao sent to reeducation camps in the remote interior.

While accepting Vietnamese guidance in the formation and administration of domestic affairs, the Lao also dutifully supported Hanoi in foreign affairs as well. On virtually all diplomatic issues, including Vietnam's conflicts with Cambodia and China, Lao policy declarations were customarily identical with Vietnam's in substance and often in wording as well, even though on some issues, such as relations with China, Laos had every apparent interest in staying out of Vietnam's disputes.

Visitors found that the easygoing Lao spirit still prevailed even under Vietnamese tutelage, and former Prime Minister Souvanna Phouma in a 1980 interview insisted that "it is not true that Vietnam has absorbed Laos. Laos and Vietnam have common interests. They have left us our own personality." If that was so, however, it was also true that whatever remained of Lao practices and social and economic arrangements survived only at Hanoi's sufferance and not because the Lao leaders had any genuine authority over their own decisions.

Unlike the subjugation of Laos, the Vietnamese occupation of Cambodia was the subject of constant and intense concern among Vietnam's regional neighbors and elsewhere. ASEAN proposed various plans for negotiating a settlement, while yearly resolutions in the UN General Assembly called for the withdrawal of Vietnamese troops. In response, the three Indochinese foreign ministers announced in August 1985 that Vietnamese forces would "conclude their withdrawal" from Cambodia by 1990. There was a king-size loophole, however: if Vietnam's adversaries took advantage of the withdrawals to undermine Cambodian peace and security, the Cambodians and their Vietnamese allies would take "appropriate measures." If almost no one took the Vietnamese timetable at face value, however, it was considered a slightly hopeful sign that at least Hanoi was committed to the principle of a military withdrawal.

In fact, the withdrawal announcement reflected an apparent sense in Hanoi that time was on its side. Its opponents in the coalition were in disarray; the Vietnamese army's successful dry-season offensive against the resistance bases had brought no reprisal from China; some of the ASEAN countries (though not Thailand and Singapore) appeared to be growing discouraged and a little disenchanted with the poor performance of the anti-Vietnamese forces; and even the weak Heng Samrin government and army, with time, seemed to be becoming modestly more effective.

Beyond its troop withdrawal schedule, Vietnam also offered various negotiating formulas in response to ASEAN proposals. What blocked peace talks was, ostensibly, the role to be played by the Khmer Rouge. But what became apparent as the decade-long conflict dragged on was that the truly intractable dispute was not among the Cambodians but between Vietnam and China.

No solution was acceptable to the Vietnamese if it meant restoring Chinese influence in Cambodia; that was the root of Hanoi's absolute determination to exclude the Khmer Rouge, in advance, from any Cambodian political settlement. Peking, however, was equally determined to prevent Vietnamese hegemony in Indochina. The Khmer Rouge, as the one armed force really challenging the Vietnamese, was the only group capable of serving Peking's strategic goal, and China had no intention of abandoning them.

Unfortunately for the Cambodians, both China and Vietnam appeared able to sustain their policies indefinitely and at acceptable cost—light for Peking, heavier but still supportable for Hanoi. In their public statements, both the Chinese and Vietnamese paid lip service to the idea of a neutral, nonaligned Cambodia. But in fact, leaving Cambodia to shape its own destiny was an unacceptable risk to both antagonists. As one Western diplomat put it in early 1985, "neither China nor Vietnam [is] ready to settle for less than total control of Kampuchea."

In the face of Hanoi's and Peking's intransigence, ASEAN's strategy was reduced to little more than a waiting game, while Washington remained on the sidelines and hopes of a Cambodian settlement rested on such vague possibilities as a new generation of leadership in Vietnam or a Sino-Soviet reconciliation leading to a withdrawal of Soviet support for the Vietnamese. In the meantime, though Vietnam had established its Indochina empire, it was an empire that knew no peace, only the endless violence and tragedy of war.

Past and present. A Vietnamese soldier sits beneath an ancient Khmer relief at Angkor Thom, a reminder of Cambodia's one-time independence and glory.

Bibliography

I. Books and Articles

Armstrong, John P. *Sihanouk Speaks*. Walker, 1964.

Batchelder, Sydney H., Jr., and D. A. Quinlan. "Operation Eagle Pull." *Marine Corps Gazette*, May 1976.
Becker, Elizabeth. *When the War Was Over*. Simon & Schuster, 1986.
Bekaert, Jacques. "The Khmer Coalition." *Indochina Issues*, September 1982.
Blaufarb, D. S. *The Counter Insurgency Era*. Free Pr., 1977.
Brown, MacAlister, and Joseph J. Zasloff. *Apprentice Revolutionaries*. Hoover Inst. Pr., 1986.
——. "Laos in 1975." *Asian Survey*, February 1976.
Burchett, Wilfred. *At the Barricades*. Times Bks., 1981.
——. *Mekong Upstream*. Seven Seas Publishers, 1959.
——. *Second Indochina War*. Lorrimer Publishing, 1970.
Butwell, Richard. "From Feudalism to Communism in Laos." *Current History*, December 1975.

Cady, John F. *Southeast Asia*. McGraw-Hill, 1964.
——. *Thailand, Burma, Laos, and Cambodia*. Prentice-Hall, 1966.
Chagnon, Jacqui, and Roger Rumpf. "Decades of Division for the Lao Hmong." *Southeast Asia Chronicle*, October 1983.
Chanda, Nayan. *Brother Enemy*. Harcourt Brace Jovanovich, 1986.
Chandler, David P. *A History of Cambodia*. Westview Pr., 1983.
——. "Revising the Past in Democratic Kampuchea." *Pacific Affairs*, Summer 1983.
——. "Transformation in Cambodia." *Commonweal*, April 1, 1977.
Coedes, Georges. *The Indianized States of Southeast Asia*. Translated by Susan Brown Cowling. East-West Center Pr., 1968.
——. *The Making of South East Asia*. Translated by H. M. Wright. Univ. of California Pr., 1967.

"Declaration on the Summit Conference of the Indochinese Peoples." *Vietnam News Agency*, May 2, 1970.
Dommen, Arthur J. *Conflict in Laos*. Praeger, 1971.
——. *Laos*. Westview Pr., 1985.
Doyle, Edward et al. *The Vietnam Experience*. Vol. 1, *Setting the Stage*. Boston Publishing Co., 1981.

Etcheson, Craig. *The Rise and Demise of Democratic Kampuchea*. Westview Pr., 1984.

Fall, Bernard. *Anatomy of a Crisis*. Doubleday, 1969.
Fallaci, Oriana. "Sihanouk." *New York Times Magazine*, August 12, 1973.
Fifield, Russel H. *The Diplomacy of Southeast Asia, 1945-1958*. Harper, 1958.
Fox, Martin Stuart. *Laos*. Hoover Inst. Pr., 1986.

"Geng Biao's Report on the Situation of the Indochinese Peninsula." *Journal of Contemporary Asia*, 1981.
Gettleman, Marvin et al. *Conflict in Indochina*. Random, 1970.
Girling, J. L. S. "Nixon's Algeria." *Pacific Affairs*, Winter 1971-1972.
The Great Geographical Atlas. Rand-McNally, 1982.

Hall, D. G. E. *A History of South-East Asia*. 3d ed. St. Martin's, 1968.
Halpern, Joel M., and W. S. Turley, eds. *The Training of Communist Cadres in Laos*. Centre d'étude du Sud-est Asiatique et de l'Extreme Orient, 1977.
Hammer, Ellen J. *The Struggle for Indochina, 1940-1955*. Stanford Univ. Pr., 1955.
Hawk, David. "Tuol Sleng Extermination Centre." *Index on Censorship*, January 1986.
Heder, Stephen R. "Kampuchea 1980." *Southeast Asia Chronicle*, February 1981.
Hilsman, Roger. *To Move a Nation*. Dell, 1967.
Holbrooke, Richard. "Conscience and Catastrophe." *The New Republic*, July 30, 1984.

Isaacs, Arnold. *Without Honor*. Johns Hopkins Univ. Pr., 1983.

Jackson, Karl D. "Cambodia 1978." *Asian Survey*, January 1979.

"Kampuchea: A Refugee's Account." *Journal of Contemporary Asia*, 1979.
Karnow, Stanley. *Vietnam: A History*. Viking/Penguin Bks., 1983.
Kaufman, Marc. "The Primitive Paradise of the Hmong." *Philadelphia Inquirer Magazine*, June 9, 1985.
Kaysone Phomvihan. "The Victory of Creative Marxism-Leninism." *Journal of Contemporary Asia*, 1977.
——. "Vingt cinq années de lutte et de victoires du Parti Populaire Revolutionnaire Lao." Speech. March 22, 1980.
Kiernan, Ben. *How Pol Pot Came to Power*. Thetford Pr., 1985.
Kiernan, Ben, and Chanthou Boua. *Peasants and Politics in Kampuchea*. Zed Pr., 1982.
Kirk, Donald. *Wider War*. Praeger, 1971.
Kissinger, Henry. *The White House Years*. Little Brown, 1979.

Lacouture, Jean. "From the Vietnam War to an Indochina War." *Foreign Affairs*, July 1970.
Lancaster, Donald. "The Decline of Prince Sihanouk's Regime." In *Indochina in Conflict*, edited by J.J. Zasloff and Allen E. Goodman. Lexington Bks., 1972.
Langer, Paul F., and Joseph J. Zasloff. *North Vietnam and the Pathet Lao*. Harvard Univ. Pr., 1970.
Lee, Chae-Jin. "Communist China's Policy Toward Laos." Paper, 1970.
Leepson, Marc. "Cambodia." *Editorial Research Report*, April 5, 1985.

Leifer, Michael. *Cambodia*. Praeger, 1967.
——. "Kampuchea 1979." *Asian Survey*, January 1980.

MacClear, Michael. *The Ten Thousand Day War*. St. Martin's, 1981.
McCoy, Alfred W. *The Politics of Heroin in Southeast Asia*. Harper & Row, 1972.
Mahbubani, Kishore. "The Kampuchean Problem." *Foreign Affairs*, Winter 1983/1984.
Masseo, Donatella, and Chiara Silvi Antonini. *Monuments of Civilization*. Grosset & Dunlap, 1978.

Norodom Sihanouk. *My War with the CIA*. Related by Wifred Burchett. Penguin, 1974.
——. *War and Hope*. Translated by Mary Feeney. Pantheon, 1980.

Osborne, Milton E. *Before Kampuchea*. Allen & Unwin, 1979.
——. *The French Presence in Cochinchina and Cambodia*. Cornell Univ. Pr., 1969.
——. *Politics and Power in Cambodia*. Longman, 1973.

PBS. "MacNeil-Lehrer Report." Broadcast January 8, 1979. Transcript.
The Pentagon Papers. Senator Gravel edition, Beacon Pr., 1971.
Pike, Douglas. "Cambodia's War." *Southeast Asian Perspectives*, March 1971.
Ponchaud, Francois. *Cambodia Year Zero*. Translated by Nancy Amphoux. Holt, Rinehart & Winston, 1978.
Porter, Gareth. "After Geneva." In *Laos*, edited by Nina S. Adams and Alfred W. McCoy. Harper & Row, 1970.
——. "Vietnamese Communist Policy Towards Kampuchea." In *Revolution and its Aftermath in Kampuchea*, edited by David P. Chandler and Ben Kiernan. Yale Southeast Asia Studies, 1983.
"Protocol to the Agreement on Restoring Peace and Achieving National Concord in Laos." *KPL*, September 14, 1973.

Quinn, Kenneth M. "Political Change in Wartime." *Naval War College Review*, Spring 1976.

Randall, R. R. *Geneva 1954*. Princeton Univ. Pr., 1969.
Rickenbach, Ron. Untitled manuscript, March 1971.
Rowan, Roy. *The Four Days of Mayaguez*. Norton, 1975.

Santoli, Al. *To Bear Any Burden*. Dutton, 1985.
Schanberg, Sydney. "The Death and Life of Dith Pran." *New York Times Magazine*, January 20, 1980.
Shackley, Theodore. *The Third Option*. Reader's Digest Pr., 1981.
Shaplen, Robert. *Bitter Victory*. Harper & Row, 1986.
Shawcross, William. *The Quality of Mercy*. Simon & Schuster, 1984.
——. *Sideshow*. Touchstone, 1979.
Simmonds, Stuart. "Independence and Political Rivalry in Laos 1945-61." In *Politics in Southern Asia*, edited by Saul Rose. Macmillan, 1963.
Simon, Sheldon W. "Kampuchea: Vietnam's Vietnam." *Current History*, December 1979.
Simpson, Alan K. "The Next Step for Indochinese Refugees." *Washington Post*, June 5, 1985.
Sisouk Na Champassak. *Storm over Laos*. Praeger, 1961.
Smith, Roger M. *Cambodia's Foreign Policy*. Cornell Univ. Pr., 1965.
——. "Laos." In *Government and Politics of Southeast Asia*, edited by George M. Kahin. Cornell Univ. Pr., 1964.
Stevenson, Charles A. *The End of Nowhere*. Beacon Pr., 1972.
Strong, Anna L. *Cash and Violence in Laos*. New World Pr., 1961.
Stuart-Fox, Martin, ed. *Contemporary Laos*. St. Martin's, 1982.
"Systematic and Increasingly Serious Violations of Vietnamese Territory by the Kampuchean Armed Forces." *Journal of Contemporary Asia*, 1978.

Tate, D. J. M. *The Making of Modern South-East Asia*. Vol. 1, *The European Conquest*. Oxford Univ. Pr., 1971.
Terzani, Tiziano. "Vietnam Revisited." *Far Eastern Economic Review*, September 19, 1985.
Thee, Marek. *Notes of a Witness*. Vintage Bks., 1973.
Toye, Hugh. *Laos*. Oxford Univ. Pr., 1968.
Turner, Robert F. *Vietnamese Communism*. Hoover Inst. Pr., 1975.

van der Kroef, Justus M. "Dynamics of the Cambodian Conflict." *Conflict Studies*, 1986.

Weatherbee, Donald E. "ASEAN." *Indochina Issues*, February-March 1986.
Westmoreland, William C. *A Soldier Reports*. Dell, 1980.

Yearbook of International Communist Affairs. Hoover Inst. Pr., 1976-1978, 1986.

Zasloff, Joseph. "Laos." *Asian Survey*, January 1970.
——. "Laos 1972." *Asian Survey*, January 1973.
——. *The Pathet Lao*. D.C. Heath, 1973.
Zasloff, Joseph, and MacAlister Brown, eds. *Communism in Indochina*. Lexington Bks., 1975.

II. Government and Government-Sponsored Published Reports

Bowers, Ray L. *Tactical Airlift*. Office of Air Force History, 1983.

"The Cambodian Operation." Report by the President. *Weekly Compilation of Presidential Documents*. June 30, 1970.

Foreign Broadcast Information Service. "LPRP History Reviewed on Founding Anniversary." Laos, March 24, 1976.
——. "Phoumi Vongvichit Speech on LPF Anniversary." January 8, 1977.

Hickey, Gerald C. *The War in Cambodia*. Internal Note. Rand Corp., September 1, 1970.

Maha Sila Viravong, trans. *History of Laos*. U.S. Joint Publications Research Service, Paragon Bk. Reprint, 1964.

Oudone Sananikone. *The Royal Lao Army and U.S. Army Advice and Support*. U.S. Army Center of Military History, 1981.

Phoumi Vongvichit. *Laos and the Victorious Struggle of the Lao People Against U.S. Neo Colonialism*. Neo Lao Hak Sat Publication, 1969.

Sak Sutsakhan, Lt. Gen. *The Khmer Republic at War and the Final Collapse*. Indochina Monograph Series, U.S. Center of Military History, 1980.
Southcay Vongsavanh, Brig. Gen. *RLG Military Operations and Activities in the Laotian Panhandle*. Indochina Monograph Series, U.S. Center of Military History, 1981.

Tran Dinh Tho, Brig. Gen. *The Cambodian Incursion*. Indochina Monograph Series, U.S. Center of Military History, 1979.

U.S. Committee for Refugees. *Cambodian Refugees in Thailand*. August 1982.
U.S. Congress. "Cambodia: An Assessment of Humanitarian Needs and Relief Efforts." Report by Inspector General for Foreign Assistance, Department of State. In *Congressional Record*. 94th Cong., 1st sess., March 20, 1975.
————. House. *The Indochinese Refugee Situation, August 1979*. Study mission report. 96th Cong., 1st sess., September 16, 1979.
————. Foreign Affairs Committee. *Military and Economic Situation in Cambodia* (confidential committee print). 94th Cong., 1st sess., March 13, 1975.
————. Subcommittee on Asian and Pacific Affairs. *1979—Tragedy in Indochina*. 96th Cong., 1st sess., February-December 1979.
————. *Refugees from Indochina*. 94th Cong., 1st sess., April 30, 1979.
————. International Relations Committee. *Human Rights in Cambodia*. 93d Cong., 1st sess., May 3, 1977.
————. *Vietnam-Cambodia Conflict*. Report prepared by the Congressional Research Service for the Subcommittee on Asian and Pacific Affairs. 93d Cong., 2d sess., 1978.
————. *The Vietnam-Cambodia Emergency, 1975*. Part II. 94th Cong., 1st sess., 1975.
————. Judiciary Committee. *Statement of Information and Hearings*. Presidential Impeachment Investigation. 93d Cong., 2d sess., 1974.
————. Senate. Appropriations Committee. *Foreign Assistance and Related Programs Appropriations FY 1974*. 93d Cong., 1st sess., 1973.
————. *Foreign Assistance and Related Programs Appropriations FY 1975*. 93d Cong., 2d sess., 1974.
————. Foreign Relations Committee. *Thailand, Laos, and Cambodia*. Staff reports. 92d & 93d Cong., 1971-1973.
————. Judiciary Committee. *Humanitarian Problems in South Vietnam and Cambodia*. Study mission report. 94th Cong., 1st sess., January 27, 1975.
————. Subcommittee on Immigration and Refugee Policy. *Refugee and Migration Problems in Southeast Asia: 1984*. Staff report (draft), 98th Cong., 2d sess., August 1984.
————. Select Committee on Intelligence Activities. *Foreign and Military Intelligence*. Bk. I, Final Report. 94th Cong., 2d sess., 1976.
U.S. Department of Defense. *United States-Vietnam Relations, 1945-67*. Bk. 10, GPO, 1971.
U.S. Department of State. *Report of the Indochinese Refugee Panel*. April 1986.
————. *The Situation in Laos*. September 1959.

Witaker, Donald P. et al. *Area Handbook for the Khmer Republic (Cambodia)*. GPO, 1973.
————. *Area Handbook for Laos*. GPO, 1972.

III. Unpublished Government and Military Sources

Air Operations in the Khmer Republic, 1 December 1971-15 August 1973. Project CHECO, PACAF HQ Directorate of Operations Analysis. April 15, 1974.
"Authority for B-52 Strikes Against Targets in Cambodia." Joint Chiefs of Staff memoranda for the Secretary of Defense. March 25 & April 2, 1970.

Cambodia Documentation Commission files.
Central Intelligence Agency. "North Vietnamese Intentions in Indochina." Special National Intelligence Estimate, 14. June 26, 1970.
Central Intelligence Agency Office of National Estimates. "Stocktaking in Indochina." April 17, 1970.
"Chronology of Significant Events—Operation Eagle Pull." Memorandum to Assistant Secretary of Defense (Public Affairs). August 25, 1975.

David Hawk interview with Kassie Neou.

Embassy cable Phnom 06061. April 8, 1975.
Embassy telegram Phnom 2925. July 15, 1971.

Interview with Col. S. H. Batchelder, Jr. USMC Oral History Collection, no. 6040.
Interviews with Ken Vong and Hom Kim.
Interview with Lee Seyla.

"Manifesto of the Khmer People's National Liberation Front." n.d.

Office of the Assistant Secretary of Defense for Systems Analysis. *Southeast Asian Analysis Report*. January-April 1971.

People's Revolutionary Council of Kampuchea. "Decree on the Establishment of the People's Revolutionary Tribunal in Phnom Penh." July 15, 1979.

Vietnamese mission to the U.N. Press release. February 22, 1979.

Winter, Roger (director of the U.S. Committee for Refugees). Private memo. June 25, 1985.

IV. The authors have consulted the following newspapers and periodicals:

Asian Wall Street Journal, 1982; *Baltimore Sun*, 1971, 1973-1975, 1979, 1985; *BBC Summary of World Broadcasts*, 1975; *Cambodia Today*, 1983; *Christian Science Monitor*, 1985; *Far Eastern Economic Review*, 1973, 1975, 1978-1979, 1985; *Journal of Contemporary Asia*, 1978-1979; *London Times*, 1985; *New China News Agency*, 1973, 1975; *New York Times*, 1973, 1975, 1978-1979, 1982, 1985-1986; *Newsweek*, 1975; *Peking Review*, 1973, 1977-1978; *Philadelphia Inquirer*, 1980; *Time*, 1975; *Vietnam News Agency*, 1972, 1975, 1978-1979; *Washington Post*, 1979, 1983, 1985; *Washington Star*, 1979.

Picture Credits

Cover Photo:
Bonnecarrere—SYGMA

Roots of Conflict
p. 9, Jean-Claude Labbé/Gamma-Liaison. p. 11, Ernst Haas—Magnum. p. 12, Philip Jones Griffiths—Magnum. p. 14, L'Illustration. p. 15, Collection Viollet. p. 16, /L'Illustration. p. 19, Collection Viollet. p. 21, Johnny Florea—LIFE Magazine, © 1945, Time Inc. p. 23, Howard Sochurek—LIFE Magazine, © 1953, Time Inc. p. 25, François Sully—Black Star. p. 26, Roger Warner Collection. p. 28, E.C.P. Armées—France. p. 29, top, Ferrari—E.C.P. Armées; bottom, Ferrari—Service Press Information, Courtesy Life Picture Service. p. 31, Keystone. p. 32, Daniel Camus—Paris Match.

The Heritage
p. 34, Eliot Elisofon—Life Picture Service. p. 36, left, Raghubir Singh—Agence ANA; right, Marc Riboud—Magnum. p. 38, Bruno Barbey—Magnum. pp. 39-41, Marc Riboud—Magnum. p. 42, Philip Jones Griffiths—Magnum. pp. 44-45, Andrew Holbrooke—Black Star. p. 46, left, Hiroji Kubota—Magnum; right, Nicolas Tikhomiroff—Magnum.

The Delicate Balance
p. 49, John Dominis—LIFE Magazine, ©. Time Inc. p. 51, E.C.P. Armées—France. p. 53, Stern—Black Star. p. 55, John Dominis—LIFE Magazine, © Time Inc. p. 56, AP/Wide World. pp. 58-59, François Sully—Black Star. pp. 60, 63, John Launois—Black Star. p. 64, Colonel Rod Paschall. pp. 67, 69, AP/Wide World.

Neutrality Lost
p. 71, Hiroji Kubota—Magnum. p. 73, Keystone. p. 75, Roger Warner Collection. pp. 76, 79, AP/Wide World. p. 80, Roger Warner Collection. p. 81, AP/Wide World. p. 83, Black Star. p. 84, Co Rentmeester—Life Magazine, © Time Inc. p. 87, Roger Pic. p. 89, Nixon Project/National Archives. p. 91, UPI/Bettmann.

Pawns of War
p. 93, Philip Jones Griffiths—Magnum. p. 95, Don McCullin—Magnum. p. 96, Roger Warner Collection. p. 99, Bunyo Ishikawa. p. 101, Philip Jones Griffiths—Magnum. p. 102, © Nancy Moran. p. 104, Photoreporters. p. 107, Keystone. p. 108, Deliveyne/Gamma-Liaison. p. 110, Ennio Iacobucci. p. 112, Borel/Gamma-Liaison.

FANK: Lon Nol's Army
p. 115, Sylvain Julienne—SYGMA. p. 116, Philip Jones Griffiths—Magnum. pp. 117-118, © Al Rockoff. p. 120, Hiroji Kubota—Magnum. p. 121, © Al Rockoff.

Liberation
p. 123, Roland Neveu/Gamma-Liaison. pp. 125-126, Bunyo Ishikawa. p. 129, Richard Dudman—SYGMA. p. 131, Bunyo Ishikawa. p. 133, Japan Press Photos. p. 135, Roger Warner Collection. p. 136, Abbas—Magnum. p. 139, Abbas. p. 140, Stern—Black Star. pp. 142-143, Gamma-Liaison.

Life in Hell
pp. 145-149, Matthew Naythons/Gamma-Liaison.

The Disinherited
pp. 150-159, Robin Moyer—Black Star.

The Third Indochina War
p. 161, Bunyo Ishikawa. p. 164, Pascal Manoukian—SYGMA. p. 166, Bunyo Ishikawa. p. 169, Bonnecarrere—SYGMA. pp. 170-171, Andrew Holbrooke—Black Star. p. 173, Roland Neveu/Gamma-Liaison. p. 175, Penelope Chauvelot—SYGMA. p. 176, Yves-Guy Berges—SYGMA. p. 180, Alain Nogues—SYGMA. p. 182, Sovfoto. p. 185, Marc Riboud—Magnum.

Acknowledgments

In addition to ackowledging the kind assistance of the following people, Boston Publishing Company gives special thanks to George Daniels, former executive editor at Time-Life Books, for his guidance and support.

Nayan Chanda, Washington, D.C.; Bob Eaton, Wendy Batson, Patricia Norland of the Indochina Project, Washington, D.C.; David Hawk of the Cambodian Documentation Commission, New York, N.Y.; Quentin R. Hardy, New York; and Terrence Maitland, Boston Massachusetts.

Index

189

Names, Acronyms, Terms

Air America—CIA-sponsored airline, often used for secret operations throughout Asia.

Angka Loeu—"organization on high." Generic name used by the CPK to refer to itself and its leaders.

Angkor—name for the Khmer kingdom established on the Cambodian plain in the sixth century A.D.

ARVN—Army of the Republic of (South) Vietnam.

ASEAN—Association of Southeast Asian Nations (Thailand, Singapore, Malaysia, Indonesia, the Philippines, and Brunei) formed in 1967.

CDNI—Committee for the Defense of National Interests. Laotian rightist organization formed in 1958 that gained power in the government due, in part, to CIA intervention.

CIA—(U.S.) Central Intelligence Agency.

Comintern—Communist International, a pre-World War II association of Communist parties controlled by Moscow.

COSVN—Central Office for South Vietnam. Communist military and political headquarters for southern South Vietnam.

CPK—Communist party of Kampuchea. Originally the KPRP and then the Worker's party of Kampuchea, the CPK was led by Saloth Sar (Pol Pot) and Ieng Sary.

Democratic Kampuchea—name given Cambodia by the ruling Khmer Rouge in January 1976.

Democratic party—moderate Cambodian nationalist party formed after World War II, opposed to King Sihanouk and favoring democratic reforms.

Doan 100—"Group 100," North Vietnamese command headquarters for Laos established on the border soon after the 1954 Geneva Conference to assist the Pathet Lao in military and political matters.

DRV—Democratic Republic of (North) Vietnam.

FANK—Forces Armées Nationales Khmères. The armed forces of General Lon Nol's Khmer Republic.

Hmong—highland tribe of Laos, also called the Meo.

Ho Chi Minh Trail—network of roads and pathways through the jungles and mountains of Laos and Cambodia that served as the principal PAVN infiltration route of men and materiel from North to South Vietnam.

ICP—Indochinese Communist party, formed in 1930 by Ho Chi Minh and others.

ICRC—International Committee of the Red Cross.

ICSC—International Commission for Supervision and Control. Mandated by the Geneva accords of 1954 to supervise implementation of the agreement, it consisted of representatives of Poland, India, and Canada.

Indochina Union—administrative grouping of France's colonial territories in Southeast Asia. Formed in 1887, it consisted of Vietnam, Cambodia, and Laos. Also known as French Indochina.

Kampuchean People's Revolutionary Council—government of Cambodia established in January 1979 following the Vietnamese takeover.

Khmer—pertaining to Cambodia or the Cambodian people.

Khmer Issarak—non-Communist independence movement formed in western Cambodia in the 1940s under Thai patronage. Aimed at expelling the French, the Khmer Issarak included a broad range of nationalist groups.

Khmer Krom—an ethnic Cambodian born and raised in southern Vietnam.

Khmer Loeu—highland tribespeople of Cambodia. Considered savages by the lowland Khmer, the Khmer Loeu traditionally resisted the authority of the central government. Many Khmer Rouge soldiers were Khmer Loeu.

Khmer Republic—Name of Cambodia under the rightist General Lon Nol, who deposed Prince Sihanouk in March 1970.

Khmer Rouge—originally members of the Pracheachon, the Cambodian leftist party. Named "Khmer Rouges" (Red Khmers) by Sihanouk to distinguish them from the right-wing "blues." Later the insurgents of the CPK.

Khmer Serei—Free Khmer. Conservative, pro-American Cambodian guerrilla force under Son Ngoc Thanh.

KNUFNS—Kampuchea National United Front for National Salvation. Front of Cambodian rebels formed by Vietnam in December 1978 to oppose the Pol Pot government.

KPNLF—Khmer People's National Liberation Front. Anti-Vietnam Cambodian resistance group formed in March 1970 under the leadership of former Prime Minister Son Sann.

KPRP—Khmer People's Revolutionary party. Cambodian Communist party formed in 1951 under Son Ngoc Minh. The previous year, Minh and his supporters had formed an umbrella group, the United Issarak Front (UIF).

Lan Chang—the "kingdom of a million elephants." Laotian kingdom established by Fa Ngum in 1353. It fell under Vietnamese control in 1479.

Lao Issara—"Free Lao" rebel government established in October 1945 under nationalist leader Prince Phetsarath.

Lao People's Democratic Republic—name given Laos by the victorious Pathet Lao in December 1975.

Lao People's National Liberation Front—Laotian resistance group formed by right-wing exiles in September 1980.

LPLA—Lao People's Liberation Army. Name of the Pathet Lao's military wing after October 1965.

LPRP—Lao People's Revolutionary party. Secret Communist party officially established on March 22, 1955, by Laotian veterans of the ICP. Headed by Kaysone Phomvihan.

National Sihanoukist Army—pro-Sihanouk guerrilla force formed from individual groups in 1981.

NLF—National Liberation Front. Officially the National Front for the Liberation of the South. Formed in 1960 to overthrow South Vietnam's government and reunite North and South Vietnam.

NLHS—Neo Lao Hak Sat (Lao Patriotic Front). Broadly based front organization created in 1956 and secretly controlled by the Communist LPRP.

NPCC—National Political Consultative Council. Created under the Lao cease-fire accords of 1973 and headed by Prince Souphanouvong.

Operation Menu—collective code name for series of covert U.S. bombings of Cambodia between March 1969 and May 1970.

OSS—Office of Strategic Services. U.S. intelligence organization of World War II. Disbanded in 1945, many of its functions were absorbed by the CIA.

Pathet Lao—Laotian revolutionary front, nominally led by Prince Souphanouvong but closely linked to North Vietnam and controlled by Lao Communists.

People's Army of Vietnam (PAVN)—originally the North Vietnamese Army (called the NVA). Later the army of unified Vietnam.

People's Republic of Kampuchea—name given Cambodia following the Vietnamese takeover in January 1979.

Pracheachon—legitimate leftist party organized by Cambodian Communists after the Geneva Conference of 1954.

Revolutionary Armed Forces of Kampuchea—military wing of KNUFNS.

RLA—Royal Laotian Army.

RVN—Republic of (South) Vietnam.

Sangkhum Reastr Niyum (Sangkhum)—People's Socialist Community. Cambodian party formed in 1955 by Prince Sihanouk to promote his rule and "Buddhist socialism."

Santiphab party—Laotian leftist "Peace party" established in 1956 by Quinim Pholsena, an ally of Souvanna Phouma.

SEATO—Southeast Asia Treaty Organization. Organized in 1954 by Thailand, Pakistan, the Philippines, the U.S., Britain, France, Australia, and New Zealand to form an alliance against Communist subversion, especially in Indochina.

Sihanouk trail—network of trails and roads connecting Cambodian ports with PAVN bases located along the South Vietnamese border. Name was derived from Sihanouk's tacit acceptance of the supply system.

U.S. AID—United States Agency for International Development. Responsible for administering American economic aid to many foreign countries, including South Vietnam and Laos.

Vietcong (VC)—originally derogatory slang for the NLF; a contraction of Vietnam Cong San (Vietnamese Communist).

Vietminh—founded by Ho Chi Minh in 1941. Absorbed by the Vietnamese Communist party in 1951.

White Star—U.S. military operation in which Special Forces advisers openly trained RLA, Hmong tribesmen, and other Laotians to combat the Pathet Lao in the central and northern mountains and in the Laotian panhandle.